The Transition from Higher Education to the Labour Market

T0316978

Holger Ehlert/Heidi Cordier (eds.)

The Transition from Higher Education to the Labour Market

International Perspectives and Challenges

PETER LANG

Frankfurt am Main · Berlin · Bern · Bruxelles · New York · Oxford · Wien

Die Deutsche Bibliothek - CIP-Einheitsaufnahme

The transition from higher education to the labour market :
international perspectives and challenges / Holger Ehlert; Heidi
Cordier (eds.). - Frankfurt am Main ; Berlin ; Bern ; Bruxelles ;
New York ; Oxford ; Wien : Lang, 2002
ISBN 3-631-37325-2

Printed with support from
Ministerium für Schule,
Wissenschaft und Forschung
des Landes Nordrhein-Westfalen

ISBN 3-631-37325-2
US-ISBN 0-8204-4840-0

© Peter Lang GmbH
Europäischer Verlag der Wissenschaften
Frankfurt am Main 2002
All rights reserved.

Printed in Germany 1 2 4 5 6 7

www.peterlang.de

Table of Contents

Introduction

Holger Ehlert and Heidi Cordier

Beginning with the observation that, in many countries, knowledge about the transition from higher education to the labour market is mostly restricted to the internal situation in each particular case, the goal of this book is to increase clarity within the international context, and in so doing to raise the level of knowledge about other countries and to stimulate international discussion.

In fact, it is still the rule in the Federal Republic today that knowledge about this process of transition and the higher education landscape in other countries is restricted to popular individual examples or phenomena, such as the institution of the Career Services[1] in Great Britain. However, these are frequently not interpreted from within their national surroundings, but are "handled" as ideal typical models. As yet, hardly any structured descriptions of the topic in the international context actually exist. Helping to bridge this gap thus had to be one of the tasks of this publication. For this reason, individual descriptions of ten countries, which we present in alphabetical order, form the focal point. The countries are *France, Germany, Great Britain, Ireland, Italy, Japan, the Netherlands, Poland, Switzerland and Sri Lanka.*

When seen from the territorial point of view, it is therefore clear that the main emphasis has intentionally been laid on Europe in order to avoid immediately counteracting the approach to the subject by rapidly making the overview too complicated from the outset. Nevertheless, we felt that it was

---

1   Cf. also Cordier, Heidi: Careers Services: Ein Modell für deutsche Hochschulen? In: Ehlert, Holger / Welbers, Ulrich (eds.): Handbuch Praxisinitiativen an Hochschulen. Berufs-orientierende Angebote an Universitäten. Luchterhand Verlag. Neuwied, 1999, pp. 303-320.

important to break up the European hegemony by including two particularly interesting examples – Japan and Sri Lanka – thus enriching the discussion by the addition of countries with completely different cultures. The inclusion of the paper on Poland is to be understood in this sense. Although the situation is different, there is nevertheless a similar basic motive. It is a country which can also be seen as an example – it is a country of the former Eastern block undergoing transformation, whose formal integration into the European Union is imminent, and which, not only in this respect, can be regarded as providing an impulse.

The profile of this collection of articles designed as a comparative study was not intended to lie, and could not possibly lie, in presenting a conclusive compendium of evaluated results within a comprehensive study.[2] On the one hand, the higher education landscapes and employment systems presented here are too heterogeneous, and, on the other hand, each of the authors was to be allowed a sufficiently free hand in order to determine his or her own individual focal points. In addition, by conceiving a catalogue of questions made available to all the authors, the editors attempted to provide systematic information about the definition and extent of the topic in order to achieve a certain "standard" in the sense of comparability for the reader. In this respect, however, it was nevertheless important to avoid reducing the reports on the individual countries to general statements that provided little information, as would have been the case with the use of a rigid grid in a questionnaire. This would have meant that there would have been no room left for the description of national idiosyncrasies and special cases. To this extent this is not a comparative representation in accordance with a strict statistical and comparative catalogue of criteria.

---

2   In contrast, the work within the framework of the THELM Higher Education Project at the Heinrich-Heine-University Düsseldorf is being continued with this goal in mind.

The editors started from the following premises: the relationship between higher education and the labour market assumes a central role, both with regard to the shaping of the degree courses and the teaching of the necessary qualifications for a changing working world, and with regard to the transition from higher education to employment and the quantitative demand for jobs requiring a university degree. In addition, vocational competence must also be maintained through contacts with the higher education institutions within the framework of lifelong learning processes.

Scientific knowledge as the basis for defining and solving problems is penetrating more and more fields of business, industry and society. The expression "knowledge-based society" postulates the increasing importance of education and qualification. At the same time, business and industry are subjected to accelerated technical and organisational change, which is having great effects on the qualifications required of the employees. In order to do justice to their responsibility to their graduates, the higher education institutions must prepare them for these processes of change within the courses they offer. However, this is not a German problem, but it concerns the demands and conditions which exist not only in the countries described here. It is therefore extremely interesting to examine how the change to a knowledge-based society is effected and regarded in other countries.

The following questions form the focal point of this survey:

* How is the labour market for graduates organised?
* How is vocational orientation achieved in degree courses in the individual countries?
* How is the transition from higher education to employment organised?

As far as the selection of the authors was concerned, from the outset the editors attempted, as far as possible, to obtain native speakers from each of the countries about which papers were to be written. For a number of different reasons it was not entirely possible to achieve this goal. In the end, however, half of the papers have been written by what one might call "natives" from the individual countries. Here, the editors were not interested in recruiting the authors with the aid of state-run institutions in the individual countries, but rather in applying knowledge of the subject and involvement with regard to the project as the primary criterion for their choice. We are convinced that this principle can be regarded as having being successful when one looks at the result.

Without wanting in advance to postulate one special feature of the German higher education system in this way, it is nevertheless essential to point out that there, more than in any other of the countries presented here, the end of the division of Germany also produced extraordinary additional national challenges from the point of view of educational policy. It is a fact that the current higher education system in the Federal Republic of Germany did not remain untouched by the historic events with regard to the ending of the division of the country. On the one hand, of course, it can be stated that the higher education system of the old Federal Republic was essentially transferred to the five states (*"Länder"*) which formerly constituted East Germany. On the other hand, however, during the past decade the East German states in particular have received a considerable amount of attention through their, in comparison, clearly innovative involvement.[3]

Another special feature must be mentioned with reference to the direct national comparison of the ten countries introduced here: the socially great

3   Compare, for example, the B.A. model at the University in Greifswald.

importance of the educational path and educational success in Japan. For the individual there, a degree course at a highly respected educational institution provides an extremely relevant precondition for successful entry into employment. Within the framework of a comparatively open educational system, higher education in Japan has extraordinarily high prestige in the later planning of a person´s occupation and life. This is because the chances of success are essentially determined during the qualifying phase. However, even in Japan a higher education degree does not automatically provide an entrance ticket to the employment being sought, since the initial phase of employment does, in the end, play a very important part in the selection process. However, the status of education and qualification before employment – at least within the modern industrial nations presented here – is clearly nowhere as relevant for talking up employment as in Japan. In their paper Ulrich Teichler and Kerstin Teicher have, in compressed form, provided the essential aspects within the context of our topic.[4] We considered it especially important to include two particularly interesting reports on countries from the Asian region by using the examples of Japan and Sri Lanka – two countries which are interesting precisely because of their differences. Thus, for example, it becomes clear that in European countries and in Japan a higher education degree protects a person against unemployment, and that the unemployment rate of higher education graduates is (in some case distinctly) lower there, but that this is not the case in Sri Lanka! Precisely the opposite is the case there.

In addition, it can be stated that even with regard to the western European education systems presented in this book – and despite far-reaching structural similarities – particular national characteristics as opposed to common features dominate here, and that the goal of improving international compatibility in

---

4   The authors have already published at length on the subject. Most recently, among others: Teicher, Kerstin / Teichler, Ulrich: Der Übergang von der Hochschule in die Berufstätig-keit in Japan. Leske & Budrich. Opladen, 2000.

the education sector still requires a great effort even here. Finally, attention must also be drawn to the fact that within the context of the topic we have given preference to a detailed description of the Careers Service in Britain rather than to the publication of a general report on higher education there. In this paper, Heidi Cordier and others discuss to what extent the Careers Service model is also an option for German higher education institutions, without putting it forward uncritically as a model for Germany.

We are extremely grateful to all the authors for their highly qualified and involved cooperation. Without this truly "boundless" involvement the book could not have been produced in this form.

We should also like to express our grateful thanks to Mr. Hugh Langridge, whose translations of almost all the papers have made an essential contribution to the success of this book.

Our thanks also to Andreas Meske for his advice and the layout of the book, which he completed under great pressure of time.

Dr. Ulrich Welbers and the Studienreformbüro Germanistik at the Heinrich-Heine-University Düsseldorf are to be thanked for the generous provision not only of the infrastructure, but also for the general support and cooperation. We are also extremely grateful to Carmen Hillebrand, a student of English and student assistant, for her reliable work, which she carried out parallel to preparing for and taking her examinations.

Our special thanks also to Univ.-Prof. Dr. Michiko Mae, Prorektorin für Lehre, Studium und Studienreform at the Heinrich-Heine-University Düsseldorf, who, as the person responsible for it, has supported and promoted the THELM project with practical help and advice since it was begun.

The editors would like to thank the Peter Lang Publishing House for its cooperation, which has always been extremely competent and professional – especially the cooperation with the staff working at the office in Essen.

This book, in particular, could not have been completed without the financial support given to the THELM[5] Research Project at the Heinrich-Heine-University Düsseldorf by the Ministry for Schools and Continuing Education, Science and Research of the State of North-Rhine Westphalia.

Holger Ehlert and Heidi Cordier

---

5   THELM: Transition from Higher Education to the Labour Market.

France

Valérie Canals and Claude Diebolt

1. The Higher Education System in France: Current Situation and Development

- More girls than boys obtain a school leaving certificate.
- Educational provision is diversified.
- The opening up of access to university from the point of view of equality is a very slow process.
- 6% of the labour force in France work in the field of education.
- A higher education degree is of importance on the labour market.
- The number of students is increasing because more of those who have qualified for university entry are willing to study.
- Individual courses react differently to the increasing student numbers.

2. The Transition of Higher Education Graduates to Employment: The Pressure of Economic Trends

- A diploma degree protects a person against unemployment.
- There are many ways of finding employment.
- Work experience in firms is frequently undertaken by students, but it is not sufficient for obtaining a job.
- Paid work while studying is a traditional practice.
- Employment opportunities are to be found essentially in private business.
- Jobs tend to be stable and are found in businesses of all sizes.
- A degree does not always guarantee work in management or in the technical field.
- Salaries are dependent on the type of degree and the course of study undertaken.

The structure of the labour force has undergone a profound change in France since the beginning of the Sixties. On the one hand the increase in particularly highly qualified positions and jobs for white-collar employees was accompanied by a decrease in jobs for manual workers and the self-employed. On the other hand, however, the level of training has constantly risen. The education sector, which was given financial support and was extended, is responsible for the increase in the level of training and qualification. Thus, in 1997 40% of those completing their education had obtained a higher education qualification, and more than half of these had completed a long course of study. Nevertheless, the lack of jobs at the beginning of the Nineties meant that the level of training of the working population rose more rapidly than the structure of jobs available. This is the origin of the worsening situation on the labour market for the highly qualified and academically trained.

In addition, the employment of young people reacts especially sensitively to the economic situation. As first-time employees, young people are particularly affected by the fluctuations of the demand for work. This sensitivity increases depending on the type of employment on offer: fixed-term contracts, little qualification, high mobility etc. This process actively leads to the lengthening and complication of the period of transition to employment. However, not all young people are "equal" with regard to the risks of the economic situation. Those with a higher education qualification suffer less from the fluctuation since, one the one hand, the qualified professions are not so susceptible (long-term employment with the demand for qualified work) and, on the other hand, the competition leads to the exclusion of those with lower qualifications.[1] Differences also exist between the various higher education courses.

---

1   FONDEUR, Y., MINNI, C. (1999) Emploi des jeunes et conjoncture, Dares, Premières informations et Premières synthèses, No.51.1, 99.12.

After a difficult start to the Nineties, when the number of young people being employed after completion of their first training was low, and access to jobs requiring medium-level or top-level qualifications was more difficult, especially for those who had completed shorter courses of study, the new upswing at the end of 1997 is making itself noticeable through the fact that the conditions for the access of young graduates to the labour market have improved, and they now have better access to leading positions. In 1998 there was a marked drop in unemployment among higher education graduates. The jobs for managers and academics is undergoing a genuine boom. This helps young first-time employees in particular.

Against this background this article is divided into two parts: the first part investigates the higher education sector in France, and the second part analyses the entry of higher education graduates to the labour market.

1. The Higher Education Sector in France: Current Situation and Development

More girls than boys obtain a school leaving certificate

Since 1970 the number of French people aged between 2 and 29 receiving education or training has stabilised at around 15 million, a figure which represents almost two thirds of the relevant age groups. The number of pupils and students older than 16 (in France schooling is compulsory until the age of 16) is about 4.5 million, and the number of students is more than 2 million. The latter comprise 14% of the population receiving education or training.[2] Moreover, participation in the education process is continually increasing: it rose from 73% in 1970 to 91% in 1997.[3] It accounts for 52% of the 16-25 age group.

2 MINODIER, F. (1999) La scolarisation des jeunes de 16 à 25 ans en 1997-1998, MENRT-DPD, Note d'information, No.99.32, September.
3 MENRT-DPD (1997) Repères et références statistiques.

Pupils and students as a percentage of their relevant age group:

Age	16	17	18	19	20	21	22	23	24	25
%	96.3	91.3	82.6	70.6	57.0	44.3	33.9	24.1	15.2	10.5

Source: MINODIER, F. (1999) La scolarisation des jeunes de 16 à 25 ans en 1997-1998, MENRT-DPD, Note d'information, No.99.32 September.

Of the female population aged between 16 and 25 54% are pupils and students. The figure for the equivalent male population group is only 51%. This difference is essentially the result of higher education, which is attended by 55% of the young women. Since girls are more successful than boys at passing the «Bac», the French university entry qualification, they start studying earlier. 40% of the young men aged 19 attend an institution of higher education, while the figure for young women is higher than 60%.

Educational provision is diversified

Higher education in France is characterised by numerous institutions with different goals, structures and entry qualifications. On the one hand, the large engineering and business schools (Grandes Écoles) each admit 10% of the students, and roughly 20% to the shorter courses respectively. On the other hand, the universities accept and train 60% of the students. Seven main criteria distinguish universities from other institutions of higher education:

Three criteria involve the nature of the training:
· the selection of the students
· the different degrees awarded
· the employment-related courses.

Four criteria involve organisational aspects of the course:
· the cost of the course
· the administrative forms of the institutions

· the student environment

· the research carried out by the teaching staff.

As far as the first three criteria are concerned, the difference between universities and other institutions of higher education are continually becoming smaller, while the situation continues to be fairly clear as far as the other criteria are concerned: nowadays, the other institutions of higher education are distinguished from the universities more by the organisation of the courses than by the degree awarded.[4]

1. The selection of students: basically, all students with a secondary school certificate can attend a university, but not one of the schools of higher education (écoles), which have an explicit and sometimes very strict selection procedure. In fact, numerous universities have introduced more or less implicit forms of selection in order to guide the number and educational level of the students. These forms of selection are either illegal (and here the universities hope that the students rejected are not aware that they can obtain entry through the courts) or legal (as, for example, in Medicine, with "numerus clausus" (a policy of restricted entry). In contrast, there are some schools, especially schools of business, which can no longer allow themselves the luxury of selecting their students and have to accept almost every applicant in order to secure their continued existence.

2. Differences between the institutions: in principle, and in contrast to degrees from the Grandes Écoles, all university degrees throughout the country are of equal value, no matter which higher education institution awarded them. With the exception of the doctorate the issuing institution cannot be recognized. In reality, however, the universities, like the Grandes Écoles, are admittedly in a competitive situation, and

---

4   ATTALI, J. (1997) Pour un modèle européen d'enseigneur supérieur, report for MENRT.

here a clear hierarchy plays a large part regarding the degrees and the institution's reputation. This is taken into account in the firms' employment procedures.

3. The vocational relevance of the courses: with the exception of certain specific disciplines, such as Medicine or Law, the goal of university training is not to learn a profession but to gain certain knowledge and research instruments which permit the student under certain circumstances to develop into a researcher or a teacher. In contrast, the training at the Grandes Écoles is job-related from the outset. Engineers and managers for private business and the public sector are trained here. However, for some years now – especially since the introduction of the Higher Education Act in 1984 – this distinction has become less and less clear: at universities students are also increasingly preparing themselves for vocational and specialist diploma degrees.

As far as the following four criteria regarding the organisation of the courses is concerned, however, the contrast between universities and Grandes Écoles is still very clear:

4. The administration of the institutions of higher education: while power at the universities is divided between the president, the teaching staff, the students and the ministry responsible, in the Grandes Écoles it generally lies in the hands of a small directorship that has extensive powers and frequently reacts with reserve to any superior authority.

5. The living conditions of the students: while the working and living conditions available at the Grandes Écoles are generally excellent, this is far from being the case at many universities. In particular, this applies to the library, the refectory, student accommodation and to the sports facilities.

6. Research undertaken by the teaching staff: while research is considered to be one of the most important components of the work of the teaching

staff at universities, at the Grandes Écoles it mostly plays only a weak or indirect role, even though the latter have good laboratories at their disposal.

7. Student fees: while the training at universities is practically free, fees have to be paid in certain Grandes Écoles, especially at the business schools. However, there are also some Grandes Écoles that provide financial support for their students.

In the following a distinction is made between three main categories: universities, Grandes Écoles and technical institutions.

The universities

Many different disciplines are frequently taught at the universities, which are divided into teaching and research units [Unités de Formation (UFR)]; each of these units deals with one particular discipline: Humanities, Natural Sciences, Languages, Law, Economics etc. In order to be matriculated at a university one must have obtained the Baccalauréat or an equivalent higher education entry qualification. In the case of the traditional degree course at a university the student begins with basic studies, which lead to the DEUG (Intermediate Examination after Two Years of Study). One can then specialise in the course of the higher levels: Licence (licentiate's degree after three years of study at a university), maîtrise (M.A. degree after four years of study at a university and the writing of a scientific paper), DESS or DEA (Diploma Degree after Five Years of Study in a Specialized Field), followed by a doctorate. Until recently, university teaching was characterised in particular by the presentation of theoretical knowledge. At universities it is now possible to receive more practice-related training that is orientated towards a later occupation. This is possible in the Instituts universitaires professionalisés (IUP), vocational institutes that are attached to the university.

The Grandes Écoles

The Grandes Écoles are specifically French. They were founded in order to teach specialist knowledge at a high level. The main subjects taught are Social Science and Economics as well as the Natural Sciences. Some of these elite institutions of higher education are government-funded and are generally under the control of a ministry, while others are private or consular. One of the characteristics of these elite institutions is the extremely strict selection procedure: it generally takes place in the form of a competition [concours]. Preparation for this selective examination is possible in Preparatory Classes for the "Grandes Écoles" (CPGE) and lasts two years. The general university entry quali-fication is necessary for participation in the CPGE.

The technical institutions

Since the Seventies there have been numerous courses which do not last so long, and which are less general in their content than those offered at the universities. The goal of these courses is to give the graduate the opportunity of rapid transition to working life. The final diploma is obtained after two years of study. Firms had definitely been waiting for the introduction of a branch of education of this kind, and these courses were immediately successful. Places are in extremely high demand because of this success. Selection is also very strict. In order to be accepted one must have obtained the Baccalauréat or an equivalent higher education entry qualification. Selection is based on an application dos-sier, and sometimes written and oral examinations are required. There are two types of technical institution: the Technical Institutes Attached to a University (IUT) and the Higher Technical Schools (STS).

In 1996-97 there were almost 4,300 institutions of higher education.

Universities		87
CPGE total		481
government-funded	*327*	
private	*154*	
Schools of engineering total		238
gov.-funded, attached to univ.	*92*	
gov.-funded, independent of univ.	*78*	
private	*68*	
STS total		1900
government-funded	*1124*	
private	*776*	
IUT		92
IUFM (Teacher Training Colleges)		26
Schools of Business and Commerce		230
Private institutions of higher education		18
ENS: Colleges of Education		4
Schools of Architecture		24
Schools of Art and Cultural Studies		225
Schools for Social Service Professions		165
Schools for the Auxiliary Medical Professions (non-university)		641
Other institutions of higher education		160

Source: MENRT-DPD (1997) Repères et références statistiques.

In 1998-1999 2,119,000 students were registered at institutions of higher education:

Universities:	1,310,000
CPGE:	78,000
Schools of engineering:	55,000
STS:	240,000
IUT:	114,500
IUFM:	81,500
Other institutions of higher education:	240,000

Source: MENRT-DPD (2000) Les chiffres clé de l'enseignement supérieur.

The opening up of access to university from the point of view of equality is a very slow process

The lengthening of the period of education (training) is noticeable at all levels of society. Even if this lengthening of education generally leads to a lessening of social differences, it is, above all, with regard to access to higher education that the educational careers of the children differ depending on their social background. The probability that the children of managers will obtain a degree from an institution of higher education is greater than in the case of children from a working-class background (Table 1).

Table 1: The social and occupational background of students in France according to type of school and sex (1996-97, as a percentage)

Occupational status of the parents	IUT	univ.	CPGE	STS	men	women
Farmers	4.0	2.8	2.4	3.2	2.2	3.3
Craftsmen, merchants, businessmen	9.6	8.9	7.4	9.5	8.7	9.0
Self-employed, managers	25.7	35.2	50.8	13.9	37.4	33.6
Occupations with a medium-level qualification	22.1	19.6	16.0	17.1	19.6	19.6
White-collar workers	14.2	12.7	8.9	16.2	12.4	12.9
Blue-collar workers	18.2	12.8	6.9	26.0	11.9	13.5
Pensioners, persons not in the labour force	6.2	8.0	7.6	14.1	7.8	8.1
Total	100.0	100.0	100.0	100.0	100.0	100.0

Source: ATTALI, J. (1997) Pour un modèle européen d'enseigneur supérieur, report for MENRT.

Since the Seventies the proportion of foreign students attending French universities has varied between 12% and 14%. In 1985 the sudden slowing down of the influx of African students led initially to the stabilisation and then to the reduction of the number of foreign students. In contrast there were distinctly more European students in 1996 than in 1982. With a figure of 36,000 Europeans (27,000 of whom were from the EU) accepted in 1996-97,

France occupies second place among European countries behind the United Kingdom with regard to the number of European students matriculated.[5]

The expenditure on education amounts to 7.2% of the gross domestic product

In 1998 the domestic expenditure on higher education amounted to FF 607 billion. The total budget for state education amounted to 21% of the national budget or 7.2% of the gross domestic product. This means expenditure amounting to FF 10,300 (1,570 Euros) per inhabitant or FF 37,200 per pupil or student (5,761 Euros).[6] In the course of the same year France as whole made available FF 100.6 billion for higher education. The government provided by far the largest proportion, representing 80% of the funding. In the period between 1975 and 1998 this expenditure increased by 122%. From 1975 to 1982 the expenditure on higher education as a proportion of the total domestic expenditure on education decreased successively from 13.6% to 13%. Since 1982 the expenditure on higher education has risen again sharply, and in 1998 it reached 16.6% of the total domestic expenditure on education.[7] Despite the increase of 84% in the number of students the average expenditure per student rose by only 21%, while the average expenditure per pupil, of whatever school type, rose by almost 72% during the same period.[8] Referred to the institutions of higher education that are dependent on the French Ministry of Education, the average expenditure per student amounted to roughly FF 50,400 in 1998. It amounted to about FF 39,000 for a student at a government-funded university and to about FF 77,800 for a student attending the preparatory class for the "Grandes Écoles".[9] This divergence is due, among

---

5   MENRT-DPD (1997) Repères et réferences statistiques.
6   MENRT-DPD (1999) L'état de l'école, 9th Edition, indicator 1.
7   MENRT-DPD (1999) L'état de l'école, 9th Edition, indicator 22.
8   MENRT-DPD (1999) L'état de l'école, 9th Edition, indicator 22.
9   MESNARD, O., RAGOUCY, C., BERREUR, C. (1999) Le coût de l'éducation en 1998, MENRT-DPD, Note d'information. No.99.37, October.

other things, to the differences in the guidance provided for students, the status of the teaching staff (remuneration and official commitments), the characteristics of each different type of training (material for technical and occupation-related training) and the relative importance of the funds invested. When seen as a trend, the development of higher education funding reveals a dynamic increase in the use of private funding (private budgets and firms) (Chart 1).

Chart 1: The development of higher education funding in France (1976-1994 in FF millions)

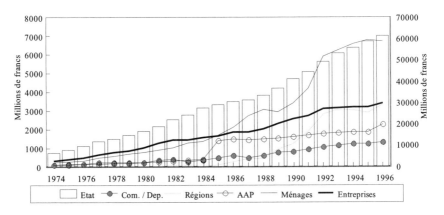

From left to right: State, Commune/Département, Regions, AAP, Private households, Firms. Source: MENRT-DPDF, Les comptes de l'éducation.

According to estimates by the OECD, the average total costs for a student's course amount to the equivalent of USD 28,930. France occupies a middle position here, with the equivalent of USD 30,750 (see Chart 2).

Chart 2: Average expenditure per student in US-Dollar (1995)

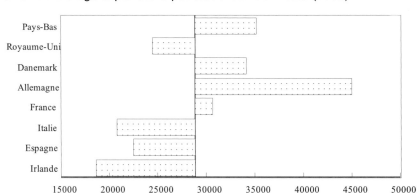

From top to bottom: Netherlands, United Kingdom, Denmark, Germany, France, Italy, Spain, Ireland.
Source: MENRT-DPD (1999) L'état de l'école, 9th Edition, Indicator 22.

6% of the labour force in France work in the field of education

The increase in the education budget is an indicator when the quality of higher education is being studied. Thus, for example, the demographic structure of the teaching staff underwent a change, since an increasing number of teachers and scientists were employed.[10] 1,540,000 people were working in schools or in higher education on January 1st, 1998, which represents 6% of the labour force in France. Women account for 66% of these employees, and their proportion within the education sector is therefore higher than in the labour force as a whole, where the proportion of women is only 45%. On average, the teachers in primary education are the youngest. They are 41 years old, while the average for teachers in secondary education is 43, and the average age of the teaching staff in higher education is 45.[11]

10   MENRT-DPD (1999) L'état de l'école, 9th Edition, Indicator 3.
11   MENRT-DPD (1999) L'état de l'école, 9th Edition, Indicator 3.

Teachers and non-teaching staff in the education sector by level in France in 1998 (in %)

Non-teaching		38%
Teachers		62%
primary level	21%	
secondary level	31%	
agricultural schools	1%	
vocational schools	1.5%	
higher education	7.5%	

Source: MENRT-DPD (1999) L'état de l'école, 9th Edition, Indicator 22.

In 1997-1998 the teaching staff in higher education numbered 76,936, split into three main groups: teaching staff required to undertake research, teachers from secondary schools working in higher education, and teachers who are not civil servants.

46,847	teaching staff required to undertake research
36%	university professors
60%	associate professors
4%	academic assistants
12,458	teachers from secondary schools working in higher education
14,631	teachers who are not civil servants
32%	with fixed-term contracts to teach and carry out research
24%	tutors who take over teaching tasks and at the same time prepare their doctoral thesis or undertake research
15%	foreign professors or associate professors
6%	lectors and academic staff members teaching foreign languages
23%	assistants in medical disciplines

Source: BIDEAULT, M., ROSSI, P., (1999) Les personnels enseignants de l'enseignement supérieur public, MENRT-DPD, Information note, No. 99.25, July.

The proportion of women continues to be very low. In 1985-1986 9% of the professors and 31% of the associate professors were women. Ten years later these figures were 14% for professors and 36% for associate professors.

A higher education degree is of importance on the labour market

In an economy that is marked by underemployment, a course of study and the massive desire to attend university is not necessarily the result of economic considerations orientated towards the possible amortization of the investment. Studying can quite simply be experienced as a way of preventing unemployment – a consideration that considerably restricts the consequences of theoretical explanations concerning human capital. A higher education degree exerts a positive influence not only on the chances of obtaining work but also on the salary. In 1996, for example, graduates from a long course who were at the start of their career (5 years after obtaining their degree) received a salary twice as high as that of employees without a degree. Where full-time employees without a leaving certificate receive FF 100, young people leaving a vocational school receive FF 111, those with a university entry qualification FF 121, graduates from a short course of study FF 156, and higher education graduates FF 202. For young graduates from a long course of study the chances of obtaining a management post are three out of four; in the case of young school-leavers with a university entry qualification the chances are three out of ten at most (MENRT-DPD 1997).

Even though the signs are that its value is depreciating, a leaving certificate continues to make its mark on the labour market (GAMEL 1998). Since the beginning of the Eighties an analysis of the relationship between training and occupation clearly shows that the formerly close connection between leaving certificate and occupation is gradually becoming looser. On the labour market the exchange value of certain qualifications is declining (AFFICHARD 1981; BAUDELOT, GLAUDE 1989). The phenomenon of the reduction in status of higher education degrees has also grown stronger: while 91% of the IUT and BTS graduates still found employment requiring medium-level qualifications or worked as managers in 1988, the figure had dropped to 73% in 1991

(MARTINELLI, VERGNIES 1995). As a result of the high level of unemployment the relation between supply and demand on the labour market is changing; employees are thus no longer in the slightly stronger position, and employers can fall back on workers who are not so demanding. Employers make use of unemployment and institutional regulations in order to "push through their own system of qualifications for workers, while at the same time putting in question the official system imposed by the education authorities" (AFFICHARD, 1981). Surveys carried out at the beginning of the Eighties, as well as the table proposed by K. Affichard, G. Gorgeot and J. Gautié illustrating the relationship between higher education degree and occupation, show that the proportion of overqualified graduates among the working population aged between 18 and 29 rose in the period from 1986 to 1995. "[...] as far as the development of the depreciation in the value of CAP and BEP graduates and those with leaving certificates from comparable schools is concerned, no clear trend can be determined. [...] On the other hand, in the same period the depreciation in the value of those fulfilling university entry requirements and of higher education graduates has greatly increased" (FORGEOT, GAUTIÉ 1997, p. 58). Beyond the situation with regard to the occupation actually carried out, this depreciation can also be observed in the development of the relative position of higher education graduates in the salary hierarchy.

According to the paper by C. BAUDELOT and M. GLAUDE, the status of education continually declined between 1970 and 1985. When seen against the background of 20 years of employment "the cost-effectiveness of education, i.e. the additional salary that a further year at school can produce had fallen from 12% for those who joined the labour market in 1950, to 10% for the generation that began its working life in 1965. If this trend were to continue, for those young people aged between 16 and 24 joining the labour market nowadays each additional year at school or attending higher education would only produce a salary advantage of 7%" (BAUDELOT, GLAUDE, 1989). As the authors of the survey state, one third of this development is due to the fact that the range of salaries in the salary hierarchy is becoming smaller, and two thirds to the competition between the graduates themselves. In addition, C. Gamel shows that between 1977 and 1993 80% of the male graduates from higher education had 50% of the best-paid posts (compared with 95% during the period from 1970 to 1985) (GAMEL 1998).

The number of students is increasing because more of those who have qualified for university entry are willing to study

From the beginning of the Eighties until now the number of those aiming for the general entry qualification for higher education has doubled; it initially rose rapidly in France, and in the past few years it has stabilised at 68%.

In 1980-1981 34% of young people of one year were admitted to Level IV (in France, %)

General university entry qualification	22.1
University entry qualification with the main emphasis on technical subjects	11.9

In 1996-1997 68% of young people of one year were admitted to Level IV (in France, %)

General university entry qualification	35.5
University entry qualification with the main emphasis on technical subjects	20.9
Vocationally-orientated university entry qualification	11.9

Source: MENRT-DPD (1997) L'état de l'école, 7th Edition.

The general university entry qualification means that general school education is completed with the main emphasis on the Natural Sciences, Economics, Social Sciences or Humanities.

The university entry qualification with the main emphasis on technical subjects means that the general school education is complemented by training in the technical field.

The vocationally-orientated university entry qualification means that a more concrete school education has been completed which leads to carrying out a particular occupation.

This development shows that the school attendance quota of the younger generations has increased to an unusually large extent and is coming very close to the goal of 80% of the pupils of a year aiming at a university entry qualification. This goal was laid down in the mid-Eighties by those responsible for the school sector. Nowadays, the university entry qualification is both the school leaving certificate and the first higher education diploma, and automatically permits entry to an institution of higher education. However, the numbers of students with a university entry qualification who then continue their studies is by no means uniform. The age of the those qualifying for university entry, and thus their school record and social background, influence the continuation of their studies (EPIPHANE, HALLIER, 1996). At the same time, the inclination to study at a higher education institution also depends on the type of university entry qualification. While almost all those with the general university entry qualification and more than 80% of those who have passed the university entry qualification with its main emphasis on technical subjects are registered immediately afterwards at a university or other institution of higher education, only 15% of the pupils who have obtained the vocationally-orientated university entry qualification enter higher education.

100% of the school-leavers with a university entry qualification subsequently
study at:

university	66%
CPGE	13%
IUT	10%
STS	9%
other institutions of higher education	7%

Depending on the type of university entry qualification, this breakdown
indicates a number of differences. While most of the school-leavers with their
main focus on arts subjects study at a university, those with their main focus
on natural sciences start studying at a university, the CPGE or at an IUT.

80% of those who have passed the university entry qualification with its main
emphasis on technical subjects study at

university	22%
CPGE	1%
IUT	10%
STS	45%
other institutions of higher education	2%

As far as the university entry qualification with its main emphasis on technical
subjects is concerned, the proportion of those who subsequently attend a
higher education institution has greatly increased: in 1980 the figure was
55%, and at the beginning of the Nineties it was more than 80%. In this field,
too, there is a gap, depending on the chosen focal point of the university
entry qualification. A large proportion of those who have specialized in
Economics study Mathematics / Physics (34%) and Natural Sciences / Biology
(25%). The third group study Law / Economics (34%) and AES (Economic
and Social Administration) (25%).

15% of those who have obtained the vocationally-orientated university entry qualification continue their studies at:

university	6%
STS	9%

The remainder of those who have obtained the university entry qualification do not start studying at a higher education institution.

A school-leaver with a university entry qualification who would like to study can either prepare for his DEUG in a general subject or in a health-related subject, or he can decide in favour of a more selective course: a preparatory class for and elite institution of higher education, a university of applied sciences, a technical institute (IUT) or a specialist school which carries out a selection examination immediately after the university entry qualification has been obtained. According to a survey carried out by the French Ministry of Education (MENRT) in 1996, most of the school-leavers with the university entry qualification study the subject of their choice. Only 16% of these are forced to study at a university because they have no alternative. They originally intended to follow a shorter course with its focal point on technology, above all (37%) a BTS, mostly in the service sector, or a course at a technical institute (IUT). Many of them would have preferred to attend a higher education institution for the health services or the social sector (16%). However, they were unable to attend these institutions because admission to them takes place by means of a selection procedure and their application was unsuccessful.[12]

12   LEMAIRE, S. (1997) Après le bac, pourquoi l'université?, in: Éducation et formations, Le premier cycle du supérieur, No.50, June, MENRT-DPD, pp. 23-31; LEMAIRE, S. (1998) Que deviennent les bacheliers après leur bac? Information Note, No.98.05, March, MENRT-DPD.

This brief overview of the development of the numbers of those obtaining a university entry qualification shows that the French goal of encouraging 80% of the young people of one year to obtain this qualification, and thus of raising the general level of education within the population, causes these school-leavers to regard the university entry qualification as the minimum school-leaving qualification and encourages them to study at an institution of higher education. The falling marginal cost-effectiveness of the training ought not to have an effect on the actual demand for training, since – as demonstrated in the so-called filter theory (ARROW, 1973) – the goal of the training is, when compared with one's competitors, to place oneself in such a position as to be able to obtain the best-paid jobs on the labour market. The trend towards studying and attending university clearly expresses one reality: a degree continues to be of importance, despite signs of depreciation (AFFICHARD 1981; BAUDE-LOT, GLAUDE 1989; MARTINELLI, VERGNIES 1995; FORGEOT, GAUTIE 1997; GAMEL 1998). Young people and their families are well aware of this phenomenon. If one takes all the forms of university entry qualification into account one discovers that nowadays half an age-group decides in favour of higher education. Nevertheless, 1996 marked a break. The rise in school attendance, which slowed down considerably after that date, can no longer make up for the drop in numbers resulting from the fact that the years with a low birthrate since 1975 mean that fewer and fewer young people have started attending a university or another higher education institution.

Individual courses react differently to the increasing student numbers

The development of student numbers according to courses reveals deviations (Chart 3). This is due, on the one hand, to the fact that young people with a university entry qualification orientate themselves differently and, on the other hand, to the fact that the higher education institutions react differently to the growing demand for training. The increase in the number of students in higher education, which was rapid after 1987, continued to develop quickly until 1993. In 1996 the number of students enrolled at institutions of higher education dropped for the first time. Not every course was equally affected by this. While the short courses (STS, DUT) were able to maintain their student numbers, the numbers attending university courses fell. The improvement in employment opportunities meant that quite a number of young people did not wait before seeking employment, as had still been the case at the beginning of the Nineties.

Chart 3: The development of student numbers in France (1982-1996, in thousands)

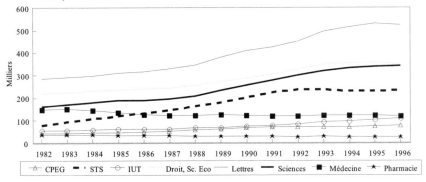

From left to right: CPGE, STS, IUT, Law and Economics, Humanities, Natural Sciences, Medicine, Pharmacy.
Source: MENRT-DPD.

After the rapid rise at the beginning of the decade the student numbers have no longer risen since the beginning of the 1996/97 academic year. In the academic year 1998/99, for the third year in succession, the student numbers also fell. While a more favourable demographic development is beginning for higher education, young people with a university entry qualification seem less inclined to attend a university or other higher education institution.[13]

13   MENRT-DPD (1999) L'état de l'école, 9th Edition, Indicator 24.

The distribution according to the stages of university studies is as follows:

	total	men	women
Stage I	47.0%	54.0%	53.0%
Stage II	37.3%	32.3%	35.5%
Stage III	15.7%	13.7%	11.5%

Women are asserting themselves. 55% of the students are women. However, their proportion becomes smaller as the level of the degree becomes higher. Apart from this, women are largely in a minority in the industrial and scientific courses of study. These facts are of significance for the transition of women to working life.

Women students as a percentage of the total number of students in France: 55%

Integrated preparations	24.5%
CPGE	39.3%
STS	50.5%
IUT	38.1%
Universities	57.6%
Schools of Engineering	22.2%
Schools of Business and Commerce	44.8%
Schools for the Medical Service or the Social Services	80.5%

Source: ROUSSEAU, B., SABOULIN, (de) M. (1998) Les effectifs de l'enseignement supérieur au cours des années 1990 (The number of students in higher education in the Nineties) MENRT-DPD, Information Note, No. 98.34, November.

Roughly 60% of the school-leavers qualifying for university entry who decide in favour of a general degree course (DEUG) reach Stage II (2ème cycle) of university studies. The remainder of the students – the majority – continue their studies at other institutions, e.g. IUT, STS, and a minority abandon their studies. However, the proportion of students obtaining entry to Stage II studies, i.e. the probability that a student in the first year of study at Stage I of a general course of study will be admitted to Stage II is to a large extent dependent on the type of university entry qualification: 66% of those with the general university entry qualification succeed, while the figure is only 21% of those who have a university entry qualification with the main emphasis on technical subjects. The latter show less inclination to study for a longer period of time. Overall, students require an average of 2.7 years to reach Stage II.[14] Here, too, there are deviations which are dependent on the type of university entry qualification. School-leavers with a qualification which has its main emphasis on technical subjects take 3.1 years to reach Stage II, while those who have a qualification with its main emphasis on the humanities or economics require only 2.6 years.

What becomes of the higher education graduates when they have completed their studies? Which position can they occupy on the labour market? How does the transition from training to employment take place? How long does this transitional phase last? These delicate and difficult questions are considered in the second part of this survey.

2. The Transition of Higher Education Graduates to Employment: The Pressure of Economic Trends

When presenting the results of this survey we consciously examine the data concerning the transition of higher education graduates to employment. On the one hand this is because this information is available;[15] on the other hand,

---

14   MENRT-DPD (1999) L'état de l'école, 9th Edition, Indicator 25.
15   Our results are based mainly on research conducted by Céreq. In the framework of a survey about the entrance into working life, Céreq conducted a study in 1999 about the first years of graduates, who had completed their studies in 1996, in the workplace. The study concerned graduates, who are French nationals under the age of 35 in 1996 and who completed their studies at either a „Institut universitaire de technologie" (IUT), a „Section de techniciens supérieurs (STS), an institue for engineering or business or who have received a *licence,* a *maitrise* or a *doctorat* (Excluded are the areas of health and social work, an apprenticeship in either the Ministry of Agriculture or Defence or institutes, that pave the way for a career in the the arts or culture.). The research covered 10544 individuals, who were randomly chosen in French institutions. Surveys of the same kind were conducted in 1987, 1991, 1995 and 1997.

the future careers of the graduates is strongly influenced by the direction of their course of study. At the end of the Eighties the transition of higher education graduates to employment took place under favourable conditions. At the beginning of the Nineties, however, the large increase in the number of higher education graduates and the economic crisis had a noticeable effect on the job market for qualified employees. The transition of higher education graduates to employment altered, and after graduation in certain subjects the qualification was no longer so highly regarded in some branches, even though a higher education course generally still continued to represent a solid guarantee against unemployment. Graduates from a DUT or BTS course in the service sector were especially hard hit by the worsening of the status of the jobs they were aiming at. The economic upswing in the past few years has not had an equally favourable effect with regard to every higher education course. The situation of the graduates from elite institutions of higher education and from Stage III of university study is more favourable because they have benefited from the upswing in the new job opportunities. In contrast, the graduates in the humanities are facing a reduction in the number of jobs for teachers.

A diploma degree protects a person against unemployment

Three years after completing their studies 9.5% of the students are unemployed (Chart 4).[16] The figure is twice as high for those leaving secondary school. As in the case of the indicators already mentioned, there are also differences here between the fields of training and courses. While less than 2% of the graduates from schools of engineering are unemployed, at the same point in time 13% of the graduates from Stage II studies are without work. These graduates are directly affected by the reduction in the number of teaching posts.

16   The unemployment figures are calculated from the relation between the number of graduates, who are looking for a job (and have not found one) and the total number of graduates on the work market, who did not continue their studies after 1996.

Chart 4: The development of the unemployment rate of higher education graduates completing their course in 1996 (in %)

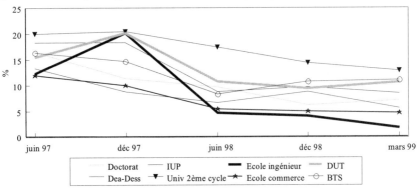

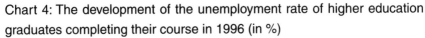

From left to right: June 97, Dec. 97, June 98, Dec 98, March 99; doctorate, IUP, school of engineering, DUT; DEAS-DESS, Stage II univ. studies, business school, BTS. Source: Céreq.

The development of unemployment rates for graduates from schools of engineering and DUT schools, which are predominantly attended by male students, is most certainly connected with the search for employment after completion of military service.

Céreq traditionally calculates two indicators of unemployment.[17] In the first the average length of unemployment before starting the first job is calculated, and in the second indicator all the months of unemployment over the entire period of the study are added together.

On average, higher education graduates are unemployed for 3.6 months before they find their first job. While this value conforms roughly to the

---

17   Unemployment is defined as the situation of looking for a job without currently being employed, while not studying, carrying out national service or while not being part of the workforce.

average in the case of DEA-DESS graduates, the period of unemployment before starting work is to a large extent dependent on the type of training and course of study. This period is distinctly shorter for graduates from a business school (2.4 months), and for graduates from the Stage II university studies it is longer (3.9 months) (Chart 5).

Chart 5: The average duration of unemployment of higher education graduates of 1966 before taking up their first job (in months)

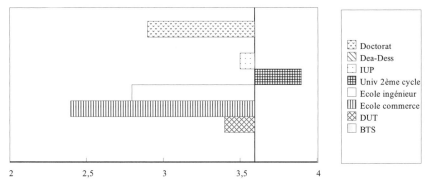

Average = 3.6 months. From top to bottom: doctorate, DEA-DESS, IUP, Stage II university studies, school of engineering, business school, DUT, BTS.
Source: Céreq.

As far as the different university courses are concerned, the graduates from a faculty of arts, whether from a DEA-DESS course or from Stage II, are unemployed for the longest period of time before they get their first job. However, more than 60% of the graduates from these courses avoid unemployment by taking up their first job quickly – essentially through a selection procedure [concours] for teachers. This result can mainly be explained by the behaviour of these graduates, which consists of continuing their studies and at the same time seeking a job. They finish studying as soon as they have found a job or have passed a selection examination.

In the first three years after completion of their training, higher education graduates are unemployed for an average of 4.9 months (Chart 6). Altogether, the duration of unemployment is 3.4 months for graduates from a school of engineering, and 5.4 months for graduates from Stage II of a university course.

Chart 6: The average duration of unemployment of higher education graduates of 1966 in the first three years after completing their training (in months)

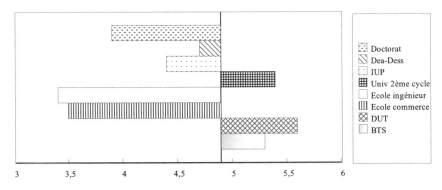

From top to bottom: doctorate, DEA-DESS, IUP, Stage II university studies, school of engineering, business school, DUT, BTS.
Source: Céreq.

The graduates from courses in Law, Economics, the Humanities and Social Sciences have the greatest problems in finding work. Thus 30% of the graduates with a "licence" or a Master's degree in the Humanities and Social Sciences had been unemployed for more than a year during the period when the survey was carried out. The DUT and BTS graduates are also unemployed for a relatively long time (Chart 7).

Chart 7: The total duration of unemployment of higher education graduates of 1966 in the first three years after completing their training (in months)

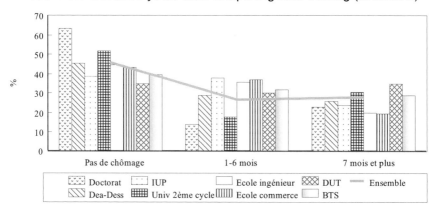

From left to right: not unemployed, unemployed 1-6 months, unemployed more than 7 months; doctorate, IUP, school of engineering, DUT, total; DEA-DESS, Stage II university studies, business school, BTS.
Source: Céreq.

There are many ways of finding employment

Higher education graduates use relatively different methods of finding employment (Graph 8). Even though, in general, mainly spontaneous applications, selection examinations and small advertisements are used, a survey differentiated according to the subjects the graduates have studied shows that there are certain differences: most university graduates (doctorate, DEA-DESS and Stage II studies) take a selection examination in order to find the appropriate job. To a lesser extent they fall back on spontaneous applications; the graduates from business and engineering schools prefer to answer job advertisements, they invest in spontaneous applications and make use of their contacts. The National Employment Agency [ANPE] and the Association for the Employment of Managers (Engineers and Technicians) [APEC] are hardly used at all.

Chart 8: The methods used by graduates of 1966 for finding employment (in %)

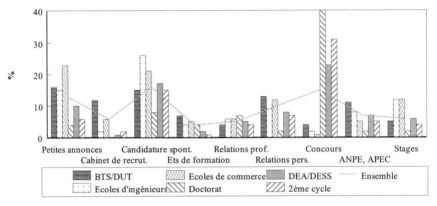

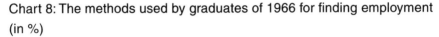

From left to right: job advertisements, spontaneous applications, business connections, selection examinations, work experience; employment office, training institutions, personal connections, ANPE-APEC; BTS/DUT, business schools, DEA/DESS, total, schools of engineering, doctorate, Stage II university studies.
Source: VERGNIES, J.-F., SIGOT, J.-C. (1998) L'insertion professionnelle des diplômés de de l'enseignement supérieur. Enquête 1997 auprès des sortants de 1994, (he transition of graduates to employment. Survey undertaken in 1997 of graduates of 1994) Céreq, Documents Observatoire, No. 137, November.

With the exception of the associations of former pupils, there are actually only very few internal facilities in France which secure and promote the employment of graduates or former students.

Work experience in firms is frequently undertaken by students, but is not sufficient for obtaining a job

Work experience in a firm can be undertaken with a number of different goals in mind. It can be a way of getting to know a firm in a few days, or with longer-term training lasting several months. On average, more than 7 students in 10 do some work experience during the last two years of their studies. Only the graduates from Stage II studies at a university have less professional experience before starting their first job: only 30% of graduates in the Humanities and Social Science have undertaken any work experience in a firm during the two years before obtaining their degree, while the proportion among Business Administration students is about 90%. This difference can predominantly be explained by the vocational goals of the Humanities students, who are aiming at the selection examinations for teachers. In no way does work experience help them to pass the selection examination. At any rate, work experience does not help them to obtain a job. Only in rare cases is work experience the first step towards lasting employment, even though the probability of being employed by the firm is greater the longer the work experience lasts.

	Total duration of work experience (%)	Probability of being employed by the firm (%)
1 to 3 months	44.9	13
3 to 6 months	25.9	21
6 to 12 months	24.5	27
More than 12 months	4.7	31
Total	100	19

Source: VERGNIES, J.-F. (1999) Les diplômés de l'université manquent-ils d'expérience? (Do university graduates lack work experience?) 10th Anniversary of OURIP, Lyon, October 4th and 5th, p. 41.

Paid work while studying is a traditional practise

The number of students who work regularly during their studies is dependent on the level of their studies.[18]

Stage I:	8%
Stage II:	24%
Stage III:	40%

---

18   VERGNIES, J.-F. (1999) Les diplômés de l'université manquent-ils d'expérience? 10th Anniversary of OURIP, Lyon, October 4th and 5th, pp. 37-46.

Students at Stage III frequently earn money as employees, and this represents genuine gainful employment. Three students out of four have jobs that are among the occupations requiring medium-level qualifications or are leading positions: supervisory teachers, researchers etc. One student in four is a blue-collar or white-collar worker: service personnel, clerk, administrative employee etc.

Employment opportunities are to be found essentially in the private sector

Three years after completing their studies, 73% of the higher education graduates are working in the private sector (Chart 9). Differences do exist, however, depending on the subjects studied. In more than 8 out of 10 cases, graduates from engineering and business schools as well as IUP, DUT and BTS work in the private sector. Only those with a doctorate are more frequently employed in the public sector (teaching and research). There are also differences depending on the type of training: while 76% of the Humanities graduates work in the public sector, the figure is only 53% for lawyers and economists. Not everyone can enter the public sector. Some graduates therefore turn again to the private sector and thus compete with graduates from schools of engineering.[19]

---

19   MARTINELLI, D., PAUL, J.-J., PERRET, C. (1998) Emploi public, emploi privé. La difficile
      reconversion des titulaires de thèse, Céreq Bref, No. 146, October.

Chart 9: Sectors in which the graduates of 1966 were employed in march 1999 (%)

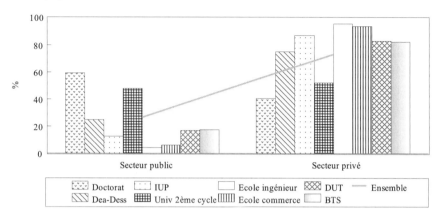

From left to right: public sector, private sector; doctorate, IUP, school of engineering, DUT, total; DEA/DESS, Stage II university studies, business school, BTS.
Source: Céreq.

The public sector includes the state and the public institutions associated with it, as well as regional authorities and hospitals. The public sector includes all private-sector businesses, and also the privatised public services (e.g France Télécom).

Access to the teaching professions is exclusively through selection procedures ("concours"). Only those with a doctorate have access to higher education. Recruitment is at the national level. The preconditions for appointment as a teacher at a primary school (academic competition) and as a teacher in the lower and upper secondary schools and as a grammar-school teacher (secondary level – national competition) are the university entry qualification plus four years of study.

Graduates from Stage II university studies work in various branches depending on their field of specialisation. Thus 91.7% of the graduates in Business Administration work in the private sector, while the greatest opportunities for Humanities and Social Science graduates continue to be within the public sector, and especially in the teaching professions. Among graduates under 30 the number of teachers in the lower and upper secondary schools as well as grammar-school teachers (the most important job opportunity for graduates from Stage II studies at a university) has trebled during the past twelve years. The increase in the number of jobs available for experts in the private sector is also an advantage for graduates under 30. Over the past 12 years the number of computer scientists has trebled and the number of development engineers has doubled.[20]

Jobs tend to be stable and are found in businesses of all sizes

Three years after completing their studies, roughly three higher education graduates out of four have a regular job (permanent contract or post as a civil servant) (Chart 10). In the case of graduates from Stage II university studies and people with a BTS/DUT degree the proportion of fixed-term contracts continues to be fairly high. Graduates with a degree in the Humanities who do not want to become teachers are hit hardest by this fact: in March 1999 barely a third of them had a permanent job.

20   MARTINELLI, D., (1999) Insertion des diplômés: avantage aux grandes écoles et aux troisièmes cycles, 10th Anniversary of OURIP, Lyon, October 4th and 5th, pp. 47-56.

Chart 10: The employment situation in march 1999 for higher education
graduates of 1996 (%)

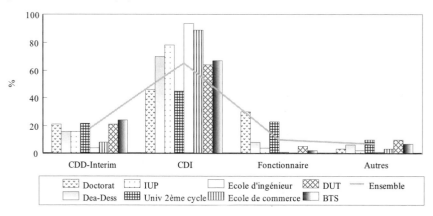

*From left to right: fixed-term contracts/temporary work, permanent contracts, civil servants,
other positions; doctorate, IUP, school of engineering, DUT, total; DEA/DESS, Stage II university
studies, business school, BTS.*
Source: Céreq.

Graduates from schools of engineering work predominantly in large firms
(Chart 11). 43.5% of them work in private-sector firms with more than 500
employees. However, large businesses are not the main career goal of higher
education graduates. Small firms also play a large part in their entry into
professional life and, in addition, they are the main employers of graduates
from Stage II university studies or with a BTS.

Chart 11: Employment according to the firm's size / the situation of the higher education graduates of 1996 in 1999 (%)

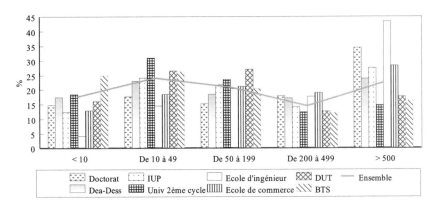

From left to right: <10, between 10 and 49, between 50 and 199, between 200 and 499, >500; doctorate, IUP, school of engineering, DUT, total, DEA/DESS, Stage II university studies, business school, BTS.
Source: Céreq.

The figures on the size of the business refer exclusively to employees in the private sector.

A degree does not always guarantee work in management or in the technical field

A higher education degree traditionally leads to jobs in two main categories. Those who have a university entry qualification and two years of study tend to have jobs requiring a medium-level qualification (technicians, technical employees and clerks etc.). Those who have studied for more than two years after obtaining their university entry qualification tend to work in leading positions and in occupations with an intellectual slant (engineers, teachers, managers in the administration and in the business sector, researchers etc.).[21]

However, a higher education degree does not automatically mean work in a leading position. In March 1998 a graduate from a longer higher education degree course had an 8 in 10 chance of obtaining a leading position or an academic job at the end of his first course of study. Despite the same level of degree, the social background and the fact of being a woman make it even more difficult to find a job that fits the level of the qualification. Women and children of manual workers who have a higher education degree make extensive use of the promotion opportunities offered by the public sector.[22]

Salaries are dependent on the type of degree and the course of study undertaken

Three years after completing their studies, 50% of higher education graduates earn more than FF 9000 (Chart 12). The graduates from the recognized engineering and business schools have the highest salaries (50% earn more than FF 12,500). Graduates from a scientific course of study after completion of Stage III, who profit from the increase in the numbers of scientific and technical jobs, are also very well paid (50% earn more than FF 11,500) when compared with the Stage III graduates who have studied a different subject. The DEA/DESS graduates who had a job in March 1999 earned an average of FF 10,700 i.e. one half earned more and the other half earned less than this sum.

---

21 MARTINELLI, D., (1999) Insertion des diplômés: avantage aux grandes écoles et aux troisièmes cycles, 10th Anniversary of OURIP, Lyon, October 4th and 5th, pp. 47-56.
22 MENRT-DPD (1999) L'état de l'école, 9th Edition, Indicator 11.

Chart 12: Average monthly net salary of the higher education graduates of 1996 in 1999 according to course of study (in FF)

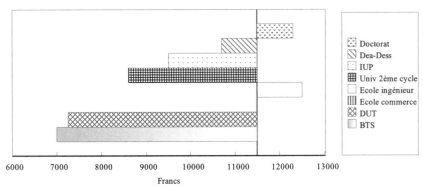

Average salary = FF 11,500. From top to bottom: doctorate, DEA/DESS, IUP, Stage II university studies, school of engineering, business school, DUT, BTS, total.
Source: Céreq.

The figures show the average monthly net salary including any possible bonus.

Conclusions

The second half of the twentieth century will go down in the history of education as a period in which higher education expanded and underwent an unusually large qualitative change. The higher education sector offers a broad range of institutions whose tasks and basic activities lie in enabling an increasing number of people to receive training at the higher education level which fulfils the expectations of a constantly changing labour market. Today, however, the French higher education sector is confronted by a number of challenges: the increasing demand for education and training, the diversification of the subjects taught, the stagnation of the expenditure on education, the rapid change in occupations and responsibilities etc.

As a result of the dramatic changes in the world of work, higher education graduates must now be prepared to change their jobs, be retrained and to obtain new qualifications in the course of their working life. Against this background the higher education sector must redefine its relations with the world of work. In the medium term the job opportunities for young managers in the private sector seem to be favourable. The new technologies as well as the fact that firms are depending more and more on consulting and advice means that the positions for engineers and managers are undergoing a continuing upswing. For the teaching professions, on the other hand, the future does not seem to be so favourable. This is due, in particular, to the falling numbers of pupils.

Abbreviations:

ANPE	National Employment Agency
APEC	Association for the Employment of Managers (Engineers and Technicians)
BTS	Higher Technician's Diploma
CEREQ	Institute for Qualification Research
CPGE	Preparatory Classes for the "Grandes Écoles" (Elite Academies)
DEA	Diploma Degree after Five Years of Study in a Specialized Field (precondition for doctorate)
DESS	Diploma Degree after Five Years of Study in a Specialized Field
DEUG	Intermediate Examination after Two Years of Study
DPD	Directorate of Futurology and Development
DUT	University Diploma on Completion of a Two to Three-Year Course at a Scientific-Technical Institution of Higher Education
IUP	Vocational Institute Attached to a University
IUT	Technical Institute Attached to a University
IUFM	Teacher Training Colleges Attached to a University
MENRT	Ministry of Education, Research and Technology
MST	Master of Natural Sciences and Technology
STS	Higher Technical School

BIBLIOGRAPHY

AFFICHARD, J. (1981) *Quels emplois après l'école : la valeur des titres scolaires depuis 1973*, in : Économie et statistique, n°134, juin, pp. 7-26.

ARROW, K.-J. (1973) *Higher Education as a Filter*, in : Journal of Public Economics, vol. 2, n°3, juillet, pp. 193-216.

ATTALI, J. (1997) *Pour un modèle européen d'enseignement supérieur*, rapport pour le MENRT.

BAUDELOT, C., GLAUDE, M. (1989) *Les diplômes se dévaluent-ils en se multipliant ?*, in : Économie et Statistique, n°225, pp. 3-16.

BECKER, G.S. (1964) *Human Capital. A Theoretical and Empirical Analysis with Special Reference to Education*, Columbia University Press, New York.

BERNADET, S. (1998) *Les étudiants inscrits à l'université en 1997-98*, MENRT-DPD, Note d'information, n°98.09, mai.

BERTHELOT, J.-M. (1990) *Les effets pervers de l'expansion des enseignements supérieurs. Le cas de la France*, in : Sociétés Contemporaines, n°4, pp. 109-122.

BIDEAULT, M., ROSSI, P. (1999) *Les personnels enseignants de l'enseignement supérieur public*, MENRT-DPD, Note d'information, n°99.25, juillet.

BIENAYMÉ, A. (1988) *La demande d'enseignement supérieur*, in : Revue d'économie politique, 98ème année, n°1, pp. 60-65.

CANALS, V. (1998) *Des motivations des étudiants. Les inscrits en première année de DEUG à l'Université Paul Valéry en 1997-98*, rapport réalisé pour le compte de l'Observatoire de la Vie Étudiante, Montpellier III.

COUET, C., LEMAIRE, S. (1997) *La rentrée 1997 dans l'enseignement supérieur*, MENRT-DPD, Note d'information, n°97.45, novembre.

DIEBOLT, C. ; EL MURR, B. (1999) *Educational Development and Labour Markets. The Case of Higher Education in Germany, 1820-1941*, First Conference on German Cliometrics, Toronto, 23-26 septembre.

DUBOIS, M., ROUSSEAU, B. (1997) *L'enseignement supérieur. Evolution de 1980 à 1996*, MENRT-DPD, Note d'information, n°97.39, septembre.

DUBOIS, M., RAULIN, E. (1997) *L'entrée dans l'enseignement supérieur : permanences et changements 1982-1996*, MENRT-DPD, Éducation & formations, Le premier cycle du supérieur, n°50, juin, pp. 11-20.

FONDEUR, Y., MINNI, C. (1999) *Emploi des jeunes et conjoncture*, Dares, Premières informations et Premières synthèses, n°51.1, 99.12.

FORGEOT, G., GAUTIÉ, J. (1997) *Insertion professionnelle des jeunes et processus de déclassement*, in : Économie et statistique, n°304-305, pp. 53-74.

FREEMAN, R. (1971) *The Market for College-Trained Manpower. A Study in the Economics of Career Choice*, Harvard University Press, Cambridge.

GAMEL, C. (1998) *Le diplôme, un signal en voie de dépréciation? Le modèle de Spence réexaminé*, Greqam, Working paper, n°98C07, juin.

LEMAIRE, S. (1997) *Après le bac, pourquoi l'université?*, MENRT-DPD, Éducation & formations, *Le premier cycle du supérieur*, n°50, juin, pp. 23-31.

LEMAIRE, S. (1998) *Que deviennent les bacheliers après leur bac?*, MENRT-DPD, Note d'information, n°98.05, mars.

LÉVY-GARBOUA, L. (1979) *Marché du travail et marché de l'enseignement supérieur*, in : Eicher, J.-C., Lévy-Garboua, L. (eds) *Economique de l'éducation*, Economica, Paris, pp. 178-210.

MARTINELLI, D. (1994) *Diplômés de l'université. Insertion au début des années 90*, Céreq, Documents Observatoire, n°100, octobre.

MARTINELLI, D. (1999) *Insertion des diplômés : avantage aux grandes écoles et aux troisièmes cycles*, 10ème anniversaire de l'OURIP, 4 et 5 octobre, Lyon, pp. 47-56.

MARTINELLI, D., VERGNIES, J.-F. (1995) *L'insertion professionnelle des diplômés de l'enseignement supérieur se dégrade*, in : Céreq Bref, n°107, mars.

MARTINELLI, D., PAUL, J.-J., PERRET, C. (1998) *Emploi public, emploi privé. La difficile reconversion des titulaires de thèse*, Céreq Bref, n°146, octobre.

MARTINELLI, D., VERGNIES, J.-F. (1999) *Diplômés de l'enseignement supérieur. La reprise de l'emploi ne profite pas à toutes les filières*, Céreq, Bref, n°156, septembre.

MARTINELLI, D., VERGNIES, J.-F., MOLINARI, M. (1999) *L'enquête Enseignement supérieur*, in : Céreq, http://www.cereq.fr

MESNARD, O., RAGOUCY, C., BERREUR, C. (1999) *Le coût de l'éducation en 1998*, MENRT-DPD, Note d'information, n°99.37, octobre.

MINNI, C. POULET-COULIBANDO, P. (1999) *L'évolution de la scolarité et de l'insertion professionnelle des jeunes (1996-1998), 1. Les sortants du système éducatif*, MENRT-DPD, Note d'information, n°99.07, avril.

MINNI, C. POULET-COULIBANDO, P. (1999) *L'évolution de la scolarité et de l'insertion professionnelle des jeunes (1996-1998), 2. Les emplois offerts*, MENRT-DPD, Note d'information n°99.08, avril.

MINODIER, F. (1999) *La scolarisation des jeunes de 16 à 25 ans en 1997-1998*, MENRT-DPD, Note d'information, n°99.32, septembre.

MENRT-DPD (1997) *Repères et références statistiques*.

MENRT-DPD (1997) *L'état de l'école 1997*, 7ème édition.

MENRT-DPD (1999) *L'état de l'école 1999*, 9ème édition.

MENRT-DPD (2000) *Les chiffres clé de l'enseignement supérieur.*

ORIVEL, F. (1974) *Le choix d'une filière universitaire : un arbitrage entre consommation et investissement ?* Colloque Credoc – Iredu, Paris.

PIROT, P., RAULIN, E. (1997) *Les étudiants inscrits à l'université en 1996-97,* MENRT-DPD, Note d'information, n°97.15, mars.

POULET, P., MINNI, C., DUCATEZ, S. (1996) *Après le baccalauréat, quelles études, quels emplois?,* in : MENRT-DPD, Note d'information, n°96.05, février.

ROUSSEAU, B., SABOULIN, (de) M. (1998) *Les effectifs de l'enseignement supérieur au cours des années 90,* MENRT-DPD. Note d'information, n°98.34, novembre.

VERDIER, E. (1997) *En France, les diplômes de l'enseignement supérieur rentre dans le rang ?* in : Formation Professionnelle, Revue européenne, Cedefop, n°10, avril, pp. 17-27.

VERGNIES, J.-F. (1997) *Diplômés de l'enseignement supérieur. Insertion des étudiants sortis en 1992,* Céreq, Documents Observatoire, n°122, janvier.

VERGNIES, J.-F. (1999) *Les diplômés de l'université manquent-ils d'expérience?* 10ème anniversaire de l'OURIP, 4 et 5 octobre, Lyon, pp. 37-46.

VERGNIES, J.-F., SIGOT, J.-C. (1998) *L'insertion professionnelle des diplômés de l'enseignement supérieur. Enquête 1997 auprès des sortants de 1994,* Céreq, Documents Observatoire, n°137, novembre.

VINCENS, J. (1999) *Les caractéristiques de l'enseignement supérieur de masse en France,* LIRHE, note n°219, juin.

Germany

Holger Ehlert and Heidi Cordier

As in other countries, the institutions of higher education and the labour market in the Federal Republic of Germany exist as autonomous systems with their own laws that have become internally independent. On the one hand, the institutions of higher education in Germany function as corporations under public law, and on the other hand, as state institutions. The institutions of higher education organize their internal processes on the basis of institutional autonomy and within the framework of performing their tasks as laid down by the state. The principle of state sovereignty in cultural affairs is laid down in the Constitution (Articles 30 and 70). The General Act on Higher Education, however, provides the Federal Government with certain responsibilities in the field of higher education. The budgets of each of the higher education institutions consist of basic funding by the state and so-called competitive additional funding by outside bodies.

The higher education system in the Federal Republic is essentially the concern of the sixteen states *(Länder)*.[1] The General Act on Higher Education *(Hochschulrahmengesetz)*, passed in January 1976, was a federal law created

---

1   On the principle of state sovereignty in cultural affairs see, for example, Oehler, Christoph: Hochschulentwicklung in der Bundesrepublik Deutschland seit 1945. Frankfurt / New York, 1989; Peisert, Hansgert / Framhein, Gerhild: Das Hochschulsystem in Deutschland, published by the Federal Ministry of Education, Science, Research and Technology (now the Federal Ministry of Education and Research). Bonn, 2nd ed. 1997, p. 5ff; Bundeszentrale für politische Bildung (ed.): Das föderative System der Bundesrepublik Deutschland. Bonn, 1977.
2   Most recently amended in August 1988. Cf. Federal Ministry of Education and Research (ed.): Hochschulrahmengesetz (HRG). Bonn, 1999.

in order to guarantee the uniformity of the higher education system.[3] In particular, the guidelines refer to the organisation of higher education institutions and their administration, admission to higher education, the personnel structure and the participation of the members in the decision-making bodies of their higher education institution. The General Act on Higher Education passed by the federal government allows the individual states room to formulate regulations specific to their needs. Amongst other things, preparation for a future occupation and the teaching of the specialist knowledge, abilities and methods required for this are laid down in the General Act on Education as the goals of a course of study.[4] In the Federal Republic of Germany the system of higher education is an integral part of the education system. This can be explained best with the aid of a diagram of the whole system:[5]

---

3   As laid down in the Unification Treaty, this also applies to the five new states which formerly constituted the GDR. See also: Hollerith, Josef: Hochschulrahmengesetz-Kompetenz des Bundes. In: Hollerith, Josef (ed.): Leistungsfähige Hochschulen – aber wie? Neuwied, 1997, pp. 243-251.
4   Cf. ibid.: Hochschulrahmengesetz §2, Para. 1.
5   Grund- und Strukturdaten 1999/2000. Ed. by the Federal Ministry of Education and Research. Bonn, 2000, pp. 10-11.

Basic structure of the education system in the Federal Republic of Germany

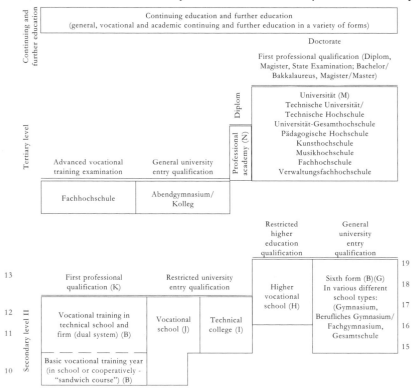

Remarks:

Schematized representation of the education system. The scheme of the secondary level is based on the distribution of the average number of pupils in the Federal Republic in 1988: Secondary school 22.8%, Secondary modern school 26.3%, Gymnasium 29.0%, Integrated comprehensive 9.3%. Interchangeability between the school types and recognition of school leaving certificates is basically guaranteed when the conditions agreed between the individual states have been fulfilled. The duration of full-time schooling (compulsory school attendance for all children) is 9 years, in 4 states it is 10 years, and the subsequent compulsory part-time schooling (compulsory vocational school attendance) is 3 years.

(A) In some states there are special forms of transition from the kindergarten to the primary school (pre-school classes, school kindergartens). In Berlin and Brandenburg the primary school lasts for 6 years.

(B) Schooling of the handicapped in accordance with the type of handicap in special forms of vocational schools and of those schools providing a general education, sometimes also together with the non-handicapped. The school type differs from one state to another (*Sonderschule / Schule für Behinderte / Förderschule*).

(C) Independent of their organizational classification, the 5th and 6th years constitute a phase of special support, observation and orientation concerning the further steps and main points of emphasis in a child's education. In some states the *Orientierungsstufe* (orientatation level) or *Förderstufe* (support level) is organized as an independent school type.

(D) School careers at the *Hauptschule* and *Realschule* are also offered at school types with several different school career types. These schools have different names depending on the state, some of which are *Mittelschule* (Saxony), *Regelschule* (Thüringen), *Sekundarschule* (Saxony-Anhalt), *Erweiterte Realschule* (Saarland), *Integrierte Haupt- und Realschule* (Hamburg), *Verbundene Haupt- und Realschule* (Hesse, Mecklenburg-West Pomerania), and *Regionale Schule* (Rhineland-Palatinate), as well as the *Gesamtschule* (comprehensive school).

(E) The *Gymnasium* (grammar school) school career is also offered at the *Gesamtschule* (comprehensive school). In the *kooperative Gesamtschule* and in the *Schulzentrum* (Bremen) the three school careers (those of the *Hauptschule, Realschule* and *Gymnasium*) are gathered under one roof both for educational and organizational purposes, and in the *integrierte Gesamtschule* they form one educational and organizational unit. The establishment of *Gesamtschulen* has been organized differently from one state to another.

(F) The general school leaving certificates after years 9 and 10 have different names in different states. It is possible to obtain these certificates later at night school.

(G) The admission requirement is the formal entitlement to attend a sixth form at a *Gymnasium*. This is normally obtained after the 10th school year. The general university entry qualification is normally obtained after the 13th school year. In Saxony and Thuringia the general university entry qualification is obtained after the 12th school year, and in other states it can be obtained after 12 years within the framework of innovatory school experiments.

(H) So far, the *Berufsoberschule / Erweiterte Fachoberschule* only exists in a few states and offers school leavers who have passed the first public examination in secondary school and who have completed vocational training, or who have worked in a job for five years, the possibility of obtaining the *Fachgebundene Hochschulreife* (restricted higher education qualification). If knowledge of a second foreign language can be provided, then it is possible to obtain the general university entry qualification.

(I) The *Fachoberschule* is a 2-year school type which, building on the first public examination in secondary school in the 11th and 12th years, leads to the *Fachhochschulreife* (restricted higher education qualification). Those who have passed the first public examination in secondary school *(Realschulabschluss)* and who have completed vocational training can enter the 12th year direct.

(J) *Berufsfachschulen* (vocational schools) are vocational full-time schools of different kinds with regard to their admission requirements, the length of their courses and their leaving certificates. There is a special form of the 2-year vocational school with the first public examination in secondary school *(Realschulabschluss)* which leads to the certificate *"staatlich geprüfter Assistent"* (state-examined assistant). There is also the one-year or two-year *Berufsfachschule* (vocational school) which provides basic vocational training. The *Fachhochschulreife* (restricted higher education qualification) can be obtained under certain circumstances, including a course lasting at least two years.

(K) In addition to the first professional qualification, under certain circumstances the *Hauptschulabschluss* (successful completion of the secondary modern school) or the *Mittlerer Abchulabschluss* (successful completion of the middle school).

(L) *Fachschulen* (vocational schools) provide vocational training (duration 1-3 years) and, as a matter of principle, require the previous completion of the relevant vocational training in an occupation with recognized training and work in the appropriate field. Under certain circumstances it is possible, in addition, to obtain the *Fachhochschulreife* (restricted higher education qualification). Within the framework of the International Standard Classification of Education (ISCED97) the *Fachschulen* belong to the tertiary sector.

(M) Including higher education institutions with single degree-level courses (e.g. theology, philosophy, medicine, public adminstration, physical education).

(N) The *Berufsakademie* (professional academy) is an institution within the tertiary sector in seven states. It links specialist training at a *Studienakademie* with practical vocational training in a firm in accordance with the dual system.

January 2000

The higher education system in Germany follows on from the primary and secondary stages; there, different school leaving qualifications are required for admission to the different types of higher education institution. The general university entry qualification *(Abitur)* or restricted higher education entry qualification *(Fachgebundene Hochschulreife)* are required for study at universities, the degree courses at the comprehensive universities, and in most cases courses at the colleges of fine arts. The restricted university entry qualification *(Fachhochschulreife)* is required for study at universities of applied sciences *(Fachhochschulen)* and the corresponding courses at comprehensive universities. In principle, the general university entry qualification *(Abitur)* permits a student to study any subject at every institution of higher education (it includes the restricted university entry qualification). The *Abitur* is predominately obtained through the leaving certificate of the general *Gymnasium*.

The classic path to the restricted university entry qualification *(Fachhochschulreife)* is via a completed course of vocational training.[6] In general, the *Fachhochschulreife* is subsequently obtained at a technical college *(Fachoberschule)*, but it can also be obtained at other institutions (e.g. at a vocational school *(Fachschule)*. In some states qualified employees without a higher education entry qualification have the opportunity of beginning a degree course on the basis of a university admission examination or an examination for the specially gifted. However, this special path still remains the exception, and less than one percent of students make use of it. In addition to the *Abitur*, special artistic talent is required (entrance examination) for a person to be able to study at a college of fine arts, and in most states there are special regulations which permit a person to start studying without the *Abitur* provided

---

6   On vocational training cf. Bundesinstitut für Berufsbildung: Berufsbildungsbericht 1999. Bonn, 2000.

that he or she has special artistic talent. In most cases, relevant work experience or the appropriate vocational experience are required before a degree course can be started at a university of applied sciences when the prospective student has the general university entrance qualification *(Abitur)*.

The *Abitur* at the *Gymnasium* is the most frequently chosen path to a degree course at an institution of higher education.[7] Quantitatively, the *Fachhochschulreife* has become less important in the last few years. Only 41% of newly enrolled students start studying immediately after leaving school. The reasons for this delay are: military service/alternative civilian service (for men), employment and work experience, time spent abroad, admission restrictions and the later desire to begin a degree course.[8] A total of 26% of all newly enrolled students in the winter semester 1998/99 had completed vocational training before they started studying; in the wintersemester 1993/94 this figure had been as high as 38%.[9] In most cases there is a connection between the apprenticeship and the subject studied.[10] For years, the average age of newly enrolled students has remained almost constant at 22.[11] In the meantime, more than half (55%) of the newly enrolled students at universities of applied sciences have *Abitur*. This means that studying at a university of applied sciences is becoming increasingly attractive for school leavers with *Abitur*; in 1975 only 19% of the students at a university of applied sciences had their *Abitur*; in 1983/84 the figure was already 34%.[12] In 1998 there were

---

7   Cf. Lewin, Karl et al.: Studienanfänger im Wintersemester 1998/99. HIS-Hochschulplanung 138. Hannover, 1999, p. 39.

8   The start of a degree course is postponed for an average of almost three years if it is not begun immediately after leaving school.

9   Cf. Hochschule-Informations-System. HIS Kurzinformation A7/99. Hannover, 1999, p. 6.

10   Cf. Cordier, Heidi: Berufsausbildung als Einstieg in das Studium: Relevant nur für bestimmte Fächer. HIS-Kurzinformation A4/95. Hannover, 1995.

11   Lewin, Karl et al.: Studienanfänger im Wintersemester 1998/99. Ibid.

12   Ibid.

roughly 327,100 school leavers with a university entry qualification in Germany, 244,900 of whom had the general university entry qualification and 82,100 the restricted university entry qualification. The proportion of the population of one age group who had a higher education entrance qualification (average for the age group of the 18 to 21-year-olds) was 36.2% in 1998.[13] This reveals the increasing participation in education – in 1980 the comparable figure was 22.4%.[14] In the academic year 1998 a total of 271,999 people in Germany began a degree course for the first time. In 1998 the number of newly enrolled students, defined as the proportion of the age group of 18-year-olds to under 22-year-olds, amounted to 30.7% within Germany as a whole (33.1% in the "old" states, and 23.5% in the "new" states). In the winter semester 1998/99 roughly 1,801,000 students were enrolled at an institution of higher education in Germany, of whom 800,927 or 44.5% were women). On average, the students were 26.7 years old.

The following table[15] provides information about students and newly enrolled students according to type of higher education institution and gender between 1980 and 1998:

---

13 Cf. Grund- und Strukturdaten 1999/2000. Ibid.
14 By comparison, until the beginning of the sixties a mere 5% of an age group decided in favour of a degree course in the Federal Republic.
15 In: Grund- und Strukturdaten 1999/2000. Ibid. p. 140.

Newly enrolled students according to type of higher education institution

	total		of whom at			
			universities	colleges of fine arts	universities of applied sciences total	of whom at civil service colleges
year	thousands	percent	thousands	thousands	thousands	thousands
Germans and foreigners						
Former Federal Republic						
1980	190.0	19.5	135.2	3.1	51.7	8.1
1990	277,9	30,4	194,8	3,1	80,0	12,5
1991	271,4	33,7	185,3	2,9	51,7	14,6
1992	257,1	33,6	173,9	2,9	80,0	15,9
1993	242,7	33,7	163,3	3,0	83,2	15,6
1994	230,0	33,1	155,3	2,9	80,4	13,4
New states						
1990	39,5	19,3	38,3	1,3	-	-
1991	36,7	19,9	31,1	1,4	4,2	0,5
1992	33,7	19,6	21,8	0,7	11,1	1,8
1993	36,9	22,9	21,2	0,7	15,0	2,2
1994	37,9	23,5	22,6	0,8	14,6	1,6
Germany						
1990	317,4	29,7	233,1	4,4	80,0	12,5
1991	308,1	31,1	216,4	4,3	87,4	15,1
1992	290,8	31,1	195,7	3,6	91,5	17,7
1993	279,6	31,7	184,4	3,7	91,5	17,9
1994	167,9	31,3	177,9	3,7	86,4	15,0
1995	262,4	30,4	176,2	3,7	82,5	14,4
1996	167,5	30,6	183,2	3,7	80,6	10,6
1997	267,4	30,0	182,3	3,9	81,3	9,8
1998	272,5	30,7	182,9	3,9	85,7	9,8
Germans						
Former Federal Republic						
1980	179,7	19,7	124,6	2,5	52,6	11,1
1990	253,6	30,9	175,0	2,3	76,3	12,5
1991	244,2	35,4	163,63	2,0	79,0	14,6
1992	227,2	35,7	149,8	1,9	75,6	15,9
1993	210,5	35,7	137,1	1,9	71,5	15,6
1994	196,7	34,6	128,5	1,8	66,4	13,4
New states						
1990	38,4	19,1	37,2	1,2	-	-
1991	35,6	19,6	30,1	1,3	4,2	0,5
1992	31,4	18,6	19,8	0,6	11,0	1,8
1993	34,2	21,7	18,81	0,6	14,8	2,2
1994	34,4	21,8	19,6	0,7	14,2	1,6
Germany						
1990	292,0	30,3	212,2	3,6	76,3	12,5
1991	279,9	32,1	193,4	3,3	83,2	15,1
1992	258,7	32,1	169,6	2,5	86,5	17,7
1993	244,6	32,7	155,9	2,5	86,2	17,9
1994	231,1	31,8	148,0	2,5	80,6	15,0
1995	125,6	30,7	146,5	2,6	76,6	14,1
1996	229,2	30,6	152,5	2,5	74,2	10,6
1997	227,3	30,3	150,4	2,5	74,4	9,8
1998	228,3	30,2	148,0	2,4	77,9	9,8

Year: summer and following winter semester.

Percent: Until 1996 as a percentage of the average of an age group of 18-year-olds to under 22-year-olds, after 1997 of the 19-year-olds to the population aged under 25.

In Germany there are currently a total of 335 institutions of higher education with roughly 1.8 million students. This figure includes 76 – mostly smaller – non-state institutions of higher education in which a total of 40,000 students (i.e. roughly 2% of all students) are enrolled.[16] This means that the higher education system in Germany consists predominantly – a figure of more than 80% – of state institutions of higher education. These institutions have been established by the individual state in which they are located, and they are funded essentially through the science budget of this state.[17] This paper will focus mainly on them.[18] As a result of numerous examples of the founding of new institutions of higher education and the refounding of old ones during the period since the unification of the two Germanies, the structure of higher education in the old and new states is now essentially identical.[19] The institutions of higher education in Germany are subdivided into academic departments, sections or faculties and can be split into three groups:

16   Cf. Federal Ministry of Education and Research: Nichtstaatliche Hochschulen in der Bundesrepublik Deutschland. Bonn, 1998.
      A good overview of the degree courses at non-state institutions of higher education can be ordered online on the internet from the Federal Ministry of Education and Research under: (http://www.bmbf.de).
17   Cf. Peissert/Framheim: loc. cit., p. 54ff.
18   The *HRK-Hochschulkompass* offers a very good overview of German institutions of higher education on the Internet, and it also provides links to the information pages of the individual institutions under: (http://www.hochschulkompass.hrk.de).
      The Federal Institute of Labour's data bank "KURS" on training and continuing education is also to be recommended. In addition to a large amount of information on vocational training and continuing education it provides information about all the courses offered by institutions of higher education. The address is: (http://www.arbeitsamt.de).
19   Cf. Buck-Bechler, Gertraude / Schaefer, Hans-Dieter / Wagemann, Carl-Hellmut: Hochschulen in den neuen Ländern der Bundesrepublik Deutschland. Weinheim, 1997.

1. Universities and institutions of higher education with comparable tasks

Universities, comprehensive universities,[20] colleges of education,[21] technical universities, theological colleges, church-sponsored colleges,[22] universities of the federal armed forces,[23] medical, veterinary and sports colleges as well as open learning universities.

Research and the right to award academic degrees, especially doctorates *(Promotionsrecht)* and the qualification to do professsorial teaching and research in a particular field *(Habilitationsrecht[24])*, are among the traditional and statutory rights of the universities which characterize their status as "academic" universities. By far the most students still study at universities.

---

20   The comprehensive universities, which have developed since 1970, are to be found only in the states of Hesse (GH Kassel) and North Rhine-Westphalia (five comprehensive universities as well as the Hagen Open Learning University as a special form). Comprehensive universities include the training courses offered at universities and universities of applied sciences and, in part, of colleges of fine arts. In addition to university degree courses and application-orientated degree courses as offered at universities of applied sciences, the comprehensive universities offer integrated courses in a number of subjects with common basic studies and qualifications at various different levels. Like universities, comprehensive universities have the right to confer doctorates and habilitations. See also Blömeke, Sigrid: Die Universität-Gesamthochschule. Eine Spezialität der nordrhein-westfälischen Hochschullandschaft. In: Ministerium für Wissenschaft und Forschung Nordrhein-Westfalen (Ed.): Gaudeamus ... Das Hochschulland wird 50. Düsseldorf, 1996. At the present time the conversion of comprehensive universities into universities is increasingly becoming a topic of discussion regarding education policy in the relevant *Länder*.

21   The colleges of education are mostly university-status institutions with the right to confer doctorates. Since 1994 they have only still existed as independent institutions in Baden-Württemberg. In other *Länder* they have been incorporated into comprehensive universities or universities.

22   Theologians are trained at the church-sponsored colleges (Protestant) and the theological colleges (Catholic) as well as at the appropriate university faculties.

23   At the universities of the federal armed forces officers and officer cadets receive a university education in degree courses as offered at universities or universities of applied sciences. The degrees obtained are of the same value as degrees from other universities.

24   The habilitation serves as the proof of a person's qualification to do professorial teaching and research. The habilitation procedure is carried out as an academic procedure and, in addition to the habilitation thesis, it includes a public lecture and an academic colloquium.

The time it takes to complete a course (nominal course length) up to the first degree at a university is in most cases between 4 and 5 years, and 6 years for medicine. The course is generally divided basic studies *(Grundstudium)* lasting 4 or 5 semesters (ending with an intermediate examination) and the main studies *(Hauptstudium)* of appropriate length. As a rule, humanities, theology, economics, law, social science, engineering sciences, natural sciences, medicine and the various teacher training courses can be studied at universities, comprehensive universities and technical universities.

2. Universities of applied sciences[25]

On the one hand, these comprise general universities of applied sciences and, on the other hand, civil service colleges for the training of future civil servants. The universities of applied sciences were established around 1970 on the basis of an agreement between the states.[26] They incorporated the former engineering colleges and other higher vocational schools, in particular for economics, social education and community work, design and agriculture, which were formerly part of the vocational secondary school system. The main focus of the universities of applied sciences still lies in these subjects, and thus their range of courses is not as broad as that of the universities. Courses at universities of applied sciences are distinguished from those at universities by their particular relevance to practice, shorter course duration and the stricter organization of the courses. Their clear focal point lies in practice-orientated and application-orientated training. Accordingly, research tasks play a smaller role at universities of applied sciences; as a rule, the laws

---

25 Roughly half the institutions of higher education in Germany are general universities of applied sciences, at which the *Diplom* is the degree awarded on completion of a student's studies. The main fields of study offered by universities of applied sciences are applied social studies, engineering, agriculture, design and, since only recently, nursing.

26 Cf. Oehler, Christoph: loc. cit., p. 103ff.

of the state in which they are situated stipulate their task of training and restrict them to application-orientated research and development. The standard course length including the time required for examinations lies mostly between three and four and a half years at universities of applied sciences. In some states this includes either one or two placement semesters. Overall, the degree courses here are shorter than at the universities with the classic *Magister* and *Diplom* degree courses. The degree course is divided into basic studies and main studies. The basic studies are completed with an intermediate or interim examination. The main studies are completed with the *Diplom*, for which oral and written examinations have to be passed and an application-orientated dissertation written. In some states a degree from a university of applied sciences provides direct access to studying for a doctorate.

3. Colleges of fine arts and colleges of music

In the whole of Germany there are a total of 48 institutions of higher education which offer courses in the artistic field. Due to their special admission procedures and the organization of their courses they are not comparable with the other types of higher education institutions. Their admission procedures differ in each particular case, and can be based on proof of special ability or on artistic aptitude tests. The possible degrees are the higher education institution's own examinations, the *Diplom*, formal recognition as a master-class artist or musician, or the state examination, or, to a limited extent, also foreign degrees.[27]

---

27   Cf. Studienangebote deutscher Hochschulen. Published by the Hochschulrektorenkonferenz (HRK). Bonn, 2000, p. 3.

Overview (in thousands) (B) of the number of students at institutions of higher education according to type of institution (A)[28]

Year (winter semester)	1992/93	1997/98	1998/99	1999/00 (C)
Students at ...				
Institutions of higher education				
total	1834,3	1824,1	1801,2	1777,8
- of whom women	728,9	794,5	801,3	804,4
proportion in %	39,7	43,6	44,5	45,2
- of whom foreign students	124,6	158,5	166,9	173,8
proportion in %	6,8	8,7	9,2	9,8
- of whom newly enrolled students	244,4	226,0	230,8	248,3
Universities and comprehensive universities (D)				
total	1385,3	1356,8	1335,0	1290,9
- of whom women	586,3	628,9	640,1	614,8
proportion in %	42,3	46,3	47,9	47,6
- of whom foreign students	99,1	122,4	132,7	133,8
proportion in %	7,2	9.0	9,9	10,4
- of whom newly enrolled students	165,9	155,5	15,2	164,0
Colleges of fine arts and colleges of music				
total	29,3	29,8	29,8	30,2
- of whom women	15,0	16,3	16,4	16,9
proportion in %	51,2	54,6	55,0	56,0
- of whom foreign students	3,8	5,5	6,0	6,3
proportion in %	13,1	18,6	20,1	20,9
- of whom newly enrolled students	3,0	3,3	3,3	3,6
Universities of applied sciences				
total	372,4	399,3	403,2	411,2
- of whom women	105,7	132,8	140,1	147,8
proportion in %	28,4	33,3	34,7	35,9
- of whom foreign students	21,7	30,5	32,3	34,2
proportion in %	5,8	7,6	8,0	8,3
- of whom newly enrolled students	59,98	59,0	63,2	68,1
Civil service colleges				
total	47,3	38,2	33,3	32,0
- of whom women	21,9	16,6	14,7	14,6
proportion in %	46,2	43,4	44,1	45,6
- of whom newly enrolled students	15,7	8,2	8,1	8,5

(A) Newly enrolled students in their 1st semester at an institution of higher education
(B) Differences from rounding up/down of figures
(C) Preliminary report
(D) Including colleges of education and theological colleges
Figure not completely cited.

28   In: Studien- & Berufswahl. Ibid. p. 52.

Deviating from a student's fundamental entitlement to study any subject at a institution of higher education of his or her choice once he or she has obtained the general university entry qualification *(Hochschulreife)*,[29] due to the increasing demand many institutions of higher education introduced admissions restrictions *(numerus clausus)* after the mid-sixties (especially in medical subjects and the natural sciences). In its judgement on *numerus clausus* in 1972, the Federal Constitutional Court laid down that admissions restrictions at institutions of higher education may only be introduced after the teaching capacity has been completely exhausted, and that the selection and distribution of scarce places must be undertaken in a proper manner and while taking into account, as far as possible, the individual's choice of location for his or her training. The perspectives and expectations of labour market policy are thus not a reason for applying admissions restrictions. As a consequence of the Federal Constitutional Court's judgement the federal states set up the Central Office for Allocating Admissions (ZVS) in Dortmund, which since then has carried out the distribution procedures for degree courses with admissions restrictions throughout the Federal Republic. In addition, there are local admissions restrictions for individual degree courses, above all at the universities of applied sciences. In this case, the institution of higher education itself decides on the admission, as a rule with the aid of the criteria of the grade obtained in the *Abitur* and the time spent waiting for the allocation of a place. In a political initiative of the federal and state heads of government it was decided in 1977 that admission to higher education institutions should generally be kept open for the subsequent years with high birthrates - despite insufficient space and personnel. This decision to "open up the institutions of higher education" consciously accepted overcrowding in order to do justice to the demand for education and training that would be made by the

---

29   Based on the free choice of place of work and training guaranteed in the German
       Constitution.

prospective students from years with high birthrates. Additional funds were made available for a fixed period of time in some of the states, and this has been complemented since the end of the eighties by higher education schemes established by the federal and state governments. It was possible in this way to avoid an overall system of admissions restrictions. A number of degree courses were subsequently removed from the central allocation process and are once again "freely" accessible. In retrospect, however, it must be stated that since the seventies no adequate adjustment of the resources for higher education in accordance with the increase in the number of students has taken place in the "old" states of the Federal Republic. For decades the institutions of higher education have thus been having to work with a situation of structural overcrowding. The assumption in the eighties that a reduction in the number of students would take place in the nineties in accordance with the demographic development has clearly proved to be empirically false. As far as the resources are concerned, the situation of structural state underfunding has actually become even worse since reunification due to the initially marked need for the institutions of higher education to catch up and be modernized in the six new states of the Federal Republic. The highest number of higher education graduates, roughly two thirds of them, come from the universities, where they have studied for a *Magister*[30], a *Diplom* or a state examination degree. At the universities, in particular, the clear orientation towards concrete fields of activity has been watered down more and more during the past few decades. Basically, however, within the German higher education landscape it is still possible to talk of three categories of degree courses with regard to their professional orientation:

---

30 *Magister* examinations usually comprise one major subject and two minor subjects or two major subjects: in contrast, *Diplom* examinations usually have only one main subject. The teacher training courses are completed with examinations similar to the *Magister*, except that they additionally contain elements dealing with education as an academic discipline and with the teaching of a particular subject.

1. The degree courses without clearly defined professional orientation. A large proportion of the university degree courses in the social sciences and the humanities comprise this category.
2. The degree courses with concrete professional orientation. These include teacher training, medicine and, in different forms, many of the courses in the natural sciences.
3. The degree courses with professional orientation towards differentiated but related fields of activity. Among others, this category includes, for example, law and public administration or economics and the engineering sciences.

The question of the orientation towards the labour market and/or the professional orientation of the institutions of higher education is controversially discussed over and over again in Germany, especially with regard to the universities. The universities stress their autonomy, academic freedom and the complementarity of research and teaching, and thus justify their detachment from training orientated towards the labour market. Any restructuring of universities into a primarily vocation-orientated training institution, with the duty to carry out research becoming less important, contradicts the way the universities see themselves. At most universities, even though it directed towards first professional qualifications, the teaching is intended primarily to be theory-orientated. In contrast, however, business and industry demand that the universities should pay greater attention to the requirements and changes in the working world.

In the past, the German higher education system initially took into account the altered role of higher education institutions within society, first of all and as far as numbers were concerned, by the establishment and expansion of the universities of applied sciences, and later also by establishment of professional academies (established outside the higher education sector). The institutional expansion of the universities of applied sciences, together with a range of subjects that is still limited, has so far led to only a small rise in the proportion of students at universities of applied sciences.[31]

The possibility of establishing courses at German institutions of higher education which end in a bachelor's or a master's degree[32] have existed since the last amendment of the General Act on Higher Education in 1998.[33] The intention of this change in the law is, above all, to improve the international compatibility of German degrees and also to reduce the total time taken to complete a course leading to a first professional qualification. The introduction of B.A. and M.A. courses is linked with the introduction of credit point systems, which are to be compatible with the ECTS system. In contrast, considerations of labour market policy have hardly played any part here. Since most of these multi-stage degree courses or short university courses in Germany are still at the experimental stage and have not been running for a sufficiently long period for them to be properly evaluated, and since no studies have been made of graduates from these courses, an objective evaluation for the whole of the Federal Republic is currently not possible. In particular, the potential labour market opportunities for the graduates from these courses cannot yet be

---

31 Despite the consensus on the priority of the expansion of the universities of applied sciences, the capacities and numbers of graduates from the former and from the universities have shifted only slightly within the last few decades.

32 Cf. Heine, Christoph: Gestufte Studiengänge und -abschlüsse im deutschen Studiensystem. HIS-Kurzinformation A3/99. Hannover, 1999. Schnitzer, Klaus: Bachelor- und Master-studiengänge im Ausland. HIS-Kurzinformation A3/98. Hannover, 1998.

33 The goal of the bachelor's degree course is training at the higher education level ending with a first professional qualification after only six semesters of study. Within the humanities this degree is usually the "Bachelor of Arts" or "Baccalaureus Artium", or in its abbreviated form: B.A. The teaching of knowledge that can be applied in subsequent employment is of essential importance for a B.A. course. The Standing Conference of the State Ministers of Education and the Arts has laid down standard course lengths for these degrees: B.A.: 3-4 years, M.A.: 1-2 years. A consecutively arranged degree programme cannot have a standard course length of more than 5 years. The master's degree corresponds to the university *Diplom* and *Magister* degrees, and the bachelor's degree with honours to the *Diploma* from a university of applied sciences.

determined in a way that is meaningful. It is to be expected that the new B.A. degree courses, mostly lasting six semesters, will in the long term only be broadly accepted by prospective future students if and when this first professional qualification has also shown that it provides the graduates with real and appropriate chances of employment in the labour market in competition with applicants with traditional degrees, and provided that the B.A. graduates do not have to obtain an additional further qualification. In the mind of the public and in the labour market in the Federal Republic the B.A. is currently still something unusual. One great advantage of the new multi-stage degree courses[34] can thus be seen in their modularised structure which, in addition, is often designed to be interdisciplinary. It thus provides students, as a rule within a period not lasting more than six semesters, with a course that is more overview-orientated, more interdisciplinary, and thus more practice and job-orientated. The introduction of new B.A. courses, the numbers of which have grown considerably in the past few years, has been accompanied by a intensive discussion both inside and outside the institutions of higher education. This has currently led to a revival of the topic of the relevance to practice and professional orientation of courses at institutions of higher education.[35]

The academic year at German institutions of higher education consists of a winter and a summer semester which, on average, add up to 28 weeks of lectures at universities and to 36 weeks at universities of applied sciences. Between the semesters, the so-called lecture-free period, there is time for independent study, practical work, field trips, and also partly time for examinations, vacation jobs etc. Traditionally, the most important teaching

---

34   In December 2000 the overview published by the Conference of Presidents and Rectors of Universities and Other Higher Education Institutions (HRK): Studienangebote deutscher Hochschulen (ibid.) reveals a renewed increase in the number of bachelor's courses (382) and master's courses (217) on offer. Source: (http://www.hochschulkompass.hrk.de).

35   Cf., among others, Welbers, Ulrich (ed.): Studienreform mit Bachelor und Master. Luchterhand. Neuwied, to be published in 2001.

forms are lectures, in which a systematic overview of a subject is presented, as well as seminars, classes and laboratory practicals, in which, in the form of discussions, special topics are dealt with as examples, often using students' seminar papers and presentations, and in which an introduction is given into the working methods of the particular subject. Practical problems within the future field of activity are handled in projects and surveys of practical work. The demanding concept of project-centred education, in which the objectives of learning through research, interdisciplinary references, cooperative forms of learning and problem-orientated relevance to practice are linked, was developed in numerous experiments. Overall, however, this still remains a marginal topic in the learning process at higher education institutions, whose model character finds its parallel above all in the humanities and social sciences.

Within degree courses at universities, phases of practical work or placement semesters are required only in individual subjects at a few institutions. Unlike the situation within the universities of applied sciences, where placement semesters or phases form an integral part of the degree course, something similar exists only in certain subjects at universities. Like the seminars, classes and practicals, the more highly developed forms of teaching and learning are in many cases based on intensified communication between the teachers and the students. There are strict limits to this intensive communication under the current conditions of the *"Massenhochschule"* (vast, faceless university), since seminars and classes with between 100 and 200 participants are not uncommon in large subjects. From the outset, the degree course is conceived as a subject-orientated course which, however, also allows students a relatively large amount of freedom. On the one hand, this refers to the fundamentally free choice of the institution of higher education and of the subject and, on the other hand, to the free choice of lectures and classes and areas of special focus, provided that this choice is in accordance with the course regulations for the subject being studied. It is also possible, as a rule, for students to organize their own course timetable to suit their individual needs, which means that they can also extend the time they require to obtain their degree. In accordance with the General Act on Higher Education, the standard course length for a course of study at a university should exceed four years only in exceptional cases. A case of this kind would be a degree in medicine with a standard course length of six years, which has been generally accepted so far. However, there are now some suggestions for reform, which would reduce the study of medicine to five years.

At the present time the standard length for *Diplom* and *Magister* degree courses is between four and a half and five years, and the actual time it takes to complete a course is generally six years or more. There is a standard course length of less than four years only for some teacher training courses (between three and four years for the lower school levels), as well as for the study of law, which has a standard course length of three and a half years, although the actual time it takes to complete a course here is, in fact, also roughly six years. Overall, the courses at universities of applied sciences are shorter and organized more strictly; regular assessments of academic achievement play a greater role here than at universities. A degree course at a university of applied sciences usually lasts for six semesters plus one or two placement semesters, depending on the different regulations laid down by the individual states. Degree courses at universities of applied sciences are divided into two different parts, as they are at universities: basic studies of between two and three semesters which are completed with an intermediate or interim examination, and the main studies comprising a further three or four semesters.

In addition to oral and written examinations, the *Diplom* examination contains a practice-related dissertation which has to be completed within two or three months. Including placement semesters and examination periods, the standard length of courses at universities of applied sciences is between three and a half and four years. In contrast, the actual time taken to study a subject averages roughly four years. Even with degree courses at universities of applied sciences there is a discrepancy between the actual length and the target length of a degree course, but it is nothing like as large as at universities. Among other things, the situation at the overfull *Massenuniversitäten* (vast, faceless universities) in the "old" federal states with their alarmingly high overcrowding is partially responsible for the actual time spent on a course, which often lies well above the standard length of a course. In addition, as many as a quarter of the students in Germany interrupt their university training "in order to gain experience outside the higher education institution."[36] It is generally the case with higher education in Germany that the ideal of full-time students is presumed, but for a long time now this has not corresponded with the everyday reality of many students.[37] As a result of this it is almost inevitable that a large number of students will study for a longer time than officially envisaged, since having a regular part-time job also temporarily makes demands on the students: "Two thirds (65%) of all German students are employed in one way or another while studying. When compared with 1994, the quota has risen once again by six percentage points. [...] Almost a quarter of the students at universities are continuously in employment (1967: only 5%), while among students at universities of applied sciences the figure is distinctly lower (19%)."[38] There are many different reasons for the increasing employment of students during their studies. For example, state funding

---

36   Cf. Bundesministerium für Bildung und Forschung (ed.): Das soziale Bild der Studentenschaft in der Bundesrepublik Deutschland. 15. Sozialerhebung des Deutschen Studentenwerks, Bonn, 1998, p. 12. This is a situation which, among other things, could indicate the lack of relevance to practice of many degree courses.

37   With the exception of the Hagen Open Learning University in North Rhine-Westphalia there is – with very few exceptions – no undergraduate level academic programme for part-time studies. See also: Leszczensky, Michael: Der Trend zur studentischen Selbstfinanzierung. Ursachen und Folgen. HIS Hochschulplanung 99. Hannover, 1993.

38   In: Sozialerhebung des Deutschen Studentenwerks. Loc.cit., p. 17.

through *(BAföG)*[39], the Federal Education Assistance Act, has declined overall during recent years.[40] As a consequence, compared with 1991 (38%), as early as in 1997 49% of students were in paid employment "because this is absolutely essential in order for students to be able to support themselves [...]. In contrast, the proportion of students earning money in order to enjoy a higher standard of living is declining."[41] It is of interest to us here that as many as 46% of the students claim that job-orientated motives, in particular, are the reason for their employment, and that they intend to obtain work experience through the jobs they are doing.[42] Nevertheless, it can be proved "that economic factors have by far the greatest influence on student employment. [...] Professional motives do not have any significant influence on employment."[43]

With the exception of the private institutions of higher education, no tuition fees[44] are currently demanded for a degree course at any of the state institutions of higher education anywhere in the Federal Republic of Germany.[45] However, in some state regulations have now come into force which demand tuition fees from "long-term" students whose studies have exceeded the standard time for completing the course.

39   BAföG = Bundesausbildungsförderungsgesetz.
40   "Of the German students enrolled in the summer semester 1997 18.6% received support
       through *BAföG* (1994: 26.8%). Cf. 15. Sozialerhebung des Deutschen Studentenwerks.
       Loc. cit., p. 10. The reform of *BAföG* comes into force on April 1st, 2001. This will increase
       the amount paid out by an additional 1.3 thousand million marks per year.
41   In: 15. Sozialerhebung des Deutschen Studentenwerks. Loc. cit., p. 17.
42   Cf.: 15. Sozialerhebung des Deutschen Studentenwerks. Loc. cit., pp. 17 and 176ff.
43   In: 15. Sozialerhebung des Deutschen Studentenwerks. Loc. cit., p. 17f.
44   On this discussion cf. Fritsche, Angelika et al. (eds.): Studiengebühren Pro und Contra
       (DUZ-DOKU). Bonn, 1996; Daxner, Michael: Ist die Uni noch zu retten? Reinbeck bei
       Hamburg, 1996. Kreklau, Carsten: Sind unsere Hochschulen noch zu retten? In: Hollerith,
       Joseph: Hochschulrahmengesetz-Kompetenz des Bundes. Loc. cit. pp. 59-72.
45   However, enrolled students pay so-called semester dues each semester, containing a student
       services fee currently amounting to approx. 100 DM per semester. At many higher education
       institutions students also pay roughly the same amount in addition for the "semester
       ticket", which provides them with cheap mobility on public transport within a limited
       area. This is based on agreements with the local integrated transport systems.

In the Federal Republic of Germany, too, the days are long past when, as a rule, a position on the labour market appropriate to the graduate's training was possible without any problem.[46] Since 1975 it has been teachers, in particular, who have been hit by unemployment, and for a long time they headed the list of unemployed graduates. Other subjects, however, such as the engineering sciences, have also had to cope with the serious problem of the shortage of jobs for their graduates in recent years. Nevertheless, when seen overall, the proportion of those in employment with a degree has continually increased since the sixties (in the "old" states of the Federal Republic).[47] Although the overall number of people in employment remained numerically relatively constant, the number of those in employment who had a degree grew comparatively drastically: in the short period between 1990 and 1997 by as much as 37%. In 1997 the group of those in employment who had a degree numbered 5.5 million, thus comprising approx. 16% of all those in employment.[48] In 1998 the figure was already 5.6 million (16.4%). In 1991 roughly every one in eight employed person had a degree from a university or a university of applied sciences – and in 1998 it was already every one in six.

In the "new" federal states, too, there was a distinct rise (16%) in proportion of those with a degree who were in employment between 1991 and 1997, while at the same time the total number of people in employment fell by 4.8%. Overall, the average income of graduates in the western and the eastern parts of the country is distinctly higher than the income of the other qualification groups. In this connection, however, it must be taken into account that the structure of many jobs has also greatly changed even for graduates from higher education institutions. Since the eighties, fixed-term employment contracts and

---

46   In Germany as many as between 10 and 25% of those in employment who have a degree do not occupy a position appropriate to their training.
47   1978: approx. 1.2 million. 1997: approx. 4.3 million.
48   Cf. Studien und Berufswahl 1999/2000. Ibid. p. 21.

part-time contracts have marked the labour market situation more and more, and they are characteristic of the working conditions of young academics at the institutions of higher education themselves.[49]

In general, however, it can be stated that in Germany a successfully completed degree course at an institution of higher education distinctly reduces the risk of being hit by unemployment at a later date. Thus the proportion of unemployed graduates was only 5% on September 1st, 1999, while the overall unemployment rate was 10.1%. On the same date 3,943,200 people were registered as unemployed. Of these, 87,900 women with a degree were unemployed. Independent of whether or not they have a degree from a university or a university of applied sciences, female graduates still have a distinctly greater (but slowly decreasing) chance of being hit by unemployment than men. Among graduates, the proportion of graduate women in employment actually rose from 31% (1991) to 35% (1998), but the unemployment rate of female graduates was nevertheless 4.6% in 1998, while the figure for the comparable group of male graduates was only 3.4%. The unemployment rate for female graduates from universities of applied sciences was 3.1%, while only 2.4% men from the same type of higher education institution were unemployed.[50] In addition,

---

49   Including fixed-term job creation schemes, in 1998 almost half, and in 1999 still 43%, of
      the job-finding activities of the employment exchanges concerning graduates ended in
      fixed-term work contracts. Cf.: Arbeitsmarktinformationsstelle der Zentralstelle für Arbeits-
      vermittlung (ZAV): Der Arbeitsmarkt für besonders qualifizierte Fach- und Führungskräfte.
      Jahresbericht 1999. June, 2000.
50   "In view of an unemployment rate of higher education graduates from university degree
      courses amounting to just under 3 percent at the end of the first year after graduation, the
      worries about the professional future of academically trained young people appear to be
      unjustified. If one takes the unemployment rate as an indicator of the chances of
      employment, the rule seems to be confirmed that a high level of education seldom results
      in unemployment. In its unspecific generality this also remains true for the current generation
      of young people; nevertheless, the quota of unemployed higher education graduates [...]
      is not a particularly precise instrument for measuring good or poor chances of
      unemployment." In: HIS Hochschulplanung Vol. 143. Hochschulabsolventen auf dem Weg
      in den Beruf. Hannover, 2000, p. 2.

women in Germany still have smaller chances of a career than men. Although the proportion of women in management has now increased from 4% to 13% during the past ten years, there is, for example, still no woman at all in the top management of the 30 DAX businesses.[51] Although, when seen overall, the number of female graduates from German institutions of higher education has continued to increase, female graduates still have advantages in the labour market over other qualification groups, and in a comparison within one sex this applies particularly to women rather than to men. In 1998 the unemployment rate of all people in gainful employment in the area of the former Federal Republic was just below 9%, and thus distinctly higher than that of the female graduates from universities with an unemployment rate of 3.5%, and more than three times as high as that of female graduates from universities of applied sciences, where the rate was 2.4%. The difference in the new states was even more marked, where with an overall unemployment rate of 17% the rate for female graduates from universities was 5.2%, and for female graduates from universities of applied sciences it was 3.8%.

As a rule, female higher education graduates usually succeed in obtaining employment at the latest within two years of obtaining their degree. It is thus mainly the group of older higher education graduates who are affected by long-term unemployment. Basically, the relatively good prospects for higher education graduates must be regarded as still being highly differentiated with regard to the individual subjects. There are even tremendous differences between the individual degree courses within a grouping of academic

---

51 Nor is the number of women employed within universities proportionate to their number within the population. In 1998 a mere 9.5% of all professors were women; the figure was only 5.9% for full professors. In addition to various other things, equal status offices and women's representatives at institutions of higher education in the Federal Republic offer everyday support of many different kinds to women who are studying or teaching. These include information and contact with professional organizations and business. For instance, functions are also offered on careers and jobs for women, and training is provided for women to help them with their applications for jobs.

departments, so that there are phases when, for example, the biologists have distinctly worse chances in the labour market than the physicists. The discussion in Germany about the so-called Green Card has made this phenomenon very clear. In certain job areas there is currently a very great shortage of graduates, which it also will not be possible to cover in the near future through the employment of German higher education graduates (e.g. in computer technology). As in other economies, the labour market opportunities – even for graduates – are always linked to the local economic development and especially in export-orientated economies like the Federal Republic of Germany also to the global economic development.

Nevertheless, it is possible to detect priorities established with relevance to particular subjects. In accordance with this, the business world is actually only expressing a small "[...] demand for humanities graduates. When asked about their concrete recruitment plans, the firms primarily mention engineers (53.9%). In second place they are seeking graduates in law, economics and the social sciences (26.9%). The natural science disciplines occupy third place (15.3%). All the other subject groups together only add up to less than 5%."[52] However, as a result of the fact that today it is not possible to predict how many graduates in which degree courses will join the labour market in 5, 10 or 15 years, and, on the other hand, how many will be required by the labour market, it will certainly not be possible in the near future to make reliable statements about the prospects for concrete employment opportunities for

---

52   Cf.: Konegen-Grenier, Christiane: Berufschancen für Geisteswissenschaftler in der Wirt-
     schaft. In: Handbuch Praxisinitiativen an Hochschulen. Berufsorientierende Angebote für
     Studierende an Universitäten. Ed. by Ehlert, Holger and Welbers, Ulrich. Luchterhand.
     Neuwied, 1999, p. 289.
     The state itself is a classic employer in the Federal Republic's employment system for
     higher education graduates. However, for a number of years now there has been a declining
     trend with regard to the employment of graduates by the state, so that its importance as an
     employer has also declined for this group of those seeking employment.

particular areas of training. In general, the requirement profile of business is high, especially for higher education graduates. Qualification in one's subject, a good degree as well as initial professional experience are elements that must be mentioned here. The so-called soft skills, such as social competence and knowledge of methods or the ability to work in a team, are becoming more and more important in addition to mobility and cognitive flexibility. The mastery of, or the readiness to obtain, various additional key qualifications[53] are becoming a precondition which is increasingly in demand. A low starting age, a knowledge of foreign languages, as well as IT knowledge and experience abroad in addition to the mastery of one's subject round off the additional essential parameters of the labour market's ideal higher education graduate.

In the course of the rapid social changes, and thus also production-orientated changes, not only in the Federal Republic of Germany, but precisely within the framework of a labour market which is continuing to become more international or more globalised, it is inevitable that the demands made on the qualifications held by higher education graduates will alter in all the countries participating in the change. The internal organisation of work within firms in Germany has also changed during the course of this macrocosmic development, and in some instances it has brought about movement within the entire structure of businesses. Almost without exception, all the work structures have been influenced by the developments in information and communication technology.

Within this context, which can be extended by various additional parameters, the demands for qualifications also made on higher education

---

53 Cf. Wildt, Johannes: Fachübergreifende Schlüsselqualifikationen – Leitmotiv der Studienreform? In: Welbers, Ulrich, (ed.): Das integrierte Handlungskonzept Studienreform. Aktionsformen für die Verbesserung der Lehre an Hochschulen. Luchterhand. Neuwied, 1997, pp. 198-213.

graduates have clearly risen. In particular, the key qualifications which are not directly orientated towards the subject or directly obtained with it, are becoming increasingly important in the labour market. In future, probably the most important qualification in the labour market will be the ability and readiness for lifelong learning, since, as the Federal Advisory Council on Science and Academic Affairs puts it, "rapid technological developments and social as well as economic changes result in the fact that in many occupations the knowledge obtained during an undergraduate degree course will become obsolete at in ever-increasing pace. The knowledge and skills acquired during the first degree course require continual renewal, complementation and expansion so that the graduate maintains his or her employability. It is thus expected that graduates from the higher education system will show the readiness and the ability to update their skills on a continual basis. This necessity is heightened by the structural change in the employment system to be expected in the future, as well as by the associated increasing loss of the guarantee of lifelong employment with just one employer. Thus it is to be expected that even in the case of uninterrupted employment with one employer the tasks undertaken will in future fundamentally change several times, and to a significantly greater extent, during the course of a working life."[54]

In the Federal Republic of Germany it is, above all, the employment offices of the individual states which have been continuously active for a number of years in each of the higher education institutions within the framework of practice and job-orientated courses and programmes. In most of the larger institutions of higher education the so-called "higher education teams" from the state employment offices, which were set up in 1995, have

---

54 Wissenschaftsrat: Stellungnahme zum Verhältnis von Hochschulausbildung und Beschäftigungssystem. Drs. 4099/99, 9th July 1999, p. 14.

even had their employees working directly on the campus.[55] It is not unusual for these higher education teams also to work together with the individual so-called placement initiatives or career services at the departmental or faculty level of the higher education institutions.[56] In addition, they are also in contact with potential employers at the regional and national level. The total number of placement initiatives throughout Germany is roughly one hundred. They are the responsibility of various providers and organized in highly different structures, but in addition to the teaching at the higher education institution they make a decisive contribution to job orientation, above all at the universities. Their goal of providing students with a better transition to the labour market is achieved in a highly differentiated way, even if the majority of them are not additional programmes that are structurally integrated into the degree courses. Thus, for example, there are programme forms ranging from the organization of work experience to courses run during the semester with speakers from business and industry, right up to the classic guidance session, all of which are well received by the students. In addition, some of these models have begun to guarantee the more job-orientated design of the degree course through the integration of the appropriate curricula into the standard programme.

As the term "initiatives" already indicates, the vast majority of these programmes are, however, not programme forms institutionally guaranteed within the higher education institution, but are mostly additional programmes which are made possible only through the involvement and enthusiasm of

---

55   The establishment of a higher education team from the employment office is required by law at institutions of higher education with more than 20,000 students. There are currently 36 higher education teams in 34 cities in Germany.

56   On this see also: Handbuch Praxisinitiativen an Hochschulen. Ibid. Here, among other things, it has been assessed that in Germany the majority of placement initiatives work directly together with the individual state employment offices (as well as with other cooperation partners).

the lecturers and the students.[57] The reference to approaches to higher education reform is characteristic of these practice-orientated activities in Germany. In addition to the higher education teams, the employment offices of the individual states support a large number of career information centres (BIZ), in which free advice and information is provided for students from all different fields of specialization. It is appropriate that the support provided by these offices is not only given to higher education graduates, but they also offer students a large number of programmes while they are still studying as well as after they have obtained their degrees. The job placement of students by the higher education teams has become such an important programme that its absence would be sorely missed. It is important not only within the framework of the ever-increasing employment of students during their studies, enabling them to support themselves financially, but also with regard to the qualified placement of what frequently is the first kind of practical experience, in particular of the younger students. Various additional programmes, such as providing training in the submission of applications, complete this multilayered programme, which differs from one region to another. Thus the higher education teams run by the employment offices of the individual states undertake tasks of many different kinds, and for a large proportion of students they have developed into an indispensable component in everyday life at their higher education institution.

---

57   "The funding of their employees is achieved on the basis of job creation schemes or on the basis of additional funds from various financial aid programmes. The fact that these jobs are based on fixed-term contracts means that the initiative will sooner or later be faced with the difficult task of retrospectively convincing "the rest" of the higher education institution of the necessity of its task, with the slight hope that its programme will be institutionalized. This, however, is a path that has been successful only in few cases so far." Cordier, Heidi. In: Handbuch Praxisinitiativen. Ibid. pp. 317, 318. Cf. also Grühn, Dieter (Ed.): Auf die Plätze, fertig, los ... mit Praxisprogrammen erfolgreich in den Beruf starten. bds-papers 1. Berlin, 1997. Perspektive Beruf. Praxisinitiativen an Hochschulen in Nordrhein-Westfalen. Published by Ministerium für Wissenschaft und Forschung des Landes Nordrhein-Westfalen. Düsseldorf, 1997. / Hahn, Silke and Ehlert, Holger (eds.): Praxisinitiativen an Hochschulen. In: die blaue reihe Nr. 37. Studienreformprojekt Germanistik. Heinrich-Heine-Universität Düsseldorf. Düsseldorf, 1997.

The General Act on Higher Education also intends that cooperation should take place between the institutions of higher education and the facilities of the Federal Labour Office. Nevertheless, the current situation still cannot be considered satisfactory. Thus, for example, the Federal Advisory Council on Science and Academic Affairs demanded in 1999 "that the counselling services at the institutions of higher education [...] must be consolidated and more closely networked with the programmes of the Federal Labour Office."[58]

In the former Federal Republic of Germany a start was already made in 1977[59] with the introduction of so-called dual degree courses. Since then more and more dual degree courses have been established, most of them at universities of applied sciences, and as a rule very successfully.[60] These degree courses are conceived together with firms and the departments at the higher education institution so that an optimum mixture of theory and practice is achieved. The average length of these degree courses is between 3 and 5.5 years at universities, and between 3 and 4.5 years at universities of applied sciences. The differences in length result from the different practices within the individual firms with regard to study release, or they are influenced by whether or not vocational training takes place parallel to the degree course. The students in these degree courses also profit almost without exception from the relative financial security which is achieved by part-time salaries or payment for placements. As a matter of principle, school leaving qualifications are required which are identical to

58 Wissenschaftsrat: Stellungnahme zum Verhältnis von Hochschulausbildung und Beschäfti-
    gungssystem. Ibid. p. 6.
59 Originally at the Rhineland-Palatinate University of Applied Sciences with the so-called
    "cooperative study scheme" (BIS).
60 Konegen-Grenier and Kramer state that in 1994 there was a total of 41 dual degree courses
    with 1718 places. As an example, see the "Berlin Model" in business administration at the
    Technical University of Applied Sciences in Berlin. Cf. also Walter, Hans-Christian: Duales
    Studium – Berliner Modell. Praxisbezug und soziale Kompetenz: Hochschule und Wirt-
    schaft im Dialog. Ed. by Konegen-Grenier, Christiane / Schlaffke, Winfried. Deutscher
    Instituts-Verlag. Cologne, 1994, pp. 237-243.

those for applicants to universities and universities of applied sciences.[61] There
are approximately one hundred dual degree courses in Germany at the present
time. The students enrolled on them already obtain an impression of the firms'
working processes while they are studying, and they can productively link this
practice-orientated experience with their academic training. In each case the
result is a gain for all three participating groups: the students increase their
employment prospects, the higher education institutions extend their programme
range, and thus their attractiveness, and the firms can count on potential young
employees who can be integrated into the appropriate working processes more
rapidly and more efficiently.[62]

In addition, centres for continuing education and technology transfer
now exist at many German institutions of higher education. Among other
things, their task is to develop and intensify contacts and cooperation between

61   "Unlike the situation in the normal higher education system, the admissions procedures
      are precisely determined: only in about one in three of the degree courses does the
      normal enrolment suffice. In all the other cases the applicant is subjected to an additional
      selection procedure, the majority of which are the joint responsibility of the higher education
      institution and the firm. In twelve cases, however, the firm is solely responsible for making
      the decision. As a rule, the firm takes the sole responsibility for admission to the degree
      course if it has to pay tuition fees to the higher education institution for the place. The
      tuition fee which firms have to pay averages 6000 DM per year. However, the firms are
      faced with costs of this kind only in nine degree courses, which are almost exclusively
      private. The same applies to the students. Apart from at one state institution of higher
      education, they have to pay tuition fees of between 6000 and 12000 DM per year only at
      eight private institutions." In: Konegen.Grenier, Christiane / Kramer, Wolfgang: Studien-
      führer Duale Studiengänge. Hochschulausbildung mit integrierter Berufspraxis. Deutscher
      Instituts-Verlag. Cologne, 1995, p. 15.
62   Outside the higher education sector (but as part of the tertiary sector) eight so-called
      professional academies in various different federal states currently award degrees which
      are recognized as being of the same value as degrees from universities of applied sciences.
      At the moment there are roughly 13,000 training places at these professional academies.
      Following the model of the dual vocational training system, the professional academies –
      together with the study academies and firms, with which the students sign a training
      contract – provide the practice-orientated training of students who will graduate with the
      necessary qualifications for employment. The curricula are developed jointly by state
      study academies and the participating employers (in committees with equal representation).

business and the institutions of higher education.[63] Generally, however, it can be stated that institutionalized cooperation between higher education institutions and the labour market is unfortunately still restricted to too few individual examples.[64]

In Germany the General Act on Higher Education now makes the reform of higher education mandatory as a permanent task of higher education institutions. It states that "the institutions of higher education have the permanent task, together with the state agencies responsible, of examining and further developing the contents and forms of study with regard to the developments in science and the arts, the requirements of professional experience and the necessary changes in the world of work."[65] The professional orientation and the organisation of the transition from higher education to the labour market must still be urgently optimized. It is, in the end, not an acceptable situation if only 16% of university graduates describe the link between theory and practice during their degree course as satisfactory, and the support by their higher education institution in the transition into employment as highly inadequate.[66] In addition, the feeling of graduates that there is a deficit in university courses with regard to abilities generally relevant to employment – apart from the gaining of purely subject-related qualifications – gives rise to considerable concern, as the following diagram demonstrates:

---

63   In addition, the "science shops" and "science parks" were founded in Germany a few years ago. They must not be equated with the primarily purely commercial "technology parks", but they try to institutionalize cooperation between higher education institutions and business within the framework of cooperation agreements.

64   "Cooperation between higher education and business mainly takes place by chance, unsystematically and at a personal level between representatives from firms and higher education institutions, and too little use is still made of the opportunities provided by institutional forms." This is how Klaus Kemmet from the Bildungswerk Hamburg expresses it. In: Hochschule und Wirtschaft als Partner in Weiterbildung und Wissenstransfer auf dem europäischen Arbeitsmarkt. Dokumente zur Hochschulreform 114. Cologne, 1996, p. 45.

65   Ibid.: Section on study and teaching, § 8 reform of higher education.

66   Cf. HIS Hochschulplanung Vol. 143. Ibid. p. 5.

The feeling of graduates that there is a deficit with regard to their university training (as a percentage)[67]

	1989	1993	1997
ability to communicate	62	54	51
reference to professional practice	55	54	52
interdisciplinary thinking	53	53	53
ability to cooperate	47	43	43
broad basic knowledge	38	41	40
knowledge of the effects of work	15	18	27
special knowledge of the subject studied	13	12	11

It is therefore to be hoped that the development will be positively influenced by the discussion about the introduction of the new multi-stage degree courses. Against the background of the fact that in future more than thirty percent of young people of an age group will probably also want to study, it will be of decisive relevance for the German higher education landscape in the new millennium that the ambitious reform goals and projects are accompanied in the long term by the appropriate and necessary increase in funding on the part of those responsible for education policy. Without this fundamental consolidation of the overcrowded institutions of higher education it would appear to be more than questionable whether or not they will be able to cope with the great challenges facing them. Business and industry, however, must also do more justice to their responsibility to higher education graduates in the future by providing greater support for the educational and training tasks of the institutions of higher education while students are still studying, and for their own tasks with regard to higher education graduates.

67   Ibid. p. 47.

Great Britain

Heidi Cordier

Introduction

Careers services[1] are central counselling offices at British universities whose task is to provide support to students at an early stage in the planning of their careers. They are frequently regarded as a model in international discussions on the subject.

This paper will illustrate the framework conditions and the goals underlying the establishment of careers services at British institutions of higher education. It is surprising that the careers services are already able to look back on more than 100 years of development. It is important to take this tradition into account in trying to provide an accurate assessment of the role of the careers services *within* and their function *for* the British higher education system.[2] The changes within the careers services since the middle of the sixties form the focal point of the paper, in particular against the background of the Dearing Report on the situation of the institutions of higher education, which was published in the autumn of 1977.

The development of the careers services ran parallel to the expansion of the British higher education system and the increase in size of a student body that was continually becoming more and more divergent (Watts 1977: 16ff.).

---

1   Sometimes also called Careers Advisory Services, University Careers Services, Careers Counselling Services etc.

2   The author is aware of the differences between the systems of higher education in England, Scotland, Wales and Northern Ireland. Since the structures of the careers services are comparable in every way, however, they will be treated as British institutions in this paper.

In 1900 no more than 20,000 students were studying at universities in Great Britain, in 1938 there were 50,000, in 1960 92,000, and in 1996 a total of 1,182,000 full-time students and 639,000 part-time students were attending higher education courses. Above all, since the beginning of the nineties there has been a considerable increase in student numbers which, however, in contrast to earlier waves of expansion, has not been accompanied by a similarly large increase in funding. An average of more than 30% of a year group now attend courses in higher education. Apart from the demographic development, the increase in student numbers is due, above all, to the increasing participation in education of women, mature students as well as students with higher education entry qualifications who come from social groups not traditionally interested in education.

The expansion of the British higher education system ran parallel to this: while Great Britain still had a relatively homogeneous university structure with 25 universities in 1960, there are now 89 universities and a further 75 institutions of higher education. The former polytechnics and colleges of higher education have a comparatively larger number of part-time students, more sandwich courses (courses of study with a considerable proportion of practical experience) and more courses orientated towards jobs and the labour market.

Framework conditions

The British universities are independent institutions with far-reaching autonomy in the running of their own affairs. This means that they alone decide on the admission of their students, the employment of teaching staff, the content of courses offered and the academic degrees to be awarded. Every department can itself decide on the number of first-year students to be admitted and on the conditions to be fulfilled for matriculation. Based on British tradition, this means that the universities "function in accordance with the rules of the market, and the rules of the market are conditioned by competition" (Pulzer: 305). In Great Britain there is thus a well-defined hierarchy of reputation among the institutions of higher education. It is obvious that the differences with regard to the distribution of funds, the admission criteria, as well as the quality and status are not without influence on the labour-market opportunities of their graduates.

A special feature of higher education training in Great Britain is the short duration of the courses. With the exception of the professional courses, such as medicine (5-6 years), the length of a course leading to the Bachelor's Degree is usually only three years, and in Scotland four years. The fact that the courses are mostly completed within this time is due, above all, to the relatively precise, somewhat school-like guidelines laid down in the course regulations. The result of this that in an international comparison British graduates are relatively young when they complete their courses, the average age being 24.4 (HIS: 136).

British universities traditionally regard their educational mandate as lying less in specific preparation for employment and specialist qualification, but rather in the imparting of broad knowledge and the furthering of the personal and intellectual development of their students. After completion of the Bachelor's Degrees a large number of graduates from the humanities are employed in business and the administration, where they are given the training specific to the job they are actually doing. Only about one fifth of the students continue their training as postgraduates after completion of their first degree.[3] Many of those who take up employment after completion of their BA participate in trainee programmes within a firm in order to obtain the (required) vocational qualifications in their chosen employment sector:

---

3   21% of all the students attending institutions of higher education (full-time and part-time) in 1996 were postgraduates aiming for a higher degree (MA, MSc, PhD).

"Vocational preparation in Britain is frequently not completed with the Bachelor's degree and the nature of the degree may be less of a determinant for subsequent employment than the equivalent qualification in other countries. Vocational preparation, being less complete, allows changes in direction for many graduates, for whom the subject of the first degree may not be crucial to employment requirements" (Brennan et al. 1996a: 52).

In a number of degree courses, however, there is greater career orientation due to the subject studied, e.g. in engineering sciences. This is a result of the significant part played by the professional associations and organizations in these fields of study; they have a considerable influence on the shaping of degree courses through the accreditation of curricula and examinations.

As far as these fields of activity are concerned, admission to a particular profession is not obtained by completion of a degree, but through special courses and examinations run by the appropriate professional association (Brennan / Shah: 171f).

The tradition of the careers services

The origin of the careers services is in Oxford. There, in 1892, a university body began an attempt to concentrate the support of the lecturers in making appointments at publicly-run schools and grammar schools. Other universities soon followed with the establishment of Appointment Services (Figure 1).

Figure 1

University	Introduction of the Appointment Service	University	Introduction of the Appointment Service
Oxford	1892	Birmingham	1930
Cambridge (M.)	1902	Cambridge (W.)	1930
Glasgow/R.C.S.T.	1903	St. Andrews	1930
Liverpool	1907	Hull	1931
London	1909	Southampton	1940
Wales	1912	Reading	1942
Manchester	1913	Durham/Newcastle	1945
Belfast	1920	Leicester	1947
Edinburgh	1920	Nottingham	1947
Leeds	1921	Exeter	1953
Bristol	1926	North Staffs	1953
Sheffield	1928	Aberdeen	1954

Source: Heyworth Report.

Until the end of the 19th century the vocational goals were generally clearly outlined for male university graduates: these 2% of a year group mostly became clergymen, teachers or civil servants. However, some graduates went into politics, joined the legal profession or practised as doctors. In brief: there was a close – above all social – link between training and the occupation chosen; a degree course was the exclusive admission criterion for the occupations mentioned here. The universities on the one hand, and trade and industry on the other hand, had no direct contact with each other. This attitude changed with the industrial developments and the establishment of the administrative society. The (technical) knowledge of higher education graduates was more and more in demand in business; this demand led to the expansion of the range of courses. The Appointment Service occupied an important position as a go-between for the two sides. Accordingly, the Career Advisers were originally, and above all, people who had been employed in business and manufacturing and who had experience which was of practical relevance. Nowadays it is more and more frequently the case that those working in the careers services are trained careers advisers. This is a development that is not only regarded as being positive (cf. Watts 1997: 17f.).

On the one hand, the Appointment Services saw their task in counselling students in their search for suitable employment and, on the other hand, in supporting employers seeking qualified personnel. Thus they pursued a public interest in placing highly qualified women and men in suitable positions as quickly as possible.

The Heyworth Report, published under the auspices of the University Grants Committee in 1964, was the first report dealing substantially with the role of the appointment services within higher education. Its recommendations had far-reaching consequences: the change made to their tasks was also followed by a change in name: careers services. The interest group entitled Standing Conference on University Appointment Services (SCUAS) was set up in 1967. This has been called the Association of Graduate Careers Advisory Services (AGCAS) since 1977, and today almost all the careers services in Great Britain and Ireland belong to it.

Tasks and organisational structures of the areers services

A careers service regards itself primarily as a service organisation for students. Its tasks can be described as follows:

"The traditional core role of careers services is helping students to manage the choices and transitions they need to make on exit from their course in order to proceed effectively to the next stage of their career." (Watts 1997: 8)[4]

---

4   For a definition of "career" cf. Brennan et al. (1996b): pp. 1-10.

Until the middle of the sixties the extensive interview formed the "core" of the appointment services' work. Many students considered that its main task was to place them in a job (Watts 1997: 15). The recommendations of the Heyworth Report, and also the increasing numbers of students without a proportional increase in financial resources led to the restructuring of the services. Nowadays every careers service incorporates three core elements: careers guidance, making information available and maintaining contacts with firms and/or job placement. The Information Room now forms the focal point; this is where students can inform themselves about possible professional and occupational fields of activity, postgraduate courses, practical training and periods of study and work abroad. The various materials available also include videos and computer-supported advisory systems (Kubik / Teichmann: 77f.).

In addition, the employees of the careers services organise, for example, discussion groups, group training for testing key qualifications, study visits and training sessions for applicants. Finally, students can take advantage of individual advice. For this purpose there is a team of advisers within the careers service (Figure 2):

Figure 2

Number of full-time students* per careers adviser	number of institutions
0 - 1000	1
1001 - 2000	38
2001 - 3000	42
3001 - 4000	15
4001 - 5000	4
5001 - 6000	2
6001 +	1

*excluding medicine

Source: AGCAS Resources Survey 1994.

The process of coming to a decision forms the focal point of the careers services. The goal is for students to start thinking about their future career as early as possible and for them to plan and prepare for it while they are still studying. This means that their plans for their own studies are indirectly furthered: knowledge about one's own career perspectives consequently also leads to a practically-orientated course of study. The careers service offers advice and help, thus supporting the students in choosing and pursuing their own career development on the basis of their individual strengths and abilities. This also takes place against the background of the majority of students starting their studies above all because they are interested in their subject; only for roughly one third are career perspectives of decisive importance for the choice of degree course.

Careers education accordingly contains four elements (cf. Watts 1992):
- recognizing individual potentials
- finding out career opportunities and spheres of activity
- decision-making
- translating and applying the decision to one's own actions.

The careers service plays no active part in arranging jobs. It does not carry out any preselection; information on open positions, about which it is informed by business and industry, is made freely available to all students. This procedure is criticised above all by smaller and medium-sized firms which are increasingly employing higher education graduates and would gladly dispense with their own time-consuming and expensive assessment procedures. In addition, the careers service organizes, for example, information fairs for graduates or information fairs on employment opportunities as well as – to a decreasing extent – the well-known milk-rounds, when potential employers come to the higher education institution in order to recruit students about to graduate. Unlike (private) offices, the careers service is relatively independent and impartial, since it has no basic interest in certain placement quotas.

In addition to these main tasks for the support of students, a careers service can also fulfil functions as an academic service and a marketing service (Watts 1997: 26). This applies, for example, within the framework of shaping a profile for the higher education institution in the competition with other institutions:

"Careers services can indeed be viewed as a means of promoting the institution, its courses and its graduates to potential employers, in ways which also enhance its marketability to students. In an increasingly competitive market, in which employers are more and more wanting to target particular institutions and even departments, an institution which fails to promote itself in this way risks losing its market position" (Watts 1997: 24).

A careers service's contacts with business and industry and with (potential) employers are characteristic of its work. This implies that changes in the labour market for graduates are initially perceived by the careers service in the higher education institution. A careers service can transport this information into the higher education institution and thus support the institution's planning.

The institutional connection of the careers services with each particular higher education establishment differs considerably. It is mostly a constituent part of student services. British experience has shown clearly that "strong" connections with the management of the higher education institution is of substantial importance for a careers service. This also applies to membership in the specialist committees of the higher education institution. In some cases the careers services are linked to the institution's committees or the committees at the departmental level. At some universities the head of the careers service is a member of the Senate. Some institutions of higher education have a Career Board, in which senior members of the university, employers and students cooperate (Watts 1997: 27).

Cooperation with the departments

Since the middle of the eighties awareness has slowly been growing in Great Britain that practice orientation and the shaping of the transition from higher education to employment must also be an integral part of the curriculum:

"The importance of careers education and guidance is now more widely recognised within higher education. The growth of interest in modular courses, in credit accumulation and transfer, and in personal transferable skills, are all giving it a more central place in relation to the higher education curriculum. This raises important issues about the respective roles of careers services and teaching departments in the delivery of careers programmes. [...] The key policy issue is how to develop an organisational structure which makes optimal use of the specialist resource offered by the careers service, and links it effectively with the rest of the institution and particularly with teaching departments" (Watts 1992).

As already mentioned, the careers services are directed towards all students. They work throughout the higher education institution and are isolated from the academic programme. This means, however, that there is a danger that they will be given the role of a "repair workshop" for the academic training: they are to remove deficits and faults inherent in the undergraduate course with regard to preparing students for employment, for it is frequently the case that job orientation during the degree course is ignored by the teaching staff. Job-orientated aspects have so far been addressed only indirectly – if at all – and only when there is direct reference to academic programme.

In this connection Watts distinguishes between three different types:
- Vocational courses are degree subjects (e.g. medicine, architecture) which prepare students directly for a future profession or for a predetermined job outline. Individual career counselling is regarded

as irrelevant, and the finding of jobs and information about opportunities for specialisation are regarded as being the task of the department.

- Semi-vocational courses are subjects (e.g. chemistry, psychology) which open up access to different professions, all of which, however, are characterised by their reference to the academic programme. The departments regard careers education, providing advice and finding jobs as a joint task with the careers service.

- Non-vocational courses are (arts) subjects whose graduates have a wide choice of jobs. Here it is, above all, the generally qualifying skills which are applied, and less the knowledge of the specific subject studied. The departments do not feel that they are responsible for preparing their students for employment and tend to direct them towards the careers service.

At present, therefore, it is above all in the area of semi-vocational courses that approaches towards cooperation are to be found. It is to a considerable extent due to the impulses from the Enterprise in Higher Education Programme (see 6) that the realization is also gaining ground in other fields that promoting the employment qualifications of students with practice-related elements can only succeed through and together with the departments, and in the end also through the integration of occupation-related elements into the academic programme. This even applies to the vocational courses where, in future, alternative employment opportunities will increasingly play a part.

For this purpose the departments require the support of the careers service, since contact with the labour market is one of its fundamental core areas: this also essentially applies to individual career counselling and the help given in choosing a career, although the departments do make a partial "contribution" here within the framework of the tutorial system and through the naming of Careers Tutors or Careers Liaison Officers (Watts 1997: 27f.).

The subjects and departments are interesting partners for a careers service, since they maintain more continuous and more intensive contact with the students. They also have the opportunity of integrating careers education and career orientation into the academic programme, and can thus make use of the information and knowledge available in the careers service. The concept of personal transferable skills[5] – not only in the non-vocational courses – plays an essential role here, since the imparting of key qualifications cannot be "produced" by teaching, but only by means of a student's own actions and experimentation. This implies, for example, the inclusion of management simulation, project and group work in the academic programme.

Thus the "shared responsibility" of departments and careers services must be aimed at, not least in order to create synergy effects. There is no easy answer to the actual form this cooperation should take; it must be negotiated and agreed upon in each individual case. A careers service can be the partner, employee or adviser of a department (Watts 1992). The British experience continues to show that it is helpful to lay down the distribution of responsibilities in a written agreement in order to increase the transparency and binding nature of the networking structure.

Government impulses for supporting career orientation and relevance to practice in degree courses

As has already been stated, the political guidelines for the university sector are minimal. However, the government uses financial incentives as external instruments of control for influencing higher education activities (Brennan / Shah: 187). One example of this is the Enterprise in Higher Education

---

5   See Pitcher / Purcell (1996) on the classification of soft skills.

programme initiated in 1987 with the goal of providing future graduates with knowledge of "entrepreneurial qualities":

"Every person seeking a higher education should be able to develop competencies and attitudes relevant to enterprise. [...] these competencies should be acquired at least in part through project based work designed to be undertaken in real economic settings and they should be jointly assessed by employers and the higher education institutions. [...] the [...] proposals should demonstrate how individual institutions would, in *partnership with employers*, embed 'learning for enterprise' within the curriculum" (Jones: 139).

The British government made additional funds available for which the higher education institutions could apply within the framework of a competition. Between 1987 and 1990 a total of 61 Enterprise Plans put forward by British higher education institutions received financial support. Cooperation with employers and their participation in the shaping of curricula is considered to be one of the cornerstones of the initiative. The current Career Management Skills Programme, which is funded by the Department for Education and Employment, is also aimed in a similar direction (Watts 1997: 43).

A National Committee of Inquiry into Higher Education was set up under the chairmanship of Sir Ron Dearing in May 1996 with the task of working out recommendations for the development of the higher education system in Great Britain in the next 20 years. The final report published in the autumn of 1997 comes, among other things, to the conclusion that at British universities teaching currently plays merely a subordinate role to research. A series of recommendations thus pursue the goal of strengthening teaching, e.g. by training and further training of the teaching staff in teaching methods and by optimizing regulations for support and criteria for promotion.

Among other things, the core points of the recommendations aim at improving the quality of teaching. New teaching and learning strategies are to be developed, the integration of key qualifications into academic programmes is to be further extended, relevance to practice in higher education is to be improved and the qualification "learning to learn" is to be taught. In the Committee's opinion the careers services are to be integrated into academic matters to a greater extent than hitherto, so that their experience can be incorporated, for instance, into the development of new academic programmes. The careers services are also to be included in the periodical evaluation carried out by the Quality Assurance Agency.

In addition, it is recommended that activities supporting the founding of firms by university graduates should be extended. The institutions of higher education are required to guarantee that their students should be able to gather practical experience – especially in firms – during their studies. In cooperation with employers' associations and Chambers of Commerce, on the other hand, firms are requested to offer more placements for students. Tax reductions, in particular, are to have a "stimulating" effect here for smaller and medium-sized businesses.

The entry of higher education graduates into employment

The career situation of higher education graduates is marked by the continuing structural changes in business and industry. The increasing mechanisation, the growing internationalisation and globalisation of production and markets, as well as the rapid growth of more and more specialised knowledge with the simultaneous networking of information flows are just a few of the aspects relevant in this connection. Firms react to these changes with an accelerated speed of innovation, quality-increasing production methods and the improved provision of services. They achieve this not least by means of a far-reaching restructuring of the management and working structures that have existed until then in the businesses and factories: from strictly specialised, clearly defined and hierarchically ordered structures to open, flexible organisational systems in which the hierarchies are flatter, the responsibility for decision-making is essentially extended to the lower levels, and the fields of work are arranged in a more inter-disciplinary and complex way.

In addition, management and working techniques are changing in the direction of new models of control and team-shaped cooperation. The fields of work are more closely intertwined, and the areas in which people work in the course of their careers will change more frequently. The traditional job for life with its predetermined career stages, which was open to most higher education graduates in the past, is rapidly disappearing. On the other hand, fields of work are opening up which in the past were not occupied by higher education graduates. Thus, for example, British graduates are much more frequently finding employment in small or medium-sized firms (Pitcher / Purcell 1998: 196).

Higher education graduates must therefore be given the ability to react flexibly to the changes in the world of work, e.g. by being taught key qualifications during their degree course. This requirement is given even more weight by the form of the employment conditions available at the end of their studies. Many of the British graduates currently take on freelance work: they place their knowledge on the market within the framework of contracts for specific tasks and short-term jobs on the basis of profit-sharing or risk-sharing.

This trend is also reflected in the results of the Great Expectation Survey of UK final-year undergraduates of the University of Warwick. In contrast to surveys of graduates[6] which are characterised by a retrospective view of

---

6   For example: University of York; Schomburg / Teichler; Brennan et al. (19976a).

things, this survey followed a future-orientated vision. When asked about their career plans, only 35.5% of the final-year students replied that they expected to find appropriate permanent employment immediately after graduation. In contrast, almost one in four (23.2%) was of the opinion that he or she would (initially) be employed for a certain fixed period of time in order to gain relevant work experience. A further 7.8% intended to take up career-related training, and 6.4% feared that they would have to work in order to pay off (a part of) the debts they had incurred while studying[7] (Pitcher / Purcell 1998: 191).[8]

Against this background it is not surprising that, in an international comparison, the quota of British higher education graduates immediately starting a career is very low, reaching only 52%.[9] The fact that only roughly half the graduates take up employment within six months of graduating cannot, however, be attributed to particularly difficult conditions in the employment market in Great Britain. The reason lies, above all, in the fact that – as already mentioned – a considerable proportion of those with a Bachelor's degree remain within the education system and for the time being are thus not available to the labour market.

Overall, the majority of the students view their career prospects optimistically, but nevertheless, against the background of the changes in the labour market sketched out above, many are worried whether their degree course has provided them with sufficient preparation for the future:

7   Following the current developments (an increase in tuition fees, the abolition of grants and the conversion of the financing of students exclusively into a loan system), it is not to be expected that the financial situation of students will improve in the future either (DUZ 15-16/1997: 27, Pitcher / Purcell 1998: 199).
8   In the other information given, the start of a full-time course of study occupies first place.
9   By comparison: in Germany 82% of higher education graduates take up employment within six months of graduating (HIS: 147).

It is [...] clear that the boundaries of the market have changed, with the development of new specialisms, but the extent to which those who have achieved graduate status as a result of widening access have been able to gain access to jobs with potential for career development in this rapidly-evolving labour market remains a crucial research issue. Will the acquisition of 'personal transferable skills' be sufficient to give all or most graduates a route into a 'graduate' career? Are the expectations of many graduates too high and is it the role of the careers advisers in institutions to temper those expectations according to the 'realities' of the labour market?" (Pitcher / Purcell 1998: 198f.)

The comparatively general direction of the degree course usually leads to the assessment that the subject studied in Great Britain less clearly than in Germany, for example, predetermines in which fields of the employment system the graduates will work (Schomburg / Teichler: 140). Roughly half of all the job offers directed at graduates are thus available for graduates with degrees in every possible subject (Watts 1997: 15).

In Britain the unemployment rate of persons capable of gainful employment who have a degree is 5.6%, and thus comparable with the rates in other Western European countries.[10] When referred to the unemployment rate of graduates aged between 30 and 44, Great Britain has a comparatively low rate[11] (OECD 1997: 103).

Much as in Germany, higher education graduates in Great Britain also continue to do better in the labour market than other groups. The expected yield from an investment in a higher education degree in the course of a

---

10   (1995), as a comparison: The Netherlands: 5.9% and Germany 5.5% (HIS: 151). This statement
      is also confirmed when observed over a period of years (1985 to 1992).
11   (1995): Great Britain: 3.0%, country average: 3.5%, Germany: 4.6%.

working life is very high in Great Britain when compared with other countries (OECD 11997: 104). The secondary analytical studies by Schomburg/Teichler and Brennan et al. (1996a) on the career situation of British and German higher education graduates include details about the employment status, income, position and use of their qualifications. Among other things, they come to the conclusion that in both countries – despite the process of beginning a career which is becoming increasingly long – two years after graduation roughly 80% (Great Britain) and roughly 90% (Germany) of the graduates are in full-time employment.

Seven scenarios for the future of the careers services

The current discussion about the future role of the careers services distinguishes a total of seven scenarios (Watts 1997: 39ff.). All the models include activities with which many of the careers services already deal in addition to their core tasks. As a rule they are not mutually exclusive, but some of them require structural separation from each other. The first four models pursue the goal of integrating the careers services more firmly within the higher education institution. In the last three models the focal point of the activities is shifted from the current main target group "students" to the higher education graduates. Its realisation is more extensive and requires additional funding. Of the latter, only the alumni model is compatible with the four scenarios that refer to higher education institutions (Figure 3).

Figure 3

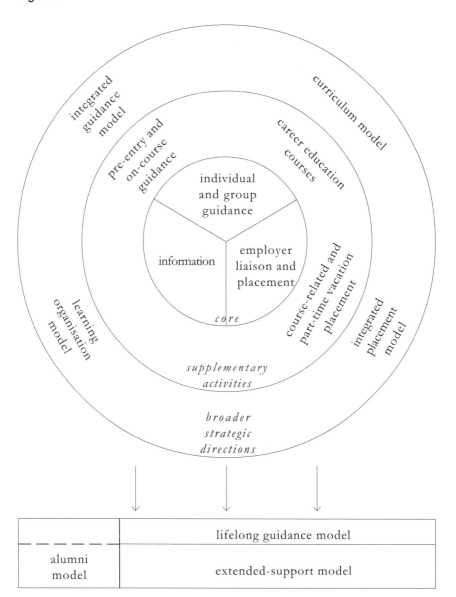

The individual models are as follows:

1. In the integrated guidance model the careers service is integrated into a continuing process accompanying the students. This includes decisions concerning the choice both of the degree course and the career. It starts before a student starts studying and lasts until graduation. The model links up with the increasing "permeability" of the British higher education system – in association with the trend towards modularisation.

2. Beginning with the premise that graduates with practical experience have distinctly better chances of employment,[12] the integrated placement model intends to coordinate the current variety of actors in the field of finding employment and placements, part-time jobs and project work for students and to provide a link with the tasks of the careers service: "At present, there is considerable fragmentation of these various services. It may be possible to find a careers service focusing mainly on job placement on graduation, an industrial placement officer attempting to co-ordinate course-related placements, teaching departments managing their own placements outside this structure, a student employment service based in the students union, and a personnel department offering part-time jobs on campus, all co-existing within the same institution, with no strategic links between them" (Watts 1997: 42).

3. In the curriculum model the careers service supports the departments in integrating employability and career management skills[13] into the undergraduate programme. There is no doubt that the importance of these key qualifications as essential additional qualifications for future higher education graduates is now undisputed (Porrer: 51), but their

---

12   Although, for reasons of financial necessity, many students have jobs while they are studying, these mostly simple jobs frequently have nothing to do with the subject they are studying and thus hardly any notice is taken of them in the labour market.

13   The following are meant here: negotiation techniques, methods for finding solutions to problems etc. (cf. Footnote 5).

inclusion in the academic programme is proving to be a complex process, as has already been illustrated.

4. While the students are the centre of interest in the first three scenarios, in the learning organisation model the careers service extends its programme to the (academic) personnel at the higher education institution. This approach is to be interpreted especially against the background that at British higher education institutions young academics are increasingly employed on the basis of fixed-term contracts. As a kind of "compensation" for this uncertainty they are to be supported by the careers service in the further development of their career.

5. Since the process of starting a career is becoming increasingly difficult for higher education graduates, within the framework of the extended support model the careers services look after their graduates for a certain period after graduation. This "support" can, however, only be provided together with other institutions. In cooperation with firms, for example, (trainee) programmes could be organised for unemployed higher education graduates.

6. The lifelong guidance model follows on from a career concept which includes the necessity of lifelong learning. In this connection careers services offer diverse services for graduates of all ages and from every higher education institution. In addition to providing counselling on the supervision of the graduate's career, continuing education segments would, for example, be integrated.

7. The alumni model regards itself as a lifelong network between the higher education institution and its graduates. Here the "pact for life" is based on reciprocity: as future employers and sponsors, the graduates remain in contact with their university and/or with the careers service and act as a go-between for the higher education institution and the labour market.

Bibliography

BRENNAN, John / SHAH, Tarla: „Hochschulpolitik in Großbritannien". In: Bertelsmann Stiftung (ed.): Hochschulpolitik im internationalen Vergleich: eine länderübergreifende Untersuchung. Gütersloh, 1993, pp. 162-193.

BRENNAN, John et al. (1996a): „Employment and Work of British and German Graduates". In: Brennan, John / Kogan, Maurice / Teichler, Ulrich (ed.): Higher Education and Work. London, 1996, pp. 47-98.

BRENNAN, John et al. (1996b): „Higher Education and Work : A Conceptual Framework". In: Brennan, John / Kogan, Maurice / Teichler, Ulrich (ed.): Higher Education and Work. London, 1996, pp. 1-24.

DfEE&AGCAS (ed.): Career & Personal Development in the Curriculum. A Resource Directory for Higher Education. 2nd edition, 1997.

DOPPLER, Christine: Zentrum für Studium und Beruf. Das Netzwerk an der Universität Bielefeld. Ein Konzept für den Aufbau eines Career Service Centers, eines Absolvent/inn/en-Vereins, einer zentralen Praktikumskoordination sowie für eine Modifizierung des Programms STUDIERENDE UND WIRTSCHAFT. (Unpublished Text) Bielefeld, May 1996.

HAWKINS, P.: Studies for Graduates in the 21st Century. Cambridge, 1996.

Heyworth Report on University Appointments Boards, HMSO, 1964.

HIS: Europäische Hochschulsysteme. Ein Vergleich anhand statistischer Indikatoren. Hochschulplanung 132. Hannover, 1998.

HRK (ed.): Hochschulabsolventen für den Europäischen Arbeitsmarkt – eine Herausforderung für die Universitäten. Beiträge zur Hochschulpolitik 4 (1997). Bonn, 1997.

JONES, Sandra: „Managing Curriculum Development: A Case Study of Enterprise in Higher Education". In: Brennan, John / Kogan, Maurice / Teichler, Ulrich (ed.): Higher Education and Work. London, 1996, p. 136-160.

KUBIK, Birgit / Teichmann, Sabine: "Die Öffnung der Hochschule zum Beschäftigungssystem hin: Einige Überlegungen und Maßnahmen zur Berufsorientierung im Kontext Hochschule und Arbeitsmarkt unter Einbeziehung britischer Erfahrungen mit dem 'Careers Service'". In: Universität Rostock (ed.) Beiträge über die Entwicklung von Studienberatung und wissenschaftlicher Weiterbildung / Fernstudium an der Universität Rostock. Heft 1. Rostock, 1996.

MINISTERIUM FÜR WISSENSCHAFT UND FORSCHUNG NRW: Perspektive Beruf. Praxisinitiativen an Hochschulen in Nordrhein-Westfalen. Düsseldorf. December, 1997.

OECD: Education at a Glance – OECD Indicators, Paris, several years.

OECD: Employment Outlook, Paris, issues of several years.

OECD: Indikatoren für Bildungssysteme. Eine bildungspolitische Analyse. Paris, 1997.

PITCHER, Jane / PURCELL, Kate (1996): Great Expectations: The New Diversity of Graduate Skills and Aspirations. Manchester, 1996.

PITCHER, Jane / PURCELL, Kate (1998): Diverse Expectations and Access to Opportunities: is there a Graduate Labour market?. In: Higher Education Quarterly, Volume 52. Nr. 2. April 1998, pp. 179-203.

PORRER, Robert: "Career Services at British Universities". In: Arbeitsgemeinschaft Career Service (ed.): Career Service. Münsteraner Modell – eine Innovationsstrategie zur Verbesserung des Übergangs vom Studium zum Beruf. Münster, 1996, pp. 48-87.

PULZER, Peter: „Wie gut schmecken Nachbars Kirschen? Bericht aus dem british-akademischen Obstgarten". In: Forschung und Lehre 6 (1997), pp. 304-306.

SCHOMBURG, Harald / TEICHLER, Ulrich: „Hochschulabsolventen im Beruf. Ein sekundäranalytischer britisch-deutscher Vergleich". In: Kehm, Barbara M. / Teichler, Ulrich (eds.): Vergleichende Hochschulforschung. Eine Zwischenbilanz. Themenband II. Werkstattberichte Nr. 50 des WZ. Universität-GH Kassel, 1996, pp. 137-163.

THE NATIONAL COMMITEE OF INQUIRY INTO HIGHER EDUCATION: Higher Education in the Learning Society. Juli 1997.

UNIVERSITY OF YORK (ed.): After a degree ...? Destinations of York Graduats. York, 1998.

WATTS, A.G. / HAWTHORN, R.: Careers Education and the Curriculum in Higher Education. Cambridge, 1992.

WATTS, A.G. (1993): Promoting Careers: Guidance for Learning and Work. National Commission on Education Briefing No. 15, Paul Kamlyn Foundation, Juli 1993.

WATTS, A.G. (1997): Strategic Directions for Careers Services in Higher Education. NICEC Projekt Report. Cambridge, Juni 1997.

Ireland

Conor Geiselbrechtinger

Introduction

As the European Union becomes a reality in everyday life and is no longer seen to be an abstract notion, the various European education systems are in the process of adapting to this new situation. Ireland is no exception here. The Irish education system has undergone many drastic changes in the last decade in order to adapt to new and wide-ranging changes in the international sphere. Ireland has faced many changes during this time and thus an adequate education system needs to be provided to accommodate these changes. Ireland is presently in the throws of what has been termed "The Celtic Tiger". Never before has Ireland experienced such economic growth and prosperity. One of the main reasons for this has always been seen to be the fact that Ireland has one of the youngest working populations in Europe. To serve this need of the economy the education system has had to be altered to provide for this young and educated working population. Universities are presently adapting to the new economic climate. The choices and accessibility of these courses have increased to a large extent. More people than ever have the chance to attend university and study. In order to assess the changes a profile of Irish students and graduates will be offered, and again the question will be asked as to whether the educational system is adequate to meet their needs in the new economic climate. Finally, a profile of the educational system will be provided, exploring the various third level institutions and the nature of the courses on offer. I shall also deal with the nature of the economic climate, since it places the educational changes within a certain context. The particular growth areas in the economy will also be highlighted. This will allow for a comprehensive study of the changes the educational system needs to make to meet these needs. The question will be to show how these courses are beneficial to the working environment in Ireland at the beginning of the twenty-first Century.

1. The Higher Education System

Matriculation into Irish universities

Before third level education is dealt with it should be mentioned how the transition from the secondary to the third level occurs in Ireland. The transition process allows for a more detailed approach to third level education and the transition to the market place. The Irish *Leaving Certificate* (equivalent of the German *Abitur*) is based on a system of point collecting. Each grade is given a value. This is necessary, since every subject is divided into honours and pass level. An honours A1[1] (in Germany 1+) is worth 100 points. A pass A1 is worth 60, which would roughly be equivalent to a C1 at honours level. Every university course offered has a certain points value. As only the best six subjects are chosen to evaluate the Leaving Certificate result, the maximum point value of any course is 600. On average, a university degree course has a value of roughly 400 to 550 points. This again depends on the faculty and the Ministry of Education. However, as I will go on to show, there are many different options to taking degree courses.

Irish universities, technical colleges and degree courses

Ireland offers post Leaving Certificate students a wide variety of study opportunities, of which the university system is the largest. The largest university is the National University of Ireland. It consists of University College Dublin,

---

1   The grades are subdivided in a very similar fashion to the German system. A 'B' grade, for
     example, can be divided into B1, B2 and B3.

University College Cork, University College Galway and St. Patrick's Maynooth. These universities are also referred to as NUI – Dublin, NUI – Cork etc. The three other universities in Ireland are the University of Dublin (Trinity College), the University of Limerick and Dublin City University. Besides these universities there are twelve Institutes of Technology in Ireland, of which Dublin (usually referred to as D.I.T. i.e. Dublin Institute of Technology) is the largest with 10,000 students. It is actually an amalgamation of six colleges run by the Dublin Vocational Education Committee, which took place in 1992. The other Technical Colleges (also referred to as R.T.C.s – Regional Technical Colleges) are in Athlone, Galway, Sligo, Letterkenny, Cork, Waterford, Tralee, Dundalk, Limerick, Castlebar and Carlow. Unlike universities, the Institutes of Technology offer both degrees as well as diplomas and certificates. This will be dealt with in more detail later. Besides the technical colleges there also a growing number of private colleges. The other main study area that is on offer involves teacher training courses, with a wide variety of private colleges in existence. Examples of such training colleges are St. Patrick's College, Drumcondra, Church of Ireland Training College, Rathmines, St. Mary's, Marino, Froebel College, Sion Hill and Mary Immaculate College of Education in Limerick. As with other countries there are also apprenticeships and other training courses. These are usually run in conjunction with the Irish employment agency FÁS.

The Irish university system is based completely on the bachelor's degree. Degrees in most universities vary between three and four years. On completing a bachelor's degree the graduate can continue to study by doing a master's degree and subsequently a doctorate. This is one reason why Irish graduates are very young on average. The average school leaver is aged between eighteen and nineteen. Unlike many other European countries, Ireland has no compulsory military service. Taking into account the length of time it takes to complete a degree, the average age of a graduate would be around twenty-two. The bachelor's degree is divided up into a year system as opposed to a semester system. Traditionally, Irish universities divided the year into trimesters. Examinations are held at the end of every academic year. The entire course is built up by students going from the first year into the second and so forth. Each year is a self-contained unit. Without passing the first year, one cannot get into second year. Besides having to pass the examinations at the end of the year the students are required to produce essays or projects throughout the year. Essays in subjects such as English and History do not tend to be long but the students are required to produce a large number of them during the term. The system can very well be compared to the American system of third level education. The advantage of a system like this is that the structure of a degree is seen as one single entity. In other words, there is a definite link between the various years of study. This also allows for the material to be followed through at a high pace; thus, as mentioned, Irish graduates are very young. The disadvantage of a system like this is that Irish students tend to have knowledge in many subjects as opposed to an in-depth knowledge of specific subjects.

Besides offering degrees like those in the universities, the technical colleges also offer other qualifications. Particular areas of study can be completed at different levels. In other words, in some cases it is not necessary finish with a bachelor's degree. The possibility of finishing with a certificate or diploma also exists. The duration of a certificate course is usually two years, whereas the diploma is finished after the third year. It should be emphasised that these are not one and the same course with different cut-off points. The courses are in the same field but with a different emphasis. Invariably, the certificate course is more practically orientated in comparison to the degree. The difference between the three lies in the entry requirements. The number of points needed to get a place on a certificate course is lower than for a degree course. The idea of this is that less academic students have an opportunity to go to college. This tiered system also has a direct effect on the subsequent job market. A very good example of this is the area of hotel and catering management in the Dublin

Institute of Technology. On the one hand there is a four-year bachelor's degree. This is primarily aimed at qualifying people as hotel managers. The diploma offers a similar course but is more practical. The certificate is called a certificate in "supervision". In other words, when a person with a diploma enters the job market the tiered system still applies. The idea of this is that there should be specific training for specific jobs. However, because the three types of qualifications are so similar, lecturers tend to lecture on all three courses. Besides full-time staff at the D.I.T. there are also many part-time positions. The maximum working hours for a part time member of staff is six hours per week. The reason for this is that the part-time staff come from industry and lecture in the college on a short-term basis, in order to give students hands-on information of working in the various industries. However, this does not mean that the split between the various qualifications is total. There are opportunities to change courses and continue on a different level. For example, somebody who has just completed a diploma may choose to enter the job market immediately or perhaps stay in college and work for a different qualification.

Funding in Ireland

Of all third level education, almost 70% is funded by the state. Private colleges are the exception; they offer post-school education but are not seen as as being part of the university system. The funding for degree courses comes in two stages. On the one hand, the government, or more specifically the Department of Education and Science, funds the courses. On the other hand, the Higher Education Authority (H.E.A.) funds special research and gives grants for postgraduate courses of study. The H.E.A. is primarily responsible for the development of third level education and acts as an advisory board to the government. It is also responsible for developing new courses which are deemed by industry to be vital in the forthcoming years. To put this into perspective, in 1996 the total expenditure on third level education was £519.7

million.[2] Of this amount £159.7 million was allocated by the H.E.A. to specialised projects. These figures can also be seen differently. Of the total budget of the Irish government, expenditure on education takes up roughly 13%. Seen in a wider context this amounts to roughly 5.8% of the entire GNP. When the expenditure on education is broken down further, almost a quarter of this is seen to be spent on third level education.

Unlike British universities, which introduced fees recently, the Irish government abolished university fees a number of years ago. In 1996 students paid half-fees, and in the following year fees were completely abolished. The basic premise for this move was to spread third level education more evenly throughout the population and not to view it as elitist. To ensure that students complete their studies in a relatively quick time, each faculty allows them a limited number of attempts at passing the examinationss. The grant system is means-tested and has nothing to do with academic results. A student can be allocated a grant for four years of college. The grant itself is not viewed as a loan, as is the case in some countries. The grant has been subjected to a lot of criticism, because it has hardly been increased, whereas the rents and the cost of living have exploded, especially in Dublin. The amount a student receives from a grant is barely sufficient to cover the rent.

EU funding in Irish universities

As far as diplomas and certificates are concerned, the funding is often provided by the EU. The EU funding is allocated to courses which have a direct link to the job market. For example, the diploma in computing is European-funded, as it is not seen generally as a degree but as a course that allows students quick and easy access to the labour market. This principle also applies to courses that

---

2   World Data on Education, 3rd. Ed. 1999: UNESCO, International Bureau of Education.

are directly involved in the tertiary sector. Many courses in the Dublin Institute of Technology are thus also funded by the EU. This also entails particular restrictions. These funded courses all have to have a foreign language component. In other words, when studying for a degree in hospitality management a student is required to have either French, German or Spanish from the Leaving Certificate. The language continues to be studied as part of the degree. As the hotel business, for example, is by its nature an international business as well as having wide European contact in terms of the job market, it would seem ideal to insert a language component in the courses, but the reality is somewhat different. This has had a negative effect on the role of languages in these courses. Languages are sometimes perceived as being forced on the students, since they are a compulsory subject. This also has a professional effect on the lecturers. Whereas most lecturers work in their own faculty, language lecturers are spread over a variety of faculties. The lecturers must therefore adapt their teaching to suit the specific aims of the course. When engineering is studied at a technical college on an EU-sponsored course the course content of German is adapted to include engineering vocabulary and text work. The main aim of these courses is to provide the student with a knowledge of the language that can ultimately be used at the workplace.

The role of languages has undergone a wide variety of changes in recent decades. The one turning point that should be mentioned is Ireland's membership of the EEC in 1973. Traditionally, Ireland has been an emigration country and the traditional emigration destinations were English-speaking countries such as Britain, the United States and Australia. But since joining the EEC the Irish have become more eurocentric, and this has been reflected in the studying of foreign languages. Foreign languages used not to play any significant role in Irish education, since the main trading partners and destinations were all English-speaking, but that has drastically changed. However, the level of foreign language competence is far behind that of other European countries.

To compete on a par with other European nations much more work is needed. The Irish government sees Ireland's future as being in Europe, and knowledge of a foreign language is an essential element of this.

Statistics show a clear rise in the number of students entering third level education. It is also interesting to note the distribution of subject choice after a student has once been accepted for the third level. In 1999 63,234 students sat the Leaving Certificate examinations. Of this number 36,500 received places on Third level courses. This is an increase of 22% since 1992. The trend in 1999 was very clear. There was a 16% increase in the number studying science / applied sciences, a 35% increase in the number studying engineering or technology and a 16% increase in the field of business and business administration. Of the 30,000 graduates Ireland produces a year, 57% are in these particular fields.[3] This can be reagrded as a clear shift towards meeting the needs of Ireland's economic climate.

2. Employment and the Labour Market for Graduates

As already mentioned, the Irish economy has done a large U-turn in the last decade or so. The annual growth rate has been consistent. The new economic climate has been dubbed "The Celtic Tiger". Unemployment is at a low (ca. 5%) and there seems to be little sign of this trend slowing. Other statistics confirm this. The annual growth of real GDP has been consistently between 8% and 9% over the last five years with the year 2000 looking like continuing this trend. Overall exports have increased by 13% from 1998 to 1999. The largest growth increases have been in the computer and technological sectors and the main increase in exports has been to the United States of America (13%) and Malaysia (248%).[4]

---

3   Ireland, Vital statistics – IDA Ireland (compiled by Marketing Services Division), Feb. 2000.

Economists have warned of "overheating". A large part in this trend is played by the gradual change from traditional industries to modern industries. Before this is dealt with in detail, other factors need to be mentioned in this connection. Firstly, with the coming of the European Union Ireland has seen a new market open up. While the United Kingdom has traditionally been Ireland's main trading partner, the European market accounts for almost twice as much today. The second major factor is the age of the population. Ireland has one of the youngest populations in the EU, almost 50% being under the age of twenty-five. This, of course, is a vital asset to a growing economy. With jobs being provided, there are large numbers of young skilled workers to take these jobs.

The effect of this is shown in the changes in the nature of work. Traditionally, Ireland has been an agricultural economy, but in 1996 only 11% of the working population were employed in agriculture. New industries have superseded this traditional industry. The strength of the economy lies in services and industry. These areas need a skilled working population, and Ireland prides itself on having a highly skilled workforce. The priority sectors are electronics, such as semiconductors, PC systems and communications. This is, of course, coupled with engineering in areas such as automotive components, aerospace and industrial electronics. Another big area of growth is in the production of healthcare and consumer items, for example medical devices, hospital products as well as sports and leisure and personal care products. Finally, another big growth area is banking, insurance and teleservices.[5] These growth areas are all specialised, and a skilled labour force is very important for continuing the growth.

4   Ibid.
5   Ibid.

3. Linking Higher Education with the Labour Market

The education and economic statistics speak for themselves. They show that the Irish economy has changed and that students are tending to enrol in courses which will give them the right qualifications to work in the labour market. This, of course, has had an effect on third level education. Universities need to adapt to this market. Whereas many vocational courses have already been in existence, universities themselves are slowly adapting to the new situation. The growing trend is to place greater emphasis on applied subjects such as the sciences and engineering. As already mentioned, the Institutes of Technology have been set up and are funded to meet this specific need. The certificates and diplomas are very practically orientated, and this is also the case with the degrees offered. All degree programmes have some element of practical training involved, from which the practical knowledge acquired is used in the continuing studies.

In recent years universities have started to take a similar approach. While the degrees offered by the universities have not really been affected, the choice of master's degrees has been widened. Universities still hold the position they do in other countries, in that they offer education in subjects that are not directly related to the labour market. Undergraduate studies have changed little and the course content is relatively abstract, but within postgraduate studies there have been a variety of changes. At the moment it is very common for graduates to study for a master's degree that has nothing to do with their original course of study. Most universities now offer these one-year master's courses. This is not to be confused with the traditional master's degree. When a person studies English, for example, he or she has a choice between two types of traditional master's courses. On the one hand, it is possible to complete a one-year taught master's course, which consists of essays, examinations and a minor thesis. On the other hand, one may wish to complete an M.Litt., which consists of two years of research and a thesis. The new one-year master's courses which are being offered are in subjects that often differ from the traditional degree in areas such as PR., journalism, business studies and multimedia technology. A good example of such a course is the one-year computer science diploma at University College Dublin. Essentially, there are no prerequisites for starting this course apart from a degree from a university in any subject, and applicants need no prior knowledge of computer science. The course is designed to be a one-year intensive computing course which gives graduates a wide variety of practical computer skills such as programming or software design. The course is very practically orientated and much of the theory, which is important in the actual degree, is dispensed with.

A very interesting point is that in many cases the practical and business orientated approach can be seen to be crossing into the general academic field. In association with the E.U. and the I.D.A. (Industrial Development Agency) many new projects are being set up to further industrial growth. The idea is to find an approach that combines industry, academia as well as entrepeneurship. A very common trend is the launching of campus companies and also protecting them with "Enterprise Ireland's Campus Companies Programme". This also includes the "Intellectual Property Assistance Scheme". The aim of this is the following: "Under this programme we provide assistance to researchers in commercialising R&D emerging from college campuses. This includes funding to enable campus based companies to assess the commercial viability of innovative technologies. Support is available in the form of both business development and financial assistance to start-up knowledge-based enterprises."[6] A similar approach has emerged in the nature of doctorate studies in Ireland. Funding for doctorates has increased, and just recently the Irish government announced a £62 million investment in third

---

6   Enterprise Ireland: Service Details – Enterprise Ireland, 1999.

level research. The aim is to promote research in fields that are applicable in industry. In many cases the research can lead to campus companies being set up. In the Forfas report the projected postgraduate research programmes were highlighted. As with enrolment at university the trend appears to be a growing amount of postgraduate research in the fields of science and technology. In the period between 1999 and 2001 the number of postgraduates is expected to be 278 as well as 140 postdoctoral students. 124 of the 140 postdoctoral students and 233 of the 278 postgraduates are expected to be in the fields of science and technology. This confirms a 1996 statistic, according to which 340 of 370 postgraduate research programmes were in these fields.[7] The problem facing Irish academia is the fact that as far as total numbers are concerned there is a shortage of third level research being carried out at the postgraduate level. Overall, Ireland awards 8.1 doctorate degrees per 100,000 of the population in science and engineering. When compared to countries such as Switzerland, where the figure is 26.1, this is a very low number. The report continues by saying, "While strong advances in the output of PhDs have been achieved, there is concern in the academic community, in specific industry sectors and amongst policy analysts that the increase in output has levelled off, primarily due to the attractiveness of alternative employment opportunities for the potential PhD students and the poor financial support given to students while undertaking research leading to a PhD."[8]

A good example of this is computer science at University College Dublin. Many of the research projects are aimed at business and industry. From 1996 to 1999 a project was underway known as "Scribble - Integrated Form - Design and Hand - Writing Recognition for Automated Data - Entry" The aim

---

7   Expert Group on Future Skills – Executive Summary – Forfas, 2000.
8   Ibid.

of this project is to produce a system by which a computer is able to recognise handwriting. The description of the project gives a clear indication of what its aim is: "In particular, research is continuing on the development of a front office, off-line handwriting recognition system which is geared towards the needs of small businesses."[9] The priority has been set to produce systems that have practical applications in the business world. This is, of course, directly linked to funding and receiving a research grant. This project, for example, was funded by the Forbairt (now known as Enterprise Ireland) Research scheme and was given £20,000. Forbairt is a government institution and thus the needs of industry will receive a lot of attention.

4. Career Orientation within the Higher Education System

As in other European countries, Irish universities offer career guidance counselling as well as other career-orientated services. The careers office in the universities plays a dual role. On the one hand, it is involved in giving students advice on what possibilities exist for graduates on the labour market, and on the other hand it informs them about further study options. The office usually has full-time staff and offers a wide range of services, one being that recently graduated students can register their name with the office, which then sends out information to the graduates for a year after completion of their final examinations. The office also deals with academic opportunities for graduates, and thus it provides information on the one-year courses mentioned above. Other information that is available concerns the possibility of studying abroad and the type of qualification needed to do so. However, in real terms the university does not actually aid students in their search for employment. As the careers office is mainly an information supplier it is up to the students themselves to find their own way after university. Although much of the content of courses

---

9   Research Projects – Department of Computer Science, University College Dublin, 1999.

in the science and technology areas has changed to accommodate industry, the faculties themselves do not directly work with industry. On the whole, students are left to their own devices, but given the economic climate in Ireland it does not actually take very long to find employment on leaving college.

Besides the careers offices, which are to be found in every university, another option when seeking employment is the state careers office known as FÁS. This agency is responsible for most of the different types of work in the country and offers a wide variety of services. Firstly, unlike the careers offices in universities, FÁS is involved in all areas of the labour market. In other words many of the jobs offered by FÁS are not necessarily academic or for people who have studied. Much of FÁS's resources is spent on working with the long-term unemployed. FÁS itself offers courses, such as computer courses, as well as apprenticeships, but the services offered go much further. FÁS is also involved in providing information on jobs abroad and the necessary bureaucratic procedures that need to be completed. Secondly, it is also involved in setting up interviews. A perfect example of this is that in the final year of the engineering course at U.C.D. FÁS brings prospective employers into the university and the students are welcomed to interviews. The advantage of this is, of course, that students then have a sense of security and a very good reason for passing their examinations at the first attempt. In other cases, FÁS also offers advice on interview techniques and presentation when graduates are dealing with prospective employers, in many cases for the first time.

5. The Transition from Higher Education to Profession

Joining the workforce

Studies have shown that the Irish situation in terms of the labour market are very good. The increase in employment, but more importantly in career opportunities, has led to almost complete employment for graduates. As has been shown, Irish industry and employers are in need of a qualified labour force, and the increase in graduates is starting to meet this need. However, the actual number of graduates is still very far below the number needed. Another major point to be mentioned is the fact that the statistics show that students are tending towards applied degrees in order to get into the labour market. A report released by the department of Enterprise, Trade & Employment confirms this. Of the men who graduated in 1999, 3.6% were unemployed. In the case of women the figure was 4.5%.[10] The actual step from third level education into the labour market is usually left to the graduates themselves. In some cases the university intervenes, as in the case of FÁS setting up interviews in the faculty of engineering but on the whole this occurs very seldom. Most employment is found through advertisements in national newspapers. As there is an abundance of places it rarely takes graduates too long to find employment. This, however, needs to be qualified. In subjects such as medicine, architecture etc. the graduates will invariably work in their chosen fields of study. As far as Arts students are concerned, the choice can be viewed as either being very wide or limited. While there are relatively few direct employment chances in the given fields of study such as history or English, many graduates go on to complete a master's course. This allows for a more flexible approach to entering the job market. The exception to this would be teachers but this is traditionally a very difficult area. In most cases Arts graduates would start at a relatively low level in a company and gradually work their way up. In cases like these the company often invests money in further education to promote their workforce. The average salaries are reflected by this. As is the case everywhere, the size of the salary depends on the level of expertise. In industry the average gross wage per hour is £ 7.77.[11] This figure is set to rise, but Ireland has one of the lowest

---

10   Ireland's National Action Employment Plan 2000 – Department of Enterprise, Trade & Employment.
11   Industrial Earnings and Hours worked, CSO Statistical Release, November 1999.

costs in all job categories in Europe.[12] In terms of contracts the labour market is relatively secure. With a demand for labour it is in the interests of the employers to give full-time contracts to their staff. The major exception to this is in education. Full-time teaching contracts are very difficult to obtain.

Working abroad

From an historical point of view there has been a very interesting change in Ireland over the last few years. Ireland has traditionally been a country of emigration. It is claimed that there are close to 70 million people of Irish descent in the world, of whom 30 million are in the United States alone. When compared to the size of the population in Ireland this is phenomenal. At present there are close to 3.75 million people in the Republic of Ireland.[13] However, with the economic growth fewer people are emigrating to foreign countries, which had been the case until the early part of the 1990s. Indeed, when the immigration statistics for last year are taken into account, over 50% of immigrants into Ireland were returned emigrants.[14] However, although little help is given in universities themselves, many Irish graduates go abroad for a certain amount of time. The skills acquired during the university degree course have always been shown to be valuable in a European and world context. It is not unusual for graduates to spend maybe two to three years in a foreign country before returning home. FÁS offers a service to provide Irish graduates with information about employment abroad. Ass with the trend mentioned above, there is a gradual shift from anglophone countries to European countries. The main problem that faces Irish students in Europe is the language barrier.

---

12   Industrial Earnings and Hours worked, CSO Statistical Release, November 1999.
13   This does not include the population of Northern Ireland.
14   Ireland: Vital Statistics – IDA (compiled by Marketing Services Division), Feb. 2000.

Prognosis

The question on many people's lips is, of course, "How long will this last?" As mentioned, there is always talk of "overheating" in the economy. Ireland has never before experienced such an economic upturn and the fear is that it will not last for ever. However, a report published in 1997[15] shows what the trend is likely to continue in the Irish labour market in the near future. On the whole, employment is to rise 23% (or 2.6% per annum) from 1995 to 2003. There will be a decline in agriculture, but the growth areas will be in areas for managers, professionals and associate professionals. The report makes the point that traditional labour is decreasing whereas there is an increase in higher positions. The report goes on to discuss this further. The main points are:

1) Increased employment will require higher qualifications.
2) There will be a large increase in employment in the services sector.
3) There will also be a decrease in employment in low skilled manufacturing.
4) The largest of the increases will be in professional, managerial, sales and personal services.
5) A decrease of 5% per annum will taken place from 1995 to 2003 in agriculture, textiles and religious services.
6) There are better opportunities for those with post secondary education or higher level skills.
7) Female employment is set to increase by more than 35% between 1995 and 2003 from 455,000 to 615,000. In this time female employment will have risen from 37% to 42%.

There are a number of conclusions to be drawn from this report. It seems that the current trend is likely to last. In other words, the universities

---

15   Occupational Employment Forecasts 2003 – D. Duggan, G. Hughes, J.J. Sexton, FÁS / ESRI Report No. 6, 1997.

have to offer a variety of programmes that will cater for the long-term future and not merely as a temporary fill-in. Heavy emphasis has been placed on the role of education. The growth areas cited in the report are all in the field of educated professionals. Traditional labour is decreasing whereas skilled employment is increasing.

Conclusion

Thus education in Ireland is gradually changing to meet the needs of the twenty-first century. The work is by no means complete, but steps have been taken in this direction. The challenge that the government of Ireland faces is to provide a growing economy with the skilled labour it requires. At present the situation has arisen that the workforce is not large enough to meet this need. But as I have tried to show, the trend in third level education is towards being practical and work-related. This not to say that the numbers of people studying traditional degrees has decreased. Actually, the opposite seems to be the case. There are record numbers of young people, and Ireland now has the prosperity to give them a wide choice in education.

Italy

Lorenzo Fischer

1. Higher Education System

The Italian higher education system is part of a model that has been defined as being "integrated homogeneous" since there is only a single institution: the university (Benadusi 1993; see also Capano 1998). In other words, it is a system without any structural or horizontal differentiation (only one organization is destined to provide higher education). As for functional or vertical differentiation (levels of education), while it was nonexistent before 1990, there is now a certain amount of diversification. Nevertheless, first-level diplomas only involve little more than 11% of the total number of students enrolled at university (ISTAT 1999b). While first-level diploma curricula (3 years) are only partially in line with the second-level (degree – 4 years or more), it is important to remember that a set of rules was issued in January 2000 that will soon radically modify the organization of the university system, a subject that will be discussed in the conclusion.

During the decade 1987/88-1996/97 the number of Centres organizing higher education increased by 41 units, from 63 to 104. Lombardia (18), Lazio (11) and Campania (9) are the regions with the greatest number of university structures (these figures also include the branch Centres located outside the province of the main university). During this same period the number of courses also increased significantly: degree courses rose from 791 to 1263, while diploma courses (created in 1992/93) increased from 420 to 756 (ISTAT 1999a). The main areas of study can be grouped together under five main headings:

- Health (Faculties of Medicine, Veterinary Science and Pharmacy);
- Science (Faculties of Mathematics, Physics, Natural Science and Agriculture);
- Technical-Engineering (Faculties of Engineering and Architecture);
- Humanities (Faculties of Letters and Philosophy, Education and Languages);
- Economic-Juridical-Political-Social (Faculties of Economics, Law, Political Science and Sociology).

Currently the national university system includes 49 State Universities, 3 Polytechnics, 3 State University Institutes, 3 State Post-Secondary Schools, 2 Universities for Foreigners, 8 Independent Universities and 4 Independent University Institutes. Therefore, private institutions are decidedly in the minority, with slightly more than 5% of the total number of students.

In the last decade the rate of transition from high school to university has been characterized by a cyclical oscillation of between 66% and 73%. On the other hand, based on data gathered from one hundred 19-year-olds, first-year enrolment at universities is constantly growing: in 1998/99, the last data available, it had reached 47% (Censis 1999).

Access to university is open. For thirty years it has been possible to enrol in any university course, as long as the prospective student has a 5-year high school diploma. However, despite open admission, it is primarily students holding a diploma from a *lycée* who enrol at university, while less than half of the technical school graduates and little more than a quarter of those from professional institutes make this choice. In addition, ever since first-level diplomas became available, it has become clear that students from technical and professional institutes prefer these briefer programmes, while *lycée* graduates tend to select degree programmes (ISTAT 1999a). In any case, equal opportunity for university enrolment remains more virtual than real, especially when we consider that students from Technical Institutes are half as likely to get a degree as students from a *lycée,* and the situation is even worse among graduates from Professional Institutes. However, it must be noted that some of the students who did not attend *lycée* drop out of university because it is easier for them to get a job. In any case, the social-cultural composition of the *lycée* differs greatly from that of the professional and technical institutes. As a matter of fact, in the fifth year of high school 78% of the students whose parents are university graduates are in a *lycée,* while about 70% of students whose parents stayed at school only until the minimum school-leaving age find themselves in technical and professional institutes.

University degree courses with limited admission hardly existed until the mid-1980s. Then, beginning with the faculties of Medicine and Veterinary Science, the regulation of admission became more widespread. Currently there is limited enrolment in the faculties of Medicine, Veterinary Science, Architecture, first-level Diploma courses and newly established courses in the initial period, as well as for those courses requiring training periods. In all of these cases student selection primarily depends on multiple-choice tests.

Between 1990 and 1996 total public funding of the University decreased from 88% to 82%, and the share of this amount coming from the Ministry for University Education and Research dropped from 78% to 67% respectively. The average total tuition paid by each student shifted in real terms from L529,000 (1986) to L921,000 (1996), which represents a 74% increase. *Per capita* public funding was L5,510,000 in 1996, meaning that student tuition now covers 17% of the cost, while it accounted for just 8% in 1986 (ISTAT 1999a). Even though only 7% of university students benefit from a scholarship in Italy, there are great regional differences: 22 students out of 100 receive scholarships in Trentino, compared with fewer than an average of 1% in

Molise. Despite the fact that expenditure on study has increased considerably in recent years, it is still insufficient. On average, over half of the students who meet the requirements regarding income or scholastic merit do not receive scholarships, even though 4 regions have been able to grant the applications from all those who are eligible.

Females students are by now in the great majority: in 1991/92 they already outnumbered males and they represented 56% of first-year students in degree programs in 1998/99 (ISTAT 1999b). However, their presence is still extremely differentiated according to which faculty they attend, being very close to 90% in Education, but reaching just 18% in Engineering. In diploma courses, on the other hand, there is an almost equal number of males and females, even though females accounted for 58% of the students receiving the university diploma in 1995/96. In addition, 29% of the women take their degrees with the maximum grade of 110/110 and *summa cum laude* as compared to 21% of the males. It is interesting to note that men achieve higher grades in degree programmes with a strong prevalence of females and vice versa (e.g. females in Engineering) (ISTAT 1999a).

The greatest problem facing the Italian university system is without doubt its low productivity. For every 100 students enrolled, only slightly more than one third finish their studies, and it takes them much longer than the prescribed time. A quarter of the students do not re-enrol after the first year, and a further 13% fail to enrol after the second year. The other very serious problem is the "behind schedule" students, i.e. those taking about 7 years to finish four-year degrees (in Italy, 27 is the average age at graduation). In 1998 only 12% had completed their degree in the prescribed time and there were considerable differences depending on the Faculty (ranging from 48% in Medicine to just 7% in Architecture) (ISTAT 1999b). However, if we consider students enrolled in the third year of a degree course, the likelihood of their finishing varies from 87% in Medicine to 44% in Engineering. This can be considered the real "success rate" for university students if we disregard those who drop out during the first two years, often as the result of choosing a course without the necessary amount of thought (ISTAT 1999a).

2. Employment and the Labour Market for Graduates

In 1998 the average employment rate was 47.6% in Italy, with a very slight increase compared to the year before, primarily due to the rise in the number of females. Nevertheless, female participation on the labour market still remains lower when compared with the situation in the other major industrialized nations. The difference between the North (almost 51%) and the South (less than 44%) is still a very serious problem despite the fact that a certain increase has been verified in the South as well. It is important to keep in mind that in Italy there is a great deal of so-called "illegal work" (various activities not officially accounted for and which therefore evade the revenue authorities), and this is especially true in the South. Southern unemployment is now four times as high as in the North (in 1994 it was three times as high) and the increase in the number of jobs is primarily due to temporary contracts, while there continues to be much less part-time work available than in other industrialized nations. Nevertheless, the labour market is slowly becoming more flexible.

The labour market for university graduates is a special case. Traditionally, almost nine tenths have been employed in the tertiary sector, less than a tenth in industry and just 3% in agriculture (ISTAT 1997). This situation is primarily the result of the Italian industrial framework, which is characterized by an abundance of medium-sized companies, and small ones in particular.

Information provided by the "Quarterly Reports on the Labour Force" reveals that there is a 34% chance of being actively employed one year after taking the degree, the rate being 37% for women, against just barely 28% for men. Female graduates are more likely than males to find employment everywhere in the country except Central Italy, where the male employment rate is 37% one year after graduation and female employment is 10 percentage points lower. There are considerable differences between the various regions, with a 52% employment rate in the Northwest, 33% in the Northeast, 30% in the Centre and only 22% in the South. It is important to emphasize that the rate of employment one year after finishing school (from the middle school certificate to the university degree) is nevertheless greater than 50% in Northeastern Italy, while in the Northwest it barely reaches 44%. This can be explained by the fact that the Northeast, with its very large number of small businesses, manages to employ relatively few people who have university qualifications (ISTAT 1999c).

Job opportunities improve with rising levels of education, and this is true at a time of both 1-2 years and 5-6 years after graduation. Within 6 years of attaining the qualification, the unemployment rate is 25% for those with only compulsory schooling, 20% for high school graduates and 13% for university graduates. People of both sexes, regardless of their qualifications, begin to work at an earlier age in the Northeast, the average age being just 19 as compared to 22 for people living in the South (ISTAT 1999c).

University graduates, particularly in the North, manage to find a job within a few months, while high school graduates have to wait for more than 2 years on average (almost 4 years for those only holding the middle school certificate). Not only do university graduates find employment more easily, but they are also hired into more well-qualified positions. More than one fifth immediately start out at the managerial level, many take up freelance positions and almost 50% become white-collar workers (ISTAT 1999c). Self-employment is also an important market for male graduates. This is especially true in the South-Central regions, where almost 15% of young people dedicate themselves to this kind of work, the majority being university graduates. The latter are also more inclined to accept "atypical contracts" (temporary, partial, etc.), as this choice means greater job flexibility, which better-educated young people often prefer.

While there has often been a discussion about intellectual unemployment in Italy, university graduates do indeed have greater advantages on the labour market since it is usually easier for them to find a job and they rarely run the risk of losing it. University qualifications also give women greater employment opportunities, particularly in the South, and graduates can generally continue working into old age (Reyneri 1996). However, youth unemployment in Italy is more widespread than in other European countries. Therefore, since younger generations are considerably better-educated than in the past, this is often erroneously viewed as intellectual unemployment. The university degree certainly reduces the risk of unemployment, but in Italy even the best prospects for university graduates (compared to high school graduates) are not as bright as in other countries. In 1995 Italy had an unemployment rate of 38% among high school graduates aged 20-24, while for university graduates aged 25-29 it was 33%, falling to 13% for the 30-34 year old age bracket (ISTAT 1999a).

In the 1970s and 1980s the educational system was the main labour market for university graduates, which is why there is a relative surplus of teachers today (the teacher-student ratio at the various scholastic levels is about 1:10 on average). It is only during the past two years that nursery school and elementary school teachers have received university training. On the other hand, after receiving their degree from the various faculties, high school teachers entered the teaching profession either after a state competitive examination or, as was often the case, through compulsory employment by law after numerous years of temporary work in the school. Now there is a two-year postgraduate degree for secondary school teachers that has been in effect since 1999/2000.

3. Linking Higher Education with the Labour Market

The Italian university system remained fairly isolated until the 1980s; concerns about job opportunities were essentially the responsibility of the new graduate and coordination of the supply and demand for employment were all but nonexistent except for a certain connection between some specific faculties and professions (Medicine, Law, etc.). In addition, the Polytechnics have traditionally had relationships with industry. In recent years, and especially following the establishment of Diplomas, the question of professionalism has taken on greater importance. It has now reached the point that nearly everywhere the so-called "job placement" offices have been set up at university faculties. Since 1994, on the initiative of the University of Bologna, the "AlmaLaurea Project" was developed, which has involved a growing number of Italian universities. 23 universities had already joined the project by January 2000, and together these accounted for roughly 40% of the Italian university graduates.

The primary objectives of the Project are:
· analysis of the internal performance of the educational activities in a given institution;
· analysis of the external performance of the degree courses offered by a given institution;
· promoting access to the labour market for new graduates;
· continuous career updating;
· extending AlmaLaurea to the European level.

The data used by the Project are gathered by means of a systematic survey, using a questionnaire that each degree candidate fills out just before completing his or her studies. The information concerns over 250 variables (e.g. university career, studies abroad, job experience, parents' level of education, language and computer skills, etc.).

Thanks to the Project the "internal" efficiency of educational institutions can be evaluated by means of specific studies of the main characteristics of graduates from a given institution and through a statistical profile of the graduate himself.

The Project also facilitates an evaluation of the "external" efficiency of the curricula offered by a given institution through systematic monitoring of the current work situation of the graduate participating in the Project, made possible by using the CATI method (computer-assisted telephone interviews).

The AlmaLaurea databank contains detailed information about all the graduates and diploma candidates (more than 150,000 in January 2000) at the universities taking part in the Project. AlmaLaurea also helps graduates to enter the labour market, assists companies in recruiting personnel and reduces the gap between the supply and demand for qualified work.

4. Career Orientation within the Higher Education System

In Italy, the transition from a university for the élite to one for the masses was not accompanied by any organizational reform for developing horizontal and vertical differentiation. Degree courses have thus maintained an approach that is still too general and segregated from the world of work except, in part, for the education of professionals. University funding has been affected as well. Even though there has been a reduction in public allocation in recent years (today down to 4/5 of the total), private contributions still only amount to a few hundred billion lire, excluding student tuition fees.

University curricula have long been, and often continue to be, a group of disciplines lacking a professionally consistent educational plan. We could even go so far as to say that scientific research has been the only real career orientation existing in higher education, and while this is a noble prospect there are certainly other duties that a university for the masses has. Unfortunately, many professors only seem capable of thinking about educating individuals in their own image. Research is certainly important, but it is not the only prerequisite for work; furthermore, it expects students to have aptitudes that many do not possess. The University Diploma has, at last, provided an initial impulse for change, as can be seen from the positive experience with *Campus*, which has demonstrated that a new relationship between the university and the world of work is indeed possible.

The Campus Project came into being in 1995 with the purpose of developing University Diplomas that would favour the employment of young people by responding to the needs of productive society. Organized mainly by The Conference of Italian University Rectors (CRUI) and the General Confederation of Italian Industry, the Project involved the participation of 26 Universities in North-Central Italy, which created a total of 67 courses in the fields of engineering, applied science, economics and the high-tech service industry. These highly professional diplomas offer important innovative features including:

- a minimum of 400 hours of laboratory practice and a required training period;
- the possibility of a dual Italian-foreign qualification;
- external teaching staff (at least 1/5) primarily from companies;
- adoption of the training credit system;
- courses in foreign languages and European culture;
- the presence of a tutor.

The most positive feature of the Campus Project is certainly the joint participation of both the university and industry from the very beginning of the curricular planning. Studies of company expectations emphasize the differences existing between small and medium-sized companies on the one hand, which are particularly interested in the university diploma, and larger companies that give preference to degree graduates (Gentili / Finocchietti / Schiavone 1996).

Joint collaboration between the university and the workplace and the broad opportunity to involve non-tenured professors from business in the teaching has gradually begun to spread. As we shall see in the conclusions, these should constitute one of the fundamental trump cards of the reform that is underway. An important example relative to the current academic year is the degree in Automobile Engineering that has been instituted at the Turin Polytechnic in collaboration with FIAT.

The University's attitude towards continuing higher education has also changed in the past decade. The traditional vision that did not consider this to be the university's mission is being altered, with specialization courses and Master's Degrees becoming more common. This change should find ample room in the reform currently in progress and will contribute to an increased rapport between the University and society.

5. The Transition from Higher Education to Employment

There were 129,000 graduates during the academic year 1998/99, which represents a considerable increase compared to the 98,000 5 years previously. Added to this number were the almost 11,000 students with the university diploma. The productivity rate of degree courses (percentage of graduates/ 100 admissions 5 years earlier) has experienced a slight upswing in the past two years, reaching 36% in 1998/99.

	1995		1998	
Degree Courses	number	%	number	%
Scientific,Geo-Biological, Chemical, Pharmaceutical	13413	12.8	14835	11.5
Medicine	7641	7.3	7090	5.5
Engineering- Architecture	15798	15.1	22093	17.1
Agriculture	2544	2.4	2630	2.0
Economics	19651	18.7	24564	19
Political Science-Sociology	7217	6.9	10056	7.8
Law	16361	15.6	19450	15.1
Letters, Psychology, Languages, Education	22252	21.2	28451	22.0
Total	104877	100	129169	100

(Censis 1999)

The most common way for a sample of students who graduated in 1992 (interviewed in 1995) to find employment is by direct contact with the employer (24% of the cases). The second way, in order of frequency (15%), is by having relatives or acquaintances mention the name to the employer (recommendation); the third (again almost 15%) is the state competitive examination; the fourth (10%) is self-employment. Newspaper advertisements occupy almost the last position, and this is true for both the graduates and the companies advertising. The only approach that is even less frequent still is direct communication between the university or professors and the employer. The main differences are that women generally undertake self-employment half as often as men and apply for teaching positions at government offices or directly to school principals with much greater frequency (ISTAT 1996).

ISTAT periodically carries out sample surveys to analyze the situation regarding university graduates 3 years after completing their studies. The last such survey looked at students who had graduated in 1995 (interviewed in 1998). In addition, graduates who had received the university diploma 3 years earlier were studied in 1999 for the first time. Only a little preliminary data is available at the moment, but it is nonetheless of great interest and reveals that 72% of degree graduates and 83% of diploma holders had jobs about 3 years after graduation. The apparent improvement made possible by the new university diploma can be explained by the fact that many students already had a job before receiving the diploma (24% compared to 12% of degree holders) (ISTAT 1999b). In terms of professional employment opportunities there is obviously a significant dissimilarity between the various types of diplomas and degrees. Therefore, the most fitting comparison can be made by only taking into account steady employment that began after the university diploma or degree.

Graduates who have had the greatest opportunities include those from Business Economics (89% employment rate), Dentistry (86%), Engineering (85%) and Computer Science (80%). Career prospects have also been good for graduates in Pharmacy (74%), Veterinary Science (73%) and the field of Economics-Statistics (73%). Graduates with the worst situation on the labour market are those from the faculties of Education (31%), Humanities (41%), Law (43%) and the Geo-Biological fields (49%). While only 38% of Medical Doctors were working, an almost equal number also admitted that they were not looking for work, but were continuing their training by studying their specialization.

Among diploma holders 80% of those from Engineering were steadily employed after graduation. The fields of Political Science and Sociology (74%),

Agriculture (67%) and Statistics (67%) also proved to have good employment opportunities. The worst situation regarding diplomas was represented by Linguistics (21%), Law (35%) and Physical Education (38%) (ISTAT 1999b).

It is important to emphasize that the job one finds is not always in keeping with the field of study. 68% of graduates found a job requiring a university qualification, while the remaining 32% carried out an activity for which the degree was unnecessary. From this perspective the least advantageous position is for Linguistics (in 68% of the cases the degree would not be necessary), Humanities (58%), Education (56%) and Political Science-Sociology (55%). The most promising situation is for the fields of Medicine (1%), Chemistry and Pharmacy (9%) and Engineering (13%).

Regarding diploma holders, only 58% had found a job for which the qualification was indispensable, while 42% were carrying out activities where the diploma would not have been necessary. In this sense, people holding diplomas from Linguistics (85%), Economics-Statistics (77%) and the fields of Science-Chemistry-Pharmacy (75%) are in the worst position, while the best situation is in the fields of Political-Science and Sociology (only 21% have jobs that do not require the diploma) and Medicine (28%) (ISTAT 1999b).

As part of the AlmaLaurea Project there is extensive, constant monitoring of graduates from the universities participating in the Project. 1998 data is available relative to 13 universities (Bologna, Parma, Modena and Reggio, Ferrara, Venezia Architecture, Trento, Trieste, Udine, Firenze, Chieti, Messina and Catania) with a total of almost 18,000 graduates (72% rate of response). 56% are employed one year after graduation. Added to this number are another 19% who are not looking for work for various reasons, the most common one (78%) being continuing their education. In conclusion, only just one quarter of the graduates are still waiting for employment. Data relative to the graduates' evaluation of the efficacy of their qualification (one year after graduation) reveal that 39% consider it of little or no benefit. This is basically comparable to the ISTAT survey, where 32% of those interviewed (3 years after graduation) judged the qualification unnecessary for their particular jobs. However, the AlmaLaurea data cannot as yet be considered representative of the Italian situation, even though this might become the case in the near future given the increasing rise in the number of universities participating in the Project.

If we consider 1997 graduates (only 9 universities made up the sample), 67% are working two years after the degree, while just 14% are still looking for employment. There are interesting differences regarding gender in this sample. If it is true that 53% of the men and 52% of the women have work one year after obtaining their degree, it is also true that the latter look for employment more frequently (almost 30%), since men have the problem of military service and since there are more men undertaking graduate studies. Moreover, a 1990 study of universities in Emilia revealed that "the gender differences in terms of postgraduate employment opportunities – all else being equal – are rather limited [...] variables, such as the kind of degree obtained, acquired work experience during the years of study and the geographical area of residence count more than sex alone" (Santoro / Pisati 1996).

These limited statistics from the AlmaLaurea Project, although very recent, lead us to an important question concerning gender differences. In Italy the income differential for *per capita* work by female graduates between the ages of 30-44 is very high compared to men (reaching 43%) while in France, for example, it is barely 29%. Generally speaking, in Italy a university qualification pays off less than in other countries, for men as well. On average, graduates have a 61% higher income than people holding a high school diploma (compared to 80% in France). However, we must once again point out that the situation for females is particularly negative. In fact, while a female university graduate in Great Britain earns more than twice as much as a high school graduate, in Italy the economic advantage is only one third.

6. Development, Trends, and Prospects

As we suggested in the introduction, the Italian university is undergoing a period of profound change.

The traditional organization of our higher educational system, which until only recently had only one degree level (chiefly the 4-year degree) is being drastically transformed in accordance with the following scheme:

· a three-year level (degree) with a large number of students;
· a five-year level (specialized degree);
· additional levels (Master's, specialization, research doctorate).

In this way it will be possible to move through a pyramidal university arrangement, which should reduce inefficiency and the consequent dispersal of students, thereby making it better suited to the current needs of society.

Within this framework, the recent provisions concerning autonomous university teaching propose four important reform objectives:

· the realization of totally autonomous teaching;
· conformity of the Italian higher educational system with the European model in accordance with the Sorbonne and Bologna agreements, which make provisions for a common first-level triennial degree that can be reciprocally recognized in the various nations;
· the transformation of university didactic principles based on students' choices and needs by means of the "credit" system;
· the realization of a flexible and self-reforming system.

In addition to university reform, integrated higher education is also being implemented. Although still at the experimental stage, it intends to develop horizontal or organizational differentiation in the Italian system of higher education. In collaboration with secondary schools, agencies for professional training, business concerns and the university, and under regional supervision, Italy is trying to establish post-secondary professional training to be achieved through learning sessions lasting from one to four semesters. Using the system of training credits, its aim is to create professional skills that are more directly applicable to the precise needs of the region so that they can be used immediately on the labour market and / or at the university.

The university training credits will be the measure of the quantity of learning (including self-study) required of each student (with the necessary prerequisites) in order to acquire the knowledge and skills provided for in each degree curriculum. On average this means 25 hours of work that can be increased or decreased by 20% (by ministerial decree) for individual categories of study, i.e. degrees with the same key educational objectives. Since it is based on the choices and needs of the students, the credit system should revolutionize university education by integrating the curriculum with students' educational objectives.

A lightened study load will have to be created aimed at making it possible for students to complete their studies within the prescribed period of time, but without lowering quality, since superficial factual knowledge will have to be abandoned and expertise (to know, to know how to do and to know how to be) will have to be developed.

The university autonomy that is being realized will be very extensive and therefore not devoid of risks at the beginning, and the qualitative differences already existing in the universities could become even more pronounced. The only antidote seems to be the introduction of effective mechanisms for evaluation aimed at fulfilling the general objectives of the faculties and the University. The State should intervene mainly by means of incentive mechanisms (Moscati 1996).

The three-year degree "has the objective of assuring that the student achieves sufficient mastery of general scientific content and methods, in addition to acquiring specific professional knowledge" (Decree No. 509 of 3/ 11/99). The student must therefore be qualified to enter the labour market directly, and for this reason there are provisions for consultation with local organizations representing industry, the service sector and the professions before drawing up the curricula. A much closer relationship between the university and the workplace is contemplated, which is also expressed by the fact that all the degrees will have to include a certain number of credits to be obtained through training periods. Another important basic characteristic of the reform is its flexibility and self-reforming nature. For a long time the university remained essentially isolated and its relatively rigid curricula were defined by law. Now however, the Italian university has acquired a great deal of autonomy that should permit it to keep its courses updated on a continuing basis. This reform, which could be beneficial for educating highly skilled labour in Italy, will be anything but easy to achieve in concrete terms. A considerable number of professors will have to modify their own outlook and attitude towards teaching, which will be a decidedly complex process. There is a need for a strong evaluation/promotion policy provided by "an intermediary organization made up of professors, in any case, that has the consensus of the interested parties and considers general and particular needs so as to reduce, at least in part, the currently hegemonic connection between the State and disciplinary organizations" (Moscati 1996).

We have seen that the university degree in Italy already reduces the risk of unemployment, even though it is less lucrative than in other countries and does not always permit one to get the desired job. It is difficult for Italian industry to take full advantage of the graduates available on the labour market, especially in the South. Expansion of the service industry is still relatively low compared to other countries (e.g. Great Britain), and this fact seems to play a negative role on the creation of employment opportunities, above all for well-trained young people.

A greater awareness of the usefulness of highly skilled labour, especially on the part of small and medium-sized companies, by coming face to face with the wide availability of very professional three-year graduates, could help to overcome the traditional difficulty Italian industry has had in offering employment to better-educated individuals. Hiring university graduates presents a real organizational challenge for an industry that finds itself forced to compete in terms of "total quality". University-educated graduates usually desire greater involvement in company matters and have career expectations that until now have often frightened off small and medium-sized companies, dissuading them from hiring. However, post-Ford production needs workers at all levels who identify with the company. Today, transversal skills are required to make the most of human resources and it is necessary to know how to work in a team and coordinate the work of others, to manage interpersonal relations and to deal with complex situations. Above all it is essential to master problem-setting and problem-solving, which currently represent the primary need in business. It is clear that the university will have to change radically in order to respond positively to these educational requirements. It will not be easy, but it is indispensable (La Mendola 1995).

Strongly spurred by entrance into Europe, the greater flexibility and diversification of the Italian higher educational system should, in any case, make it more efficient, and this should result in greater benefits both for students and for society.

Bibliography

Benadusi, L. (1993) (ed.), *L'istruzione superiore di primo livello*, Angeli, Milano.

Capano, G. (1998), *La politica universitaria*, il Mulino, Bologna.

CENSIS (1999), *33° Rapporto sulla situazione sociale del paese*, Angeli, Milano.

Gentile, C. / Finocchietti, C . / Schiavone, N. (1996), *Minerva e Vulcano. I diplomi universitari e le imprese*, CRUI, Roma.

ISTAT (1996), *Inserimento professionale dei laureati. Indagine 1995*, Roma.

ISTAT (1997), *Rapporto sull'Italia*, il Mulino, Bologna.

ISTAT (1999a), *Lo stato dell'Università*, Roma.

ISTAT (1999b), *Università e lavoro*, Roma.

ISTAT (1999c), *Rapporto sull'Italia*, il Mulino, Bologna.

La Mendola, S. (1995), *Con gli occhi di Caronte. Le imprese e i neolaureati*, Clueb, Bologna.

Moscati, R. (1996), *Prospettive per l'autonomia universitaria*, in Staropoli et al., *Modelli di Università in Europa e la questione dell'autonomia*, Fondazione Giovanni Agnelli, Torino.

Santoro, M. / Pisati, M. (1996), *Dopo la laurea*, il Mulino, Bologna.

Japan

Ulrich Teichler and Kerstin Teicher

1. Institutions and Enrolment

When the structure and organisation of the Japanese education system was reformed after World War II closely in tune with the US education system, universities (daigaku) were established initially as the only type of higher education institution. In 1994, the total number of universities was 552, and they enrolled altogether about 2,480,000 students (Monbushô 1995).

As Table 1 shows, the number of universities in 1994 was almost two and a half times as high as in 1955, i.e. the time when the new postwar system of higher education had consolidated. During the same period, the number of students increased from about 523,000 to almost 2.5 million, i.e. almost quintupled (see the statistical overview in Hiroshima Daigaku, Daigaku Kyoiku Kenkyü Senta 1995).

Japan is the only industrial society in which the private sector of higher education clearly outnumbers the public sector (see Geiger 1986). In 1994, 406 universities were private, 98 were national, i.e. supervised and primarily funded by the national governments, and 48 local, i.e. primarily funded and supervised by the provincial or city governments. As Table 2 shows, about 73 per cent of the university students were enrolled at private institutions. As a rule, universities provide four-year course programmes to students who have completed 12 years of primary and secondary education. The programmes lead to a gakushi, which is considered internationally equivalent to a bachelor's degree. In medical fields, the course programmes require six years of study.

Table 1. Number of institutions of higher education in Japan 1955-1994

	Universities			Junior colleges			Colleges of technology		
Year	Public*	Private	Total	Public*	Private	Total	Public*	Private	Total
1955	106	122	228	60	204	264	-		
1960	105	140	245	66	214	280	-		
1965	108	209	317	68	301	369	47	7	54
1970	108	274	382	65	414	479	53	7	60
1975	115	305	420	79	434	513	58	7	65
1980	127	319	446	85	432	517	58	4	62
1985	129	331	460	88	455	543	58	4	62
1990	135	372	507	95	498	593	58	4	62
1994	146	406	552	92	501	593	59	3	62

*Source: Ministry of Education, Science and Culture 1995, pp. 70-73. *National and Local.*

Three hundred and seventy-one universities, i.e. about two thirds, had established graduate schools (daigakuin). Of them, 252 awarded doctoral degrees (hakushi), whereas 119 conferred master's degrees (shûshi) only – many not in all the fields of study provided in undergraduate education. Master's courses take two years as a rule, and doctorate courses three years. It is possible, though, to be awarded a doctoral degree upon submission of a thesis without prior enrolment at the daigakuin. In 1994, altogether about 139,000 students were enrolled at daigakuin. The transfer ratio from undergraduate to postgraduate study of less than ten per cent can be considered as low in comparison to other industrial societies in which the first university degree is equivalent to a bachelor's degree.

Junior colleges (tanki daigaku) were initially established on a provisional basis in 1950 because not all the institutions possibly upgrading to universities in the new postwar system could comply with the standards of a university.

Table 2. Number of students* at institutions of higher education in Japan 1955-1994

Year	Total number			Percentages of private institutions		
	Universities	Junior colleges	Colleges of technology	Universities	Junior colleges	Colleges of technology
1955	523,355	77,885	-	59.7	81.1	-
1960	626,421	83,457	-	64.4	78.7	-
1965	937,556	147,563	22,208	70.5	85.3	20.0
1970	1,406,521	263,219	44,314	74.4'	90.1	16.5
1975	1,734,082	353,782	47,955	76.4	91.2	12.1
1980	1,835,312	371,124	46,348	75.0	90.9	6.7
1985	1,848,698	371,095	48,288	*11.1*	89.7	7.0
1990	2,133,362	479,389	52,930	72.7	91.4	6.0
1994	2,481,805	520,638	55,938	73.4	92.5	5.2

*Source: Ministry of Education, Science and Culture 1995, pp. 70 and 74f. *All students (including part-time students, graduate students, etc.).*

In 1965 they became a permanent feature of the higher education system. They mostly provide two-year courses, and in some fields three-year courses, to students who have completed 12 years of primary and secondary education. In the 1990s, an associate degree (jungakushi) was introduced in tune with U.S. practice. In 1994, altogether about 521,000 students were enrolled at 593 junior colleges, of which the private sector comprised 84 per cent (501 as compared to 36 national and 56 local) of the institutions and 93 per cent of the students.

Colleges of technology (kôto senmon gakkô) were established in 1962 as a third type of higher education institution. Upon completion of the middle school and altogether nine years of school education, students are provided with a five-year programme in which the final two years are considered to be part of higher education, as Chart 1 shows. The 62 colleges (54 national, 5 local and 3 private) have altogether about 56,000 students, among them only five per cent at private institutions.

Since 1976, the better equipped among the so-called "miscellaneous schools" (kakushu gakkô) have been upgraded to special training colleges (senshû gakkô). The 3,437 special training colleges in 1994 (155 national, 206 local and 3,076 private) are considered to be part of the post-secondary education system in Japan. They provide one-year to three-year predominantly full-time courses for specific vocational areas, mostly requiring 12 years of prior education. Of the total of about 837,000 students, 94 per cent were enrolled at private institutions.

In recent overviews, miscellaneous schools have also been called post-secondary institutions. There were altogether 2,934 institutions of that type (among them 3 national and 70 local) with about 339,000 people enrolling (among them 98 per cent at private institutions). The institutional type comprises such different activities as driving schools, "crammer" schools for entrance examinations, vocational schools, and even foreign educational institutions residing in Japan (for example branch campuses of U.S. universities, or colleges for the Korean minority in Japan) etc.

There are some colleges for special professions which are not under the supervision of the Ministry of Education, Science, Sports and Culture (Monbushô), but under other ministries, for example the Ministry of Labour and the Self-Defence Agency. A few years ago, the Ministry of Education, Science, Sports and Culture established the National Institution of Academic Degrees, i.e. an office in charge of examining the qualifications acquired at these institutions and the possibility of awarding a higher education degree.

Chart I: The present system of education in Japan

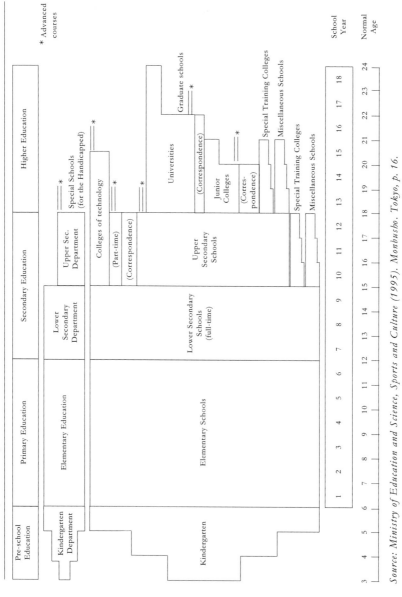

Source: Ministry of Education and Science, Sports and Culture (1995). Monbusho. Tokyo, p. 16.

2. Some Basic Information on Education and Employment in Japan

2.1 Institutional framework of education

Compulsory education in Japan lasts for nine years. The curriculum in every primary school is the same. In the following three years in the middle school pupils have the choice between English and teaching related to vocational training. The former is chosen almost exclusively, since more than 95 percent of those leaving the middle school transfer to upper secondary education.

Success in entrance examinations decides on a person's future educational career. Roughly 75 percent of those receiving upper secondary education (kôto gakkô) take general courses and roughly 25 percent takes courses with a vocational emphasis. The level required for admission to upper secondary schools varies greatly; publication of the percentage of graduates from individual schools who later start studying or have been admitted to a famous university contributes towards stabilising the school hierarchy.

The proportion of young people starting to study was approximately 35 percent in the mid-Seventies, and rose to more than 40 percent in the course of the Nineties. Roughly two thirds attend universities (daigaku), most of which provide four-year courses, and six-year courses for medicine; master's courses lasting two years and doctorate courses lasting three years are attended by only relatively few graduates with first degrees. Almost a third – mainly women – attend universities providing short courses (tanki daigaku) with mostly two-year courses. Finally, there are colleges of technology (kôto senmon gakkô), above all for technical subjects, which combine the three-year upper secondary period and a short period of study into a five-year programme under one institutional roof. Only about one percent of each year group actually makes use of this.

Roughly one fifth of the upper secondary school leavers decide in favour of vocational schools before they start employment. Higher vocational schools (senshû gakkô) provide specialised subject-based programmes lasting between one and three years. A large proportion of the "miscellaneous schools" (kakushu gakkô) specialise in programmes providing a vocational qualification.

2.2 The qualification of those taking up employment

The Japanese Ministry of Education annually publishes detailed statistics on the whereabouts of graduates from the most important types of schools and higher education institutions right at the beginning of the following school year. The data are gathered by questionnaires sent to the educational institutions which, for their part, request their pupils and students to inform them of their whereabouts. According to these statistics, of those taking up employment for the first time in April 1994 who had completed their schooling or higher education immediately beforehand, 52 percent had completed a course in higher education, 45 in the upper secondary school and three percent in the middle school.

However, a comparison between the figures of graduates and school-leavers in 1994 with the corresponding figures for those starting their courses a few years previously permits the conclusion that the dropout rate at upper secondary schools was 6 percent, at institutions of higher education with short courses it was three percent, and for students attending their first course of study at universities it was six percent. This means that at least eight percent of an age group leave the education system after breaking off their schooling or their course of study.

In addition, the statistics on the whereabouts of the young people reveal that after completing the middle school roughly one percent of the age group, and after completing the upper secondary school more than 25 percent, transfer to higher vocational schools or other schools providing vocational qualifications. However, no statistics are available on the transition from these schools to the employment system.

Finally, the statistics do not cover delayed transitions. If we assume that the school-leavers and higher education graduates who can be said to be unemployed at the beginning of the following school year do, in fact, generally take up employment at a later date, then we find a quota of delayed transition of nine percent of all the successful school-leavers and higher education graduates in 1990, and 12 percent in 1994. Until recently it was the case that the schools and institutions of higher education did not provide any support in helping their former pupils and graduates to seek or find employment (see the later comments on this). Recently, however, a number of institutions of higher education have been reporting that they also offer their usual services to those graduates of the previous year who did not take up employment immediately after completion of their studies.

Overall, we can state that the traditional analyses for the transition from school and higher education to the employment system, which also form the basis for the following description, only reflect the situation for little more than half the young people. There is no doubt, however, that the following description takes in the processes of transition which are considered to be typical.

2.3 The significance of starting employment

In Japan the transition from the education system to the employment system is considered to be particularly important. Ideally, the person does not change employers since the principle of "permanent employment" prevails: Japanese firms make a greater effort than is the case in other industrial societies to secure employment for a person's entire working life; in return, they expect greater willingness to adapt to changes in the tasks to be performed during the employee's working life.

In fact, comparative international statistics actually reveal that occupational mobility in Japan lies below the average level of that of western European countries, but that it is similar to that in some of these countries (cf. Teicher 1955, p.38 ff.). At the beginning of the Nineties a survey revealed that 66 percent of the middle-school leavers in employment, 47 of the upper secondary school-leavers, 40 percent of the short-course graduates and 28 percent of university graduates changed employers within the first three years (Ôe 1994, p. 115). Occupational mobility in the initial years is therefore hardly any lower than in Germany. Those, however, who find employment in a business which is considered to be particularly attractive – usually a large firm – hardly move at all. "Lifelong" employment does actually occur under ideal circumstances; this underlines the value of the process of seeking and finding a job for school-leavers and higher education graduates.

3. The Process of Transition in Japan

The mechanisms of the transition from the education system to the employment system in Japan (cf. the overviews in Kariya 1994; Yoshimoto 1996) are by no means uniform. We find differences depending on the educational courses attended and between the private and public employment sectors. There are, however, a number of common features, which will be dealt with initially.

Firstly, the time phase for seeking and finding employment takes place fairly early. As a rule, the decision concerning the employer is already taken a number of months before the end of school attendance or graduation from a higher education institution – the school and university year officially ends in March, and firms always employ people taking up their first job from April 1st.

The last months until graduation may possibly lead to corrections here and may offer a last chance to those for whom the search has until then been completely unsatisfactory. Until recently there was no systematic opportunity in Japan to seek employment only after graduation – something that is widespread among German higher education graduates because the grade of the final examination is often an important employment criterion.

Secondly, in Japan the institutions participating in the process of seeking and finding are jointly making great efforts to restrict this process to a very short period of time. The fairness of the competition is to be increased in this way, and thus a limit is to be imposed on the effort expended on the transition process. It has become clear, however, that the activities of those involved do not all take place within this official framework; the interest in gaining an advantage through earlier activities is too great.

Thirdly, the schools and institutions of higher education play a conside-rable role in the transition process. Apart from the employing organisations and the graduates it is clear that the educational institutions themselves are the most important actors. By contrast, the public employment service plays a much more modest role; in the case of the transition from the institution of higher education to employment, private institutions which take on the task of providing information are of far greater significance than the employment service.

This, however, is where the common features end. The individual mechanisms of the transitions differ very distinctly according to whether the school-leavers or graduates are able to apply to a large number of employing organisations independently of the support of their educational institutions, or whether they are dependent on the support of the educational institutions and can only apply to a moderate number of organisations. We call the former the "open procedure" and the latter the "closed procedure".

Figure 1: Fields of application of the different employment procedures

Application procedure	Field of employment/career	Typical educational qualification/ Subject/Sex
closed university	manual technical field of work (ginôshoku)	upper secondary school leavers (male), graduates in engineering and natural sciences
open	higher administrative work (sôgôshoku)	university graduates in the arts and social sciences (male), graduates from colleges of technology
semi-closed	simple office work (ippan shoku)	female graduates from short university courses, partly graduates from upper secondary schools or universities

3.2 The closed procedure for school-leavers

It is clear that there is a closed procedure for young people leaving the middle and upper secondary schools who want to take up employment in private business after obtaining their school leaving certificate (cf. Tsuchiya 1992; Kariya 1994). The characteristics of the seeking and placement procedure which probably applies to roughly 90 percent of those school-leavers who want to take up employment after leaving school, can be illustrated best in chronological order.

In the first two months of the school year, i.e. April and May, the employment offices offer information events for those pupils from the last class in middle and upper secondary schools who want to take up employment after obtaining their school-leaving certificate. Firms can advertise their job vacancies within the framework of these events. However, in accordance with the annual agreement on job placements, in which the education and employment authorities as well as representatives of the firms participate, during this period it is forbidden for them to advertise the job vacancies through visits to schools or by inviting pupils. During this time it is also forbidden for them to accept applications already and to select from among those who have applied.

In June firms must generally enter on a special form the job vacancies that they want to make known to the pupils through the schools, and they have to hand in these forms to the employment office. This registration system (kyûjinhyô) for job vacancies with the employment authorities was introduced in 1970. In the first place its goal is to guarantee that pupils receive a sufficient amount of information about the employment tasks and the employment conditions to be expected. Secondly, in this way – as already stressed – it is to be guaranteed that the process of seeking employment and making vacancies known is restricted to a certain period of time.

It is only at the beginning of July that firms are permitted to turn directly to the schools in accordance with the rules of the agreement mentioned above. In most cases they do not advertise their vacancies openly for all pupils. A system of relations over many years between individual firms and schools (jisseki kankei) is much more typical, through which firms make their vacancies known only to certain schools and provide them with concrete information on how many of their pupils they will probably employ. The security of expectation which the firms grant the pupils of the particular school has its counterpart in the efforts on the part of the school to provide the firm with pupils who are as suitable as possible.

In the summer an exchange of information and a selection process takes place between teachers, parents and pupils. The teachers who have the task of maintaining contacts with the firms and helping the pupils to find jobs play an important role here. To what extent the wishes of the pupils and the parents are fulfilled and to what degree the teachers provide guidance may differ from one school to another. When questioned, roughly 70 percent of the pupils stated that they had found the firms themselves, while the teachers had decided on their own in less than 10 percent of the cases (cf. Rikurûto Risâchi 1995).

One of the preconditions of the placement system for school-leavers from middle schools and upper secondary schools is that the school initially issues only one letter of recommendation to each pupil in the last school class, and that each pupil should initially apply to only one single firm (hirtori isshashugi). Only when an application attempt has failed after the firm has turned the applicant down can the pupil receive a new letter of recommendation and apply to another firm.

Schools issue letters of recommendation (suisen) to their pupils at the beginning of September. After that the firms invite the applicants who have been recommended to an interview in the firm. Offers of employment are made as early as in September. There is then sufficient time left to solve the minority of the cases in which the firm does not make an offer of employment to the recommended applicants or when the applicants turn down offers made to them.

3.3 The open procedure and the mixed procedure

Until well into the Seventies a similar, i.e. closed, procedure had existed for students at institutions of higher education (cf. Azumi 1969; Teichler-Urata 1975). However, the procedure was criticised again and again precisely with regard to the higher education graduates because it created an almost automatic mechanism of entry to the most attractive firms for the graduates from famous universities, and thus contributed to overheating the competition for entry to the most famous universities. In the mid-Seventies a procedure of open application (jiyû ôbo) was therefore set up for university graduates in the field of business and administrative positions in private firms. At the beginning of the Nineties it was shown that roughly 40 percent of higher education graduates take up employment in private business by means of this procedure (cf. Ôe 1994).

The open and mixed procedures at institutions of higher education are interconnected with each other in many respects, and follow the same schedule (cf. Teicher / Teichler 1996). The universities offer information and advice sessions to students as early as during their third year of study – mostly in the second half of their penultimate year (cf. Yoshimoto / Kosugi 1993). It can be stated overall that the vocational advice and placement offices (shûshokubu and others) of the private universities participate much more actively in the transition process than the corresponding offices at state-funded universities.

Firms start sending out prospectuses during the last few months of the third year of study. The students also receive handbooks – without requesting them and free of charge – from publishers specialising in activities of this kind. In these handbooks the individual firms describe their job vacancies, in each case in a predetermined format. The handbooks are accompanied by bound piles of reply cards (seikyû hagaki) with which, in an easy form, the students can signal their interest in additional information and a possible application.

Until 1996 the framework for the official part of the employment procedure was laid down in the Agreement on Employment (shûshokukyôtei). In it, under the overall control of the Association of Japanese Employers' Organizations (Nihon Keieisha Dantei Renmei, abbreviated to Nikkeiren), the Japanese Employers' Organizations – after consultations with the higher education institutions and the Ministry of Education – each year determine the dates for the most important steps in the procedure for filling vacancies for graduates from universities, short-course universities and colleges of technology. Analogous with the recommendations that Nikkeiren informs the firms about, the Ministry of Education addresses the institutions of higher education and requires them to observe the procedures and the scheduled dates.

During the Eighties it was usual to reserve the months of May and June for contacts between the higher education institutions and firms in order for the latter to provide more precise details of the job vacancies and for the former to make the information about job vacancies they had received from the firms available to the students. From August onwards the firms were free to run information sessions and to begin interviews with applicants. Finally, the Agreement on Employment fixed the date on which the informal job offers (sayô naitei, often abbreviated to naitei) were permitted to be made for the first time. At the end of the Eighties this was generally at the beginning of October.

In the case of the open procedure, which applies to the highest career levels of the business and administrative field, in which only university graduates are employed, the students can make direct contact with the firms. This also applies even when firms request individual universities to recommend a certain number of students. The firms' handbooks and prospectuses encourage students to make open contacts, and in this field the firms generally accept applicants without a recommendation on the part of the university.

The firms evade the agreements on dates for contacts by seeing to it that their personnel departments do not officially participate in contacts that take place prematurely. Larger numbers of younger employees take over the task of making the initial contacts as temporary "recruiters"; they phone the students – mostly students from their own alma mater who have contacted the firm by means of reply cards or in other ways – as OBs (Old Boys) or, more rarely, as OGs (Old Girls), and have informal conversations with them. Firms also rent external rooms for information sessions (e.g. in hotels), so that these sessions on premature dates can be considered as informal.

University graduates wanting to work for private firms in the fields of natural science and technology are informed in the same way as students wanting to apply for jobs in the field of business and administration. This is generally done with the aid of handbooks and prospectuses about all the job vacancies the firms have. For the most part, however, they require a letter of recommendation from the university in order finally to be regarded as an applicant; more than two thirds of them find their job through recommendations made by the higher education institution or the professors. The recommendation system means that the interviews for the applicants usually take place later than those for students applying for jobs in the fields of business and administration. In general it can be stated that the more open the procedure is, the earlier the placement begins.

People who apply for the general career track (ippan shoku) in the field of business and administration – especially women who have completed a short course of study choose this middle career level – can apply to most of the firms either without restriction or with a recommendation from their higher education institution. Many firms inform the short-course universities about how many applications they will accept from them with recommendations. Those graduates who apply with the support of a recommendation generally appear to have better chances of obtaining a job than those who apply direct. Roughly half do, in fact, take up employment with the aid of recommendations.

According to a survey carried out at the beginning of the Nineties, 44 percent already had an informal job offer in June, i.e. nine months before completing their studies. The proportion rose to 66 percent by the end of July (cf. Tsuchiya 1992). The employment procedure is thus evaded in the majority of cases.

However, the offers of employment are only announced after the start of the period during which recruitment is officially allowed to take place in accordance with the agreement. This then happens so quickly, however, that it is hardly possible to conceal the fact that the interviews and negotiations took place prematurely. The last six months before the date set for the start of employment – April 1st – thus only serve to permit additional application procedures: if a graduate has not found a job by then, or when students are seeking something better, or firms want to entice them away from other firms.

3.4 The procedure for employment in the civil service

Examinations must be passed in order for a person to qualify for most areas of the civil service – i.e. for the general state administration, the judicial authorities and work as a schoolteacher. These examinations are usually held in the summer. In most cases two examinations take place roughly one month apart, and only the most successful in the first examination are admitted to the second. It is, above all, students in their last year of study who participate; it is possible, however, to repeat the examination, and some students participate only after completion of their studies.

Students generally find the basic information about the examinations and the further application procedure in the brochures (tebiki) compiled each year by the employment advice and placement offices of the individual institutions of higher education for their students seeking employment; the brochures also contain basic information about applications within the private sector. Students usually receive these brochures during the second half of their third year of study.

A far greater number of applicants participate in the examinations than are finally employed in the civil service. The reason for this is partly that the success rate in some examinations even lies well below 20 percent. In addition, success in a particularly selective state examination can certainly prove to be an advantage for applications in the private sector.

As a rule, the individual public authorities carry out the selection of their applicants at the same time as the firms which strictly abide by the guidelines of the Agreement on Employment. The vacancies are always advertised publicly and can be obtained without the intermediate hurdle of a recommendation from the institution of higher education. It is generally the case that the results of the qualifying examination have the greatest weight in the selection of the applicants.

3.5 The personnel selection procedure

Firms and public authorities always employ first-time employees from April 1st each year. The number of higher education graduates expected to be employed is determined more than a year in advance, and the number of school-leavers at least nine months in advance. In the case of firmly established contacts between schools and firms, as well as in the case of the particularly well-known institutions of higher education, the firms employ all the recommended applicants, since the number of recommendations made by the institutions of higher education corresponds to the quantitative demands made by the firms. In the case of the open procedure the firms inform the institutions of higher education about how many people they have employed from the individual institutions of higher education in the recent past; the students are given this information selectively through the handbooks and in detail through portfolios on the individual firms, which the institutions of higher education make available in their employment advice and placement offices. In the case of mixed procedures the firms often request the institutions of higher education to name a slightly larger number of applicants than they intend to employ from these institutions.

At the time of the official application both pupils and students merely submit a curriculum vitae on a prescribed form. In many fields, as already mentioned, a letter of recommendation from the school or institution of higher education must be produced. Apart from this it is not customary to formulate the application by means of an accompanying letter or to produce additional documents in support of the application.

In the case of the open procedure the recruiters in the firms have the task of providing the students with information to help them in making a decision, of encouraging interesting applicants, and of making an initial assessment of the applicants. They are not infrequently given the task of suggesting to ambitious women that they ought rather to withdraw their application for the highest career level (sôgôshoku), and instead that they should follow the safe path of taking up a middle-level career (ippan shoku).

Finally, in the case of the open procedure the firms invite the more interesting applicants, and in the case of the closed or mixed procedures the applicants with letters of recommendation, to an interview, and under certain circumstances also to entrance examinations. Selection interviews generally do not last longer than half an hour and are complemented by discussions about employment conditions etc. Entrance tests are especially widespread in the selection procedure for the middle-level career in the firms – the so-called general (ippan shoku) career – which is taken up almost exclusively by women, of whom most are short-course graduates. Some tests examine general knowledge and knowledge of foreign languages; in addition, there are tests for specific specialist knowledge, e.g. in the field of data processing.

Finally, an informal undertaking to employ the applicants is given. It is expected that they will either accept or reject it. Firms, can, in fact, withdraw their undertaking without having to fear legal consequences. However, the withdrawal of an undertaking of this kind is considered to be detrimental to a firm's image; the firm must fear that it will have fewer good candidates in future. Some applicants withdraw their acceptance or simply do not appear on the first day of their planned employment. The less open the procedure is, the less unlikely it is that an even more favourable opportunity will offer itself to them, and thus they are subjected all the more to moral pressure by their educational institutions not to withdraw their acceptance under any circumstances, in order to avoid harming the chances for future generations of graduates from this institution.

Some firms offer seminars for graduates from higher education institutions even before they take up employment. These serve to provide an introduction to the business. Seminars take place most frequently and are most impressive during periods of a strong demand for higher education graduates, since they also have the function, as far as possible, of preventing the candidates from backing out.

4. Employment and Expected Qualifications

There is much speculation about the weight of the different criteria in the selection of applicants by Japanese firms. In Japan, for example, there are journals which have specialised in providing information to pupils and students concerning the transition from education to the employment system. They are full of articles in which experts, managers or younger employees in firms discuss their impression of what is most important in the selection of applicants. The number of empirical studies on this subject is, however, comparatively small (on the state of research cf. Teicher et al. 1996).

Both for the higher education graduates and school-leavers it can be stated that an important part is played by the institution of higher education or the school they attended. Even if many firms stress that they do not pay so much attention to the rank of the educational institution, as is commonly asserted, there seem to be no serious doubts among all those involved that the institution attended is of great importance in this selection procedure.

With regard to the transition from the higher education institution to employment in particular, firms do, in fact, frequently give assurances that the institution of higher education attended is not of decisive importance. However, in the end it is the preselection by the Old Boys which underlines the status of the institution of higher education that has been attended. The recommendations of the institutions of higher education are by no means always made in accordance with the results a student has achieved: in some state-funded faculties recommendations are intentionally given in the order in which enquiries were received from students, after informal discussions between the students themselves, or even by chance, so that the preselection on the part of the institution of higher education is restricted as far as possible; by contrast, there are private institutions of higher education which recommend students in accordance with the presumed criteria of the firms – e.g. in accordance with simulated entrance examinations by the firms. At any rate, many students – especially those in the fields of the arts and social sciences – have the impression that, once they have enrolled at a higher education institution, their chances of employment are no longer dependent to a great extent on the results they achieve during their studies.

Within the framework of the Group Project "A Comparative Perspective of Relationships between the Education and Employment Systems in Japan" we have attempted to obtain a more precise picture of the skills expected. In a written questionnaire in the summer of 1993, 80 large Japanese firms that are members of the Japanese Employers' Association, Nikkeiren, provided information about the skills they expect from their new employees

- at the time they are employed (i.e. recruitment criteria)
- after the initial phase of learning and training in the firm and
- at the time of the first large promotion (cf. Teichler 1995).

In Figures 2 and 3 those careers are characterised as being higher careers for which a university degree is generally expected. Middle-level careers are those for which the completion of a short course of study is expected, and simple careers are those for which an upper secondary school leaving certificate is a precondition in most cases.

As the diagrams show, when new applicants with a university degree are employed the large Japanese firms lay the most emphasis on
- hard work and the readiness to work,
- the willingness to communicate,
- the ability to work in a team, and
- the willingness to learn.

General cognitive skills, social qualifications and positive attitudes to work have almost the same weight for those being employed in the technical field as for those in the business and administrative field. Additionally, in the former field there is also the expectation that the employee will have basic and specialist knowledge of the subject and mathematical abilities.

Figure 2: Skills expected of employees in the business and administrative field of Japanese firms (arithmetic mean)

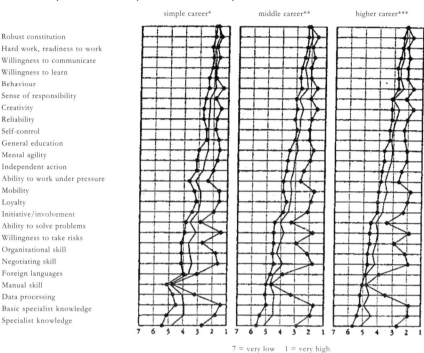

simple career*   middle career**   higher career***

Robust constitution
Hard work, readiness to work
Willingness to communicate
Willingness to learn
Behaviour
Sense of responsibility
Creativity
Reliability
Self-control
General education
Mental agility
Independent action
Ability to work under pressure
Mobility
Loyalty
Initiative/involvement
Ability to solve problems
Willingness to take risks
Organisational skill
Negotiating skill
Foreign languages
Manual skill
Data processing
Basic specialist knowledge
Specialist knowledge

7 6 5 4 3 2 1   7 6 5 4 3 2 1   7 6 5 4 3 2 1

7 = very low   1 = very high

• on employment, – after the initial training phase, ♦ at the time of the first large promotion

*   usually upper secondary school or middle school leavers
**   usually graduates from short courses or colleges of technology
*** usually university graduates

Source: Group Project: "A Comparative Perspective of Relationships between the Education and Employment Systems in Japan".

The picture for middle and simple careers is not essentially different. The order of precedence of the desired skills is similar, the only difference being that the expectations are slightly more moderate.

Figure 3: Skills expected of employees in the technical field of Japanese firms (arithmetic mean)

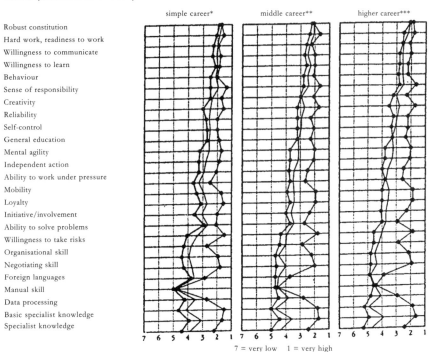

simple career*   middle career**   higher career***

Robust constitution
Hard work, readiness to work
Willingness to communicate
Willingness to learn
Behaviour
Sense of responsibility
Creativity
Reliability
Self-control
General education
Mental agility
Independent action
Ability to work under pressure
Mobility
Loyalty
Initiative/involvement
Ability to solve problems
Willingness to take risks
Organisational skill
Negotiating skill
Foreign languages
Manual skill
Data processing
Basic specialist knowledge
Specialist knowledge

7 = very low   1 = very high

• on employment, – after the initial training phase, ♦ at the time of the first large promotion

* usually upper secondary school or middle school leavers
** usually graduates from short courses or colleges of technology
*** usually university graduates

Source: Group Project: "A Comparative Perspective of Relationships between the Education and Employment Systems in Japan".

These findings from the written questionnaire and interviews carried out later underline the fact that at the start of employment value is laid, above all, on a "raw material" of skills. In the initial training period on the job it is not usually expected that there will already be any crystallization of marked specialist skills and greater specialist knowledge; in so far as it is regarded as necessary at all, this is left, above all, until the phase of employment that lasts until the first large promotion.

5. More Recent Developments in Japan

In the Nineties it was possible to observe changes in the relationship between the education and the employment system in Japan. On the one hand, the situation of a clear shortage of labour during the boom at the end of the Eighties and the beginning of the Nineties, which was subsequently termed the "bubble economy", was replaced by economic problems and a lack of job vacancies. It is true that firms are trying to solve the problems primarily by placing their employees in firms with which they have good relations, or that they are terminating the employment of older employees prematurely; nevertheless, for the first time for more than three decades school-leavers and graduates from institutions of higher education are facing serious difficulties in finding employment.

On the other hand, some long-term rethinking can be found in the firms both with regard to their expectations concerning qualifications and to their employment concepts. Experts are in agreement that greater importance has been attached recently to the specialist orientation of training and employment than was previously the case. At the same time the principle of lifelong employment seems to be slowly collapsing. It is also possible to detect some rethinking among the employees. Great importance was attached to the findings of an international comparative study, according to which Japanese employees appear to be particularly dissatisfied with their employment (cf. Ministry of Labour 1995). Vocational mobility seems to have increased during the Nineties, not only as a result of the worsened situation with regard to job vacancies, but also because of the increasing willingness to change employers due to discontent with the work (cf. Teichler 1995).

Here it cannot be precisely explained to what extent long-term structural changes and current shifts in labour-market constellations are contributing to the complete change of mood mentioned above. It is also not possible to determine whether or not the changes in the course of the Nineties are of a long-term nature. It is clear, however, that the recognition of specialist qualifications is gaining in importance. A study by the Japanese Employers' Association, Nikkeiren, dating from 1995 (Nihon Keieisha Dantai Renmei 1995) certainly reflects the prevailing mood: the emphasis on the all-round readiness for work and the principle of lifelong learning are to be maintained for the majority. In addition, however, those with specialised knowledge appear as a second type of no little weight.

6. A Comparative Balance

Regarding the transition from the education system to the employment system in Japan it is certainly remarkable, above all, how it works with so little friction. Most pupils and students already know many months before the end of their time at school or of their studies where they will be employed. Unemployment while they are seeking a job after the end of their education only becomes a certain problem if – as has been the case since 1992 – unemployment becomes a notable problem in general; in this case, however, concern seems to increase very suddenly if the expectation of security that has existed until then is disturbed by frictions, which nevertheless appear to be relatively small in an international comparison.

It is difficult to explain why a "closed procedure" exists in Japan for the transition from the school to employment, and why the recommendations of the schools have a high standing with regard to the chances of obtaining employment. For the transition from the short-course universities and from universities into tasks within the fields of natural science and technology it is also difficult to explain why a "semi-closed" procedure prevails with limited importance of the recommendations, and that for the transition from the university to tasks within the business and administrative field an open procedure has become established which attaches no importance at all to recommendations. In the transition from the school to a firm the regional limitation of the recruitment, and thus the greater personal familiarity with the interlinking relationships certainly play a role. With the opening up of the procedure for university graduates who want to work in business and administrative fields it may be that, in addition to the frequently large numbers of vacancies to be filled and to national recruitment, a role may have been played by the fact that firms regard the academic performance only to a very limited extent as providing predictions for a successful career; however, the latter certainly does not provide a satisfactory explanation, since this also applies in a similar way to the academic performance of graduates from short-course universities.

In each case the repercussions of the transition mechanisms on learning in the school and the institution of higher education differ. In the case of the schools, Japanese experts point out that by relying strongly on the recommendations of the schools when employing school-leavers the firms underline the high value of learning success. For graduates from institutions of higher education the early and intensive search for the best job is regarded rather as a burden which draws their attention away from their studies. Many students of arts and social science subjects also have the impression that success during their studies – in contrast to the success of entering the institution of higher education – is of little significance for their chances of finding employment.

The strong emphasis on general skills and social qualifications can, of course, result in the "cultural capital" passed on by the family being of considerable value. In Japan, however, there is no doubt that the worry is more marked that the more or less automatic reward for the rank achieved in the hierarchy of education certificates leads to the "overheating" of the competition for educational success, rather than that entry into the employment system provides too few open opportunities for those who make an effort to be successful in the educational competition.

In Japan the concept prevails to a lesser extent than in Germany that with the transition from the education system to the employment system a balance has to be achieved in the conflict between individual inclinations and skills on the one hand, and the demands of the employment system on the other. Either the harmony between the two sides is stressed, or it is expected to a greater extent that the individuals will adapt to the demands of the employment system. The low level of friction during the transition also has its price if individuality and the firm's demands are not directly in harmony.

In recent years it has no longer been possible to maintain the simple description of the Japanese situation, according to which during the transition from the education system to the employment system everything is concentrated on establishing a close relationship between the educational and occupational rank, or of seeking small deviating advantages in the face of the distribution of an educational meritocracy. Not everything is concentrated on status selection, to which the relationship between learning and employment with regard to content would be completely indifferent. The high degree of discontent with the work done and the frequent changes of employing organisations within the initial years of employment are, at least, interpreted as a sign that the information process at the time of the search for employment is not carried out in an optimum way. It is often the case, however, that the change of employer, which has become more frequent, is regarded as a sign that a change in values has taken place, in which there is an increasing claim to useful or sensible work and a visible relationship between skills and the work done. At the same time firms are attaching increasing significance to the value of specialised qualification and the understanding of professional work.

In contrast to this, the importance of general skills, social qualification and the readiness to make changes during the course of one's working life appears to be growing. Doubts are now being expressed more loudly about whether or not the mechanisms of seeking a job and placement in a job that have prevailed so far are actually worth maintaining. It would, therefore, not be surprising if the considerable differences between Japan and Germany which do, in fact, continue to exist with regard to the firms' expectations concerning qualifications, as well as in the processes of transition from the education system to the employment system, were to be further reduced.

In Japan it is regarded as a milestone that in 1996, for the first time for decades, no further agreement was concluded for regulating the employment procedures for graduates from institutions of higher education. However, it is too early to assert that the character of the processes prevailing so far concerning the transition from the education system to the employment system has thus undergone a fundamental change. It may be that this merely means that the de facto early search and employment activities are no longer considered to be indecent; however, it cannot be excluded that many trusted practices may be becoming less a matter of course.

Bibliography

Azumi, Kôya: Higher Education and Business Recruitment in Japan. New York, 1969.

Kariya, Takehiko: Gakkô, shokugyô senbatsu no shakaigaku. Kôsotsu shûsoku no nihonteki mekanizumu [Sociology of the Choice of School and Profession: The Japanese Mechanism of the Transition from the Upper Secondary School to Employment]. Tôkyô, 1991.

Kariya, Takehiko: Vom Bildungssystem in die Erwerbstätigkeit [From the Education System to Employment]. In: Demes, Helmut and Walter Georg (eds.): Gelernte Karriere. Bildung und Berufsverlauf in Japan. Munich, 1994, pp. 65-91.

Ministry of Labour: White Paper on Labour. Tôkyô, 1995.

Nihon Keieisha Dantei Renmei [Association of Japanese Employers' Organizations] (ed.): Shinjidai no "nihonteki keiei" – chôsen subeki hôkô to sono gutaisaku ["Japanese Management" on the Path to a new Age: The Coming Challenges and Concrete Strategies for Overcoming them]. Tôkyô, 1995.

Ôe, Atsuyoshi: Arbeitsvermittlung durch Bildungsinstitutionen [Job Placements by Education Institutions]. In: Demes, Helmut and Georg (eds.): Gelernte Karriere. Bildung und Berufs- verlauf in Japan. Munich, 1994, pp. 93-122.

Rikurûto, Risâchi [Recruit Research]: Saiyô tôkei benran 1995 [Handbook of Employment Statistics 1995]. Tôkyô, 1995.

Teicher, Kerstin: Zwischenbetriebliche Mobilität in Japan im Kontext personalpolitischen Wan- dels. [Mobility between Firms within the Context of Changes in Personnel Policy] Kassel: Dissertation, 1995.

Teicher, Kerstin et al.: Bildung und Beschäftigung in der japanischen Forschungsliteratur [Education and Employment in Japanese Research Literature]. Munich, 1996.

Teicher, Kerstin and Ulrich Teichler: Der Übergang vom Bildungs- in das Beschäftigungssystem: Erfahrungen in Deutschland – Vergleiche zu Japan [The Transition from the Education to the Employment System: Experience in Germany – Comparisons with Japan]. In: Demes, Helmut and Georg (eds.): Gelernte Karriere. Bildung und Berufsverlauf in Japan. Munich, 1994, pp. 35-64.

Teicher, Kerstin and Ulrich Teichler: Vom Studium zum Beruf. Die japanische Situation in ver- gleichender Perspektive [From Study to Employment. A Comparative Perspective of the Japanese Situation]. In: Japanisch-Deutsches Zentrum Berlin (ed.): Symposium. Übergang vom Bildungs- in das Beschäftigungssystem und der Berufsstart – Veränderungen in Japan und Deutschland in den 90er Jahren. Berlin, 1996, pp. 15-43.

Teichler, Ulrich: Bildung und Berufsstart in Japan – Impressionen aus einem japanisch-deutschen Vergleich [Education and Starting up Employment in Japan – Impressions from a Japanese- German Comparison]. Europäische Zeitschrift "Berufsbildung" No. 5, 1995, pp. 67-74.

Teichler, Ulrich and Yôko Teichler Urata: Der Arbeitsmarkt für Akademiker in Japan [The Labour Market for Graduates in Japan]. Göttingen, 1975.

Tsuchiya, Hiroshi: Shinsotsu saiyô no jissai [On the Practice of Employing School and Higher Education Graduates]. Tôkyô, 1992.

Yoshimoto, Keiichi: Transition from School to Work in Japan. OECD, Paris, 1996 (duplicated manuscript).

Yoshimoto, Keiichi and Reiko Kosugi: Daigaku shûshokushidô to daisotsusha no shoki kyaria [Vocational Guidance at the Universities and University Graduates Starting Employment]. Tôkyô, 1993.

Netherlands

Roland Richter

A. Initial Situation

1. The higher education system

The development of the higher education system in the Netherlands is closely linked with the post-Reformation conflicts between the Catholic regents and the European regents who had converted to Protestantism. Seen from this point of view, the first university founded in the Protestant northern part of the Netherlands in 1575, the University of Leyden in the province of Holland, was a Calvinist bulwark against the University of Leuven in the Catholic southern Netherlands, which had been founded 150 years earlier. Other provinces like Frisia, Groningen, Utrecht and Gelderland followed this example in the first half of the 17th century and founded their own universities within the framework of the regionalisation of higher education: in Frisia there were Franeker (1585 - 1818), Groningen (since 1614), Utrecht (since 1636), and in Gelderland there were Harderwijk (1647 - 1843) and Nijmegen (1656 - 1679). Two more universities followed in the 19th century: in 1876 the Athenaeum founded in 1632 became the University of Amsterdam, and as a reaction to this the founding of the Free University of Amsterdam as the first private, Calvinist foundation took place in 1880. Finally, the 20th century saw the founding of the majority of the existing universities. The Royal Academy for Technology, founded in 1842, became the Technical University of Delft in 1905, and in 1917 the State School of Agriculture, which had opened in 1876, became the Agricultural University of Wageningen. These were followed in 1923 and 1927 respectively by the Catholic universities of Nijmegen and Brabant in Tilburg. Due to the constantly increasing student numbers, after the Second World War the Technical University of Eindhoven was established in 1957, then the Technical University of Twente in Enschede in 1961, followed by the University of Rotterdam in 1973 and the University of Limburg in Maastricht in 1975. Finally, in 1981 the last university, the Open University in Heerlen, was opened for distance learning. It was only in 1986 that the higher vocational colleges, which previously had been organized as private foundations, were raised to the status of universities of professional education (*Hogescholen*) and made part of the tertiary education sector.

All of the 13 state-funded „attendance" universities today still carry out basic scientific research and the training of young scientists, as they always have done. They have strongly differentiated profiles. Apart from the Agricultural University in Wageningen and the three technically orientated universities in Delft, Eindhoven and Twente, the four state universities in Leyden, Groningen, Limburg and Rotterdam focus more strongly on the liberal arts and the social sciences. In contrast, the universities in Amsterdam and Utrecht have a profile focused rather on the liberal arts and the natural sciences. This also applies to the three private (some of them Catholic) universities. The 65 universities of professional, which are predominantly organised as foundations, but are also state-funded, offer training courses that are consciously based on practical work and are vocation-orientated; they pursue mainly application-orientated research, and thus are in much more direct contact with the business world around them. It is possible to participate in seven different courses of study there: agriculture, teacher training for primary schools and lower secondary schools, technology, economics, social work, health care and art. For a long time, many of the universities of professional education offered only one course of study. In the meantime, however, as a result of the amalgamation of universities of professional education undertaken since 1986 more and more of these universities are offering two and more different courses of study.

According to data provided by the Central office for Statistics *(CBS)*, in the academic year 1999/2000 there were 162,754 full-time students enrolled at the universities on the set date 02/02/2000, of whom 77,255 were women, and 30,609 were first-year students. On the set date 04/11/99 a total of 242,083 full-time students were enrolled at the universities of professional education, of whom 123,389 were women. In addition, 44,617 part-time students were enrolled there. The proportion of female students has risen rapidly during recent decades, and with the exception of the technical courses of study (16%) the proportion of male and female students is almost equal. On the set date 01/12/1998 6.2% of the 160,480 full-time students enrolled at the universities at that time were 18 years old and younger, and 66.4% of the students were between 19 and 24 years old; the 21-year-olds and 22-year-olds formed the largest group, totalling 38,575 students. 17.9% of the full-time students were between 25 and 29 years old, and 9.5% were older than 30. The picture is similar at the universities of professional education. According to older figures already published in 1998 for 1997/98, 10.7% of the 236,790 full-time students were 18 years old and younger, 78% of those enrolled were between 19 and 24 years old, and here the 21-year-olds formed the largest group with 17%. Only about 10% were between 25 and 29 years old, and 1.5% were older than 30. The group of part-time students more than 30 years old then amounted to more than 60% at the universities of professional education. The average time spent studying a subject until being awarded a degree dropped by an average of two months from 71 to 69 months between 1993/94 and 1996/97, i.e. in four years. Here the corresponding value for female students was from 69 to 67 months, and for male students by only one month from 72 to 71. The average time spent studying a subject thus amounts to 5 years and 9 months.

The 1998 version of the Higher Education Law of 1993 regulates the first phase of the course of academic study at universities and universities of professional education. The admission requirement for studying at a university of professional education is generally the successful completion of the eight-year elementary school, including two years of preschool, as well as the five-year „Continued Higher General Instruction" (HAVO) or the six-year „Scientific Propaedeutic Instruction" (VWO). In order to be admitted direct to a university a student has to successfully complete the eight-year elementary school as well as one of several branches of the six-year VWO course. Those who have completed the HAVO can, after the first year of study (*propedeuse*) at a university of professional education, change to the *propedeuse* at a university. Apart from these general admission requirements, and according to national regulations, the proof of having fulfilled additional subject-relevant admission requirements can be demanded for certain subjects. If certain requirements have not been fulfilled, however, the university can examine in each individual case whether admission can be granted on the basis of other or additional achievements. In addition, aptitude tests are permitted for certain courses of study. Admission to a course of study can be refused if the existing teaching capacity at the university in question is exhausted, or if the labour-market situation means that it does not appear sensible to admit more applicants for places on particular courses of study. Both cases are regulated by the Ministry of Science. For applicants applying for a place who are older than 21 and who do not have any „normal" certificate qualifying them for entrance into higher education, there is the opportunity, which has already existed for a long time, for them to take a separate admission examination, the so-called *colloquium doctum*. Admission to all study programmes is carried out by the Central Office for the Allocation of University Places (CBAP) in Groningen. The Central Office determines annually for which subjects the number of places must be restricted. Because they are predominantly subject to private law, the universities of professional education themselves decide on admission to their courses of study. The academic year begins on September 1st.[1]

---

1   Cf. Richter, R.: Der niederländische Weg zur Modernisierung der Hochschulen. Ein Bericht über die Hochschulreform der 80er und 90er Jahre. Ed. GEW Frankfurt a.M., 1998.

As far as the financing *of* studies is concerned, since 1986 children's and tax allowances have been added together as one sum and paid to the full-time students direct as basic funding for their monthly budget. Part-time students receive no money to finance their studies, since they are generally in employment and study while they work. Since the beginning of the Nineties both this state share for covering the cost of living as well as the additional allowance for students whose parents have a low income have been paid as a scholarship, as previously, but its size was initially reduced, and since 1993 it has had to be repaid if the student's performance is not satisfactory (*tempobeurs*). Since 1996, however, students have as a rule received the state study grant and additional funds for studying only as a four-year loan, which has to be paid back with interest only if the course of study has not been completed successfully within six years (*prestatiebeurs*). Moreover, students have the opportunity to receive a loan on which they pay interest. In the near future the study funding for 4 years (48 months) is to be extended to 10 years, but the amount is to remain unchanged. This state funding of a course of study, however, only covers part of the monthly budget. The level of the monthly budget is orientated toward the general cost-of-living index and is newly determined each year by the Ministry of Science. The budget includes the expenses for living, teaching materials, tuition fees and health insurance. In addition, since 1990 every student has received a semester ticket for use on buses and trains. For 1999/2000 the monthly budget has been fixed at 1294,46 guilders for students not living at home, including the monthly portion of the annual study fees amounting to 2816,20 guilders. The basic state funding, which has now been indexed, is currently 444,25 guilders per month. In order to cover the remaining 850,20 guilders, provided that their parents remain below certain income levels, students can receive an additional grant amounting to a maximum of 457,15 guilders, dependent on the parents' income. In addition, they can take out a loan at a current interest rate of 5.92% to make up the remaining sum that is not yet covered. Of course, the

850,20 guilders can also be provided partially or entirely by the parents or by the students themselves (loans/jobs). Students are allowed to earn up to a maximum of 15,000 guilders per year. If the basic and additional funding has to be repaid, this means that interest has to be paid after completion of the course of study. As stated above, in future the funding of studies and study fees can be requested or paid by the student flexibly within a 10-year period, in accordance with the situation of each individual student regarding his or her life and course of studies.[2]

2. Employment and the labour market for university graduates

During the past 20 years the labour market in the Netherlands has undergone a fundamental change. Due to „corporatist governance" of labour-market policy, through which „state officials are able and willing to share political authority with functionally organized interest groups in society, and the interest groups are willing and capable to mobilizing the support of their constituent membership in exchange for political influence" (Visser 1997,[3] p. 64) the unemployment rate has been halved since the beginning of the Eighties: „from almost 14 per cent in 1983 to slightly more than 6 per cent in 1992, distinctly below the sad average of 11 per cent for the European Union". Therefore „Mr. Jean-Cluade Trichet, president of the French Central Bank, recommends a ´Dutch miracle´ of fiscal rectitude, welfare and labour market reform, social consensus and job growth to his compatriots" (Visser 1997, pp. 9, 10). Since this trend has even increased during the second half of the Nineties, especially in the labour-market segment for university graduates, the Ministry of Science is at present making efforts with the aid of suitable measures to alleviate the shortage of labour that is starting to develop (see below).

2   Cf. Richter, R.: Mehr Zeit zum Jobben. In: DUZ 5/2000, p. 26ff.
3   Cf. Visser, J; Hemerijk, A.: "A Dutch Miracle" Job Growth, Welfare Reform and Corporatism in the Netherlands. Amsterdam, 1997.

The total population of Netherlands citizens was 15.7 million in 1998, of whom 10.6 million were aged between 15 and 64. Of these, 6.9 million men and women, i.e. 66%, formed the so-called working population, who were working for at least 12 hours per week, or who were seeking employment of this kind; 3.6 million, i.e. 34% were not considered as belonging to the working population because they were neither employed, nor were they seeking work (e.g. schoolchildren, students, people who had retired early). Among the working population in 1998 there were 6.6 million, i.e. 75% of the 15 to 64-year-old men, that is 4.0 million, and 49% of the 15 to 64-year-old women, i.e. 2.5 million, who were working for at least 12 hours per week. 348,000 Netherlands citizens, i.e. 5.0% of the working population between 15 and 64 were unemployed.

If one compares the working population actually in employment (6.6 million) with the group of so-called „working people", which in addition to the working population also includes those Netherlands citizens who were working for less than 12 hours per week, then it is noticeable that the proportion of women among the 7.7 million working people amounts to 43.1%, and that among the working population amounts to 38.8%, i.e. a above-average proportion of women were employed for less than 12 hours per week.

If one looks at the group of people aged between 15 and 64 (10.6 million) and the working population (6.9 million) with reference to their grouping according to qualification and their type of training as well as to the proportion of women in each case, the following picture is provided by Table 1 for 1998:

Table 1

Level of training/ Type of training	population: 15-64 year-olds x 1000		working population x 1000						proportion of those employed as a percentage of the relevant population group	
			total		employed		unemployed		column 4:2	
1	2		3		4		5			
	men	women	men	women	men	women	men	women	men	women
15 to 64 year-olds of whom are:	10.604		6.957		6.609		348			
	5.369	5.235	4.196	2.761	4.047	2.562	149	199	75	49
of whom have a degree from a university of applied sciences,	829	758	705	557	689	532	16	25	83	70
including: technical/natural sciences	265	37	223	23	218	21	<5	<5	82	57
economics	244	146	215	117	210	113	5	<5	86	77
social sciences	317	571	265	415	259	396	7	19	82	69
of whom have a degree from a university,	449	243	418	207	407	198	11	9	91	81
including: technical/natural sciences	131	29	122	24	119	23	<5	<5	91	79
economics	136	51	129	46	126	44	<5	<5	93	87
social sciences	180	163	165	137	160	131	5	6	89	80

Source: Centraal Bureau voor de Statistiek: Personen van 15-64 jaar naar arbeidspositie, geregestreeerde werklozen, participatiegraden en werkloosheidspercentages, geslacht en onderwijsniveau en -richting, 1998. (Table PE0320_98.XLS).

Column 2 shows that the population of the Netherlands aged between 15 and 64 was divided almost equally between the sexes (m 50.7%, w 49.3%). However, this ratio no longer applied as far as the working population was concerned, for here the proportion of women totalled only 39.7% (Col. 3), those in employment 38.7% (Col. 4), and it was above average among the unemployed at 57.1% (Col. 5). However, it is interesting, and it must be specially stressed, that the number of women in employment corresponded to their percentage of 49% within the total population of 15 to 64-year-olds (Col. 4:2).

If one looks at the distribution of the population group with a degree from a university of professional education according to sex, then it is noticeable that women are almost equally represented when referred both to the group of the population aged between 15 and 64 (Col. 2: 47.7%), to that of the working population overall (Col. 3: 44.1%) and to that of those in employment (Col. 4: 43.5%), and that women are clearly over-represented when referred to their proportion of the population (49.3%), the working population (39.7%) and those in employment (28.7%). With the group of the population with a university degree the picture is different, for here women in the categories mentioned are represented by roughly one third in each case (Col. 2: 35%; Col. 3: 33.1%; Col. 4: 32.7%), and are thus clearly under-represented. If one looks at the group of female graduates from universities of professional education and universities in accordance with their distribution among the three courses of study mentioned, then it becomes clear that the degree of female participation in the population, the working population and those in employment is essentially due to the over-proportional participation of women from the fields of the social sciences: in the case of female graduates from universities of professional education the figure is more than 60% in each case, and with female graduates from universities it is more than 45% in each case. Approximately 10% of female graduates from universities of professional education and approximately 17% of female university graduates come from the technical and natural science fields; approximately

35% of female graduates from universities of professional education and approximately 26% of female university graduates come from courses of study in economics.

In 1998 the unemployment rate (Col. 5:2) among the working population between 14 and 64 was 3.5% among men and 7.2% among women. In contrast, it was distinctly lower among female graduates from universities of professional education: among women with degrees from universities of professional education the figure was 4.4%, and thus exactly twice as high as that for the corresponding male group; 4.3% of women with a university degree were unemployed, compared with 2.6% of the men with the corresponding degree. It is noticeable, despite the general impression, that women with degrees in technical and natural science subjects from universities of professional education and from universities hardly play any role in the relevant unemployment rate, while women with degrees from the social sciences respectively constitute 73% and 54% of the relevant unemployment rate.

If one places these data in the development context of the past 15 years, then it can be added that since 1987 the labour force participation rate among women in particular has risen from 35% to 49%, and that the number of people not considered to be part of the working population has fallen from 4.3 million to 3.6 million. Thus when compared with 1987, when just under half were employed for more than 12 hours per week, almost two thirds (62%) are now employed. In the end, the general unemployment of 8.5% in 1987, after a temporary rise at the beginning of the Nineties, then fell to 5% in 1998. Job-hunting for graduates from both university types currently lasts an average of 2.8 months – even when the situation for many fields, which is still difficult, is taken into account.[4]

4   Cf. Centraal Bureau voor de Statistiek: Tweederde bevolking aan het werk, 21/02/2000, (www.cbs.hl./nieuws/artikelen); Ministerie van Onderwijs Cultuur en Wetenschappen: Hoger Onderwijs en Onderzoek Plan 2000 (HOOP 2000). Zoetermeer 1999, p. 21.

According to the prognoses of the Research Centre for Education and Labour Market (ROA) at the University of Maastricht the increasing demand for graduates in all fields cannot currently be met in some segments of the labour market – in distinct contrast to the labour-market situation at the beginning of the Nineties, when graduates had difficulty finding the appropriate jobs.[5] This shortage applies, in particular, to teaching, the natural science and technical jobs and to ones in economics. Among other things, the reason for this is to be seen in the consequences of the increasing ageing and the lack of support for young people in the past few years on the one hand – the effects of which will be felt even more strongly in the coming years – and, on the other hand, in the start of a wave of retirements from 2005 onward, with simultaneous cuts in the funding of people to replace those retiring. Due to the unforeseeable social and economic influences on the development it is hardly possible to make a more precise prognosis. Nevertheless, the Socio-Economic Council, for example, assumes there will be a shortage of 50,000 university graduates and 150,000 graduates from universities of professional education by the year 2003.[6] This shortage will arise, in particular, in the health services, teaching and in the information and communications field. Here the situation is now so dramatic that many businesses have started „buying up" students even before they graduate.[7]

---

5   Cf. Van der Loo, P.J.E.; Van der Velden, R.K.W.: De arbeidsmarktpositiie van HBO'ers. In: Tijdschrift voor Hoger Onderwijs Nr.2 1995, pp. 72-88.
6   MOCW: Groeiend tekort aan hoger opgeleiden dwingt instellingen tot „maatwerk". In: Uitleg 21 1999; cf. Sociaal-Economisch Raad: Samenvatting Advies Hoger onderwijs en Onderzoek Plan 2000. (www.ser.nl/adviezen/ADV9904.html).
7   Van Heffen, Oscar; et al.: Overheid, Hoger Onderwijs en Economie. Ontwikkelingen in Nederland en Vlaanderen. Utrecht, 1999, p. 62.

B. Initial Situation

3. Linking university training with the employment system

As recently as during the Seventies and Eighties the universities and the job market which, however, was to take on the university graduates, were still complete strangers to each other. It was only at the end of the Eighties and, above all, during the course of the Nineties that the relation between study programmes and orientation towards practical work and the labour market were increasingly discussed.[8] While the government registered almost 1 million unemployed university graduates in the middle of the Eighties, based on the appropriate prognoses it was at the same time able to announce that, with the forward projection of the economic growth at that time, by the year 2000 there would be a clear shortage of university graduates in the technical and economic fields as well as a similar surplus in the social fields[9] – a prognosis that has, in fact, proved correct in the meantime. Since the end of the Eighties an intensive discussion has thus taken place whether, in the face of a shortage of funds, it perhaps might be a waste of public money if, on the one hand, a large amount of money and a large portion of their lives is spent on the academic education of young people who, on the other hand, later assume functions in a competition for markets that until then have been carried out by less qualified people. At the same time, however, it was pointed out that the demands for qualifications in the labour market were rising at an even faster rate, and that for this reason the problem of the surplus, at least of university graduates, would presumably not arise to the extent feared. Nevertheless, precisely in the sense of saving resources and of an efficient labour-market policy, as early as in 1991 the government saw the necessity of more effectively shaping the fitting of higher education and labour market,

8   Van Heffen, loc. cit.
9   Ministerie can Onderwijs Cultuur en Wetenschappen: Hoger Onderwijs en Onderzoek
     Plan 1988 (HOOP 1988). Zoetermeer, 1987, p. 35.

e.g through improved preparation for the course of study and the choice of profession, the provision of academic further training for employees and the development of so-called dual study programmes, which means study programmes with integrated phases of practical work.[10] Precisely in the universities of professional education, which have always had good contacts with the later fields of work of their graduates, pilot study programmes for connecting studies and work were already carried out at an early stage, whereas the universities were very reticent for fear of undermining the academic character of their courses of study.[11] Since the mid-Nineties the Ministry of Science has more and more clearly emphasized the mutual dependence of higher education and labour market – this was also most probably done under the impression of the increased demand for graduates that was becoming clear. Thus the programme of the 1998 Higher Education Development Plan stated:

„Qualitatively good science and research are of vital interest for the socio-cultural and economic development of the Netherlands. In order to fulfil their social function in the best way it is necessary for the curricula of studies at the higher education institutions to be marked by strong social orientation. In the long term an open higher education system must develop that is characterised at all levels by intensive interconnections with society." (HOOP 1998, p. 30)

In accordance with this, the Ministry of Science has since been making efforts to remove the legal hurdles wherever they existed, and to promote cooperation between higher education and labour market in the provision of work experience placements (*stages*) or the development of so-called dual study programmes (see below) in order to facilitate impulses for innovation of the curricula themselves by means of feedback from the world of work to

---

10   Ministerie van Onderwijs Cultuur en Wetenschappen: Hoger Onderwijs en Onderzoek Plan 1992 (HOOP 1992). Zoetermeer, 1991, p. 20.
11   Van Heffen, loc. cit., p. 66ff.

courses of study.[12] It goes without saying that these efforts can only be put into practice following consultation and cooperation between the higher education institutions, which are largely autonomous in the shaping of their courses of study, and the employers' associations and trade unions, as well as with the individual firms. In connection with the Higher Education Development Plan 2000, which is valid until 2004, the Socio-Economic Council also supports the recommendations put forward by the Ministry at an earlier stage. Among other things, it supports the further opening up of the higher education system and the raising of the quota of successfully completed courses of study by making the study programmes more flexible and by strengthening orientation towards the labour market (e.g. by means of dual study programmes). The purpose of this is to solve the social and economic problems needing to be dealt with and to avoid the shortage of labour for highly qualified jobs. In its current Higher Education Development Plan 2000 for the time until 2004 the Ministry stresses that this orientation must, above all, be an instrument for the reform and renewal of teaching and research.[13]

One of the results of a discussion that has been taking place in the Netherlands since the beginning of the 20th century, and increasingly so since 1945, about the structure of the university and its role in society is, in fact, manifested in this higher education policy, which is closely orientated toward the social and economic needs of the society. While the universities in the Netherlands were committed to the Humboldt model of the research university well into the 20th century, according to which the requirements and demands of science determine university teaching, and independent and research-orientated learning is to be practised by the students, after World War 2 university policy was orientated along the lines of the Ameri-

---

12   Ministerie van Onderwijs Cultuur en Wetenschappen: Hoger Onderwijs en Onderzoek
     Plan 1998 (HOOP 1998). Zoetermeer, 1997, p. 32.
13   Ministerie van Onderwijs Cultuur en Wetenschappen: Hoger Onderwijs en Onderzoek
     Plan 2000 (HOOP 2000). Zoetermeer, 1999, p. 22.

can university system which, with its different levels of courses on offer in the colleges, initially prepares the students for working life, and, based on this, provides for more detailed occupation with science only at the university level. It is generally attributed to the influence of the American model that, in addition to the traditional task of carrying out research and teaching, since 1960 „the furthering of the sense of social responsibility and of social and political knowledge have become a goal of the universities in the Netherlands" (Rupp 1997, p. 345).[14] The universities carried out this new task to the same extent as the state withdrew from the detailed regulation of the higher education institutions, and this also applies to their own activities. This is due to the fact that after the mid-Eighties, when public funding was being reduced and the pressure of legitimation towards society was becoming greater, they developed internal and external procedures of quality evaluation and assessment in order to be able to provide justification of their achievements for public opinion. The quality evaluation that has been taking place regularly since then refers just as much to research as to studying and teaching and their framework conditions, i.e. the study conditions for newly enrolled students, as well as the employability of the graduates. The goal of this quality evaluation is to discuss and agree upon the demands and necessities of the sciences and the needs of society on a regular basis, and in accordance with this to further develop higher education training at a high level.

4. Professional orientation during the course of study

As a rule, full-time study lasts four years and is divided into the one-year *propedeuse* and the three-year *doctoraal* course. The *propedeuse* is completed with a cumulative examination, the *doctoraal* course is completed at the universities

---

14   Rupp, J.C.C.: Van oude en nieuwe universiteiten. De verdringing van Duitse door Ameri-
      kaanse invloeden op de wetenschapsbeofening en het hoger onderwijs in Nederland,
      1945-1995. Den Haag 1997; Baggen, P.: Vorming door wetenschap. Universtair onderwijs
      in Nederland 1815-1960. Delft, 1988.

with the title *doctorandus (drs.), ingenieur (ir.)* or *meester (mr.)*, and at the universities of professional education with the title *baccalaureus (bc.)* or *ingenieur (ing.)*. After the first year of studies the university has to provide compulsory advice for all students concerning their further studies. As a result of the 1999 Declaration of Bologna on the creation of the European area of higher education, which recommends the adoption of a system essentially based on two main cycles, undergraduate and graduate, a larger number of new bachelor's and master's courses are now being established in the Netherlands.

As far as formalised part-time study is concerned, the corresponding right to study lasted for nine years. With the abolition of the six-year term this provides more flexible opportunities for arranging studies and part-time employment. Part-time studies are not intended for regular school-leavers with permission to study at a higher education institution, but for applicants for study places who – for social reasons (providing for a family) or because they are already in employment – are unable to participate in the full-time course of study. Students must deliberately decide to undertake full-time or part-time study. However, this decision can also be reversed.

The study requirements for a course of study are described by a number of so-called *Studiepunten.* One „study point" covers 40 hours (including class hours, preparation and further study time for classes, preparation time for examinations, private study). As a rule, a course of study has study requirements amounting to 168 study points. This corresponds to a four-year course of study, since with 42 weeks per year – after deduction of time for vacation and illness – it is assumed that the average study load will be 1680 hours per year, which amounts to a total of 6720 hours. However, for the courses in dentistry and philosophy, and since 1997 also for the engineering sciences at the Technical Universities of Delft, Eindhoven and Enschede as well as the Agricultural University of Wageningen a five-year study programme with 210 study points is provided for. The courses of study in human medicine and veterinary medicine, and also pharmacy, have a six-year study programme with 252 study points. As stated above, the distribution of these points will be possible over a period that has now been extended to 10 years. The relative importance of the individual classes, lectures of part-disciplines in the study programme is indicated by the number of study points and by the time required for their successful completion. Each study module is finished with examinations or with evidence of fulfilment of the requirements, which confirm successful participation. Courses can be repeated. No study points are awarded for courses that have not been successfully completed. As a rule, the graduate diploma is awarded when the formal proof of all the required study points, including those for the final thesis, has been provided. There is no standard length of time laid down for completion of the final thesis. It is rather the case that this is determined by the number of study points dependent on the complexity of the subject and the effort necessary for its completion. The level of difficulty of the topic and the defined length of time for its completion are related to each other. In practice this means: from the outset the subjects of the final theses are to be formulated with regard to the time actually required for handling them: as a rule, a demanding thesis requires 1000 hours, i.e. roughly 6 months, but there are also subjects for 480 hours, i.e. approximately 3 months. If the period of time laid down for the thesis is exceeded unduly, then under certain circumstances this can have a negative effect on the mark.

After completion of their studies most of the graduates leave higher education. Only a small proportion continue their vocationally orientated training as vocationally orientated preparation for certain fields of work (doctors, teachers etc.). Depending on the subject, these courses of study last between 1.5 and 4 years. The government envisages that only a maximum of 30% of graduates from the first phase of study should be admitted here.[15]

15   Cf. Richter, R.: Der niederländische Weg zur Modernisierung der Hochschulen. Ein Bericht
      über die Hochschulreform der 80er und 90er Jahre. Ed. GEW Frankfurt a.M., 1988.

Within these structures for courses of study, which can be flexibly organised in many different ways, the institutions fulfil not only their task of providing students with knowledge, methods and abilities in their chosen subject, enabling them to critically order and further develop their knowledge, but at the same time, and with great personnel and financial effort, they pursue the task given to them by society – that of preparing the students for their later vocational occupation.

At present, vocational orientation during the course of study takes place at higher education institutions in the Netherlands essentially in three kinds of ways by:

- orientation to working life and the vocational orientation of the content of the courses as well as by the integration of practical phases into the normal curriculum;
- the introduction of so-called dual study programmes (*„duale leerwegen"*);
- the wide range offered by the so-called Career Advice Centres (*„Loop-baan Advies Centra"*) at the universities and the universities of profes-sional education.

Probably the most widespread approach for preparing students for their profession and for the labour market while they are still studying lies in the practical phases or work experience programmes. Depending on the subject, these are either in public administration, commerce or industry, which in many cases provide the appropriate places in the sense of supporting possible future employees. As far as cooperation with the labour market is concerned, the universities – mindful of their reputation as research institutions – are slightly more reticent than the universities of professional education. Phases of practical experience are not provided for in all the courses of study; so far this has partly been justified by the fact that the curriculum in particular subjects is so tightly organised that no time is available for practical experience during the period during which a course must be completed. This applies, in particular, to law and medicine, in which the practical phase is structured to follow on in the form of a traineeship after graduation. Work-experience placements, however, are to be found not only in the obvious fields of the natural sciences and engineering sciences and economics, but also, for example, in philosophy. The study programmes for future teachers are an exception here to the extent that the courses for teaching in primary schools and lower secondary schools are designed to be closely practice-orientated at universities of professional education, with a large number of periods of practical experience spread over the whole course of study. Students who want to become teachers at upper secondary schools, first have to complete a purely subject-orientated course of study. After that they are prepared for the teaching profession in a one-year postgraduate course of study in education, didactics etc., which contains a high proportion of practical training.

Obviously, the form of practical work experience differs greatly depending on the subject studied and future field of work. In general, however, it can be stated that for courses of study that have compulsory or optional periods of work experience integrated into them the students are usually required to gather this practical experience, which is supervised by the higher education institution, during the third or fourth years of the course of study. Depending on how they are conceived, a period of up to six months is required as rule, but in exceptional cases it can last 12 months. In many cases the examination theses are written in the fourth year during a work experience placement. In some university courses, participation in defined research projects is organised as a kind of period of practical experience within the university. Depending on the level of difficulty, a work experience placement can be weighted with a few study points or with more than 20 points. The trainee students usually receive monthly payments, which can lie between 400 and 1256 guilders per month, depending on the branch of industry; Procter & Gamble, for example, even pay 70-80% of an average starting salary. Some businesses also attract students for longer projects with even more lucrative offers, in which they can easily earn 4,000 guilders per month.[16]

The trainee students are supported in their search for work experience placements by the institutions, and they are supervised by their lecturers during the placements. Surveys within the universities have revealed that, in practice, friction losses have sometimes occurred between the higher education institutions, firms and students, since, for example, the lecturers are mainly interested in the result of the work and do not spend enough time supervising the students during the course of the placement, or because too much is asked of the university and the lecturers regarding continuous contact with commerce and industry in finding suitable work experience placements for all the students, or because the universities regard the firms providing work experience placements merely as providing a service and not as equal partners.[17]

Another approach to the practical orientation of courses of study is the so-called Problem Based Learning (,,*problemgestuurd onderwijs*") which, instead of first providing the basic knowledge of a science in lectures given by professors, and instead of then coming to its practical application, starts the other way round with problems faced in practice, and from the very outset in small student working groups opens up the basic knowledge required for their solution. The University of Maastricht, in particular, is very well known for following this approach.

16   De marktwaarde van de student. In: Nobiles Magazine, Feb./Mrt. 2000, p. 58f.
17   Vereniging van Samenwerkende Nederlandse Universiteiten (VSNU): Stages in het universitaire onderwijs: doel, frequentie en omvang; een voorlopige onventarisatie. Utrecht 1997; Steenkamp, F., Maljaars, W.: Keuze Gigs Hoger Onderwijs. Amsterdam 1999; Ministerie van Onderwijs, Cultuur en Wetenschappen: Hoger Onderwijs en Onderzoek Plan 1998 (HOOP 1998), Zoetermeer, 1997, p. 33ff.

A second variant of the vocational orientation of courses of study can be seen in a structured link between study programme and work, the so-called dual study programmes. The corresponding initiatives are currently receiving a large degree of support from the Ministry, on the one hand because the link between theory and practice can improve both the classes provided in these courses of study themselves and also the chances of these graduates in the labour market, and, on the other hand, because in this way the existing paid work undertaken by many students parallel to their studies can usefully be integrated into their studies. In cooperation between the university / faculty, students and firms curricula are drawn up for which all are responsible. These provide for work phases in a firm at certain stages of the curriculum, in which the students can perform a function relevant to their course of study. The basis of this is a proper contract of employment between the students and the firms which also provides for appropriate wages for the „employee students".

Within the universities of professional education two models have so far been developed and successfully implemented since 1997/98: one of the models provides for alternating periods of study and work lasting six months after the first year of full-time study; the other, the so-called *MKB-leerwerkroute*, refers to the last year of study, which in this case must be completed after a maximum of three years, in which the students occupy a function relevant to their course of study in a medium-sized or small firm and also study part-time. The universities are currently developing dual courses of study after the third year of study in association with the representatives of employers and employees. Since 1998/99 students undergoing study programmes for future teachers have had the opportunity during their last year at a university of professional education or during the one-year graduate course at a university to spend a period of five months with a proper contract of employment and to work as a so-called „teacher in training" (*Leraar in opleiding*) in a school as a member of the teaching staff with equal rights (including independent teaching without supervision, awarding marks, school conferences, parents' meetings etc.).[18] While universities of professional education in the meantime have 350 registered dual study programmes with approx. 5,000 students for the academic year 1999/2000, the universities, with 28 courses of study, are still at the experimental level. The figures for universities of professional education make it clear that students in the dual study programmes recognise the highly motivating possibility of effective and target-orientated study which, in addition, can provide them with an advantage in the labour market over the full-time students.[19]

The third possibility during one's studies of orientating oneself towards later fields of work is provided at universities in the Netherlands by student deans or by independent so-called Career Advice Centres as central facilities. Above all, the centres direct their attention to students and student representative bodies, but also, among others, to student advisers and coordinators, coordinators of work experience placements, employers, job centres and university graduates already in employment. In accordance with these very heterogeneous target groups, what the centres have on offer stretches from general information about the labour-market situation and individual study and vocational advice via the offer of study and vocational orientation workshops for students, graduates and graduates studying for their doctorate, right up to the arrangement of work experience places and vacant positions in the labour market. In addition, the centres participate, among other things, in organising temporary job fairs. Obviously,

---

18   Leraar in opleiding kan ervaring opdoen met arbeidsovereenkomst. In: Uitleg 12/1997, p. 18; Onderwijs krijgt 549 miljoen extra. In: Uitleg 12/1988, p. 15.
19   Ministerie van Onderwijs, Cultuur en Wetenschappen: Hoger Onderwijs en Onderzoek Plan 2000 (HOOP 2000). Zoetermeer, 1999, p. 74f.

these many different tasks require not only close contact with the students and student advisers, but also with the representatives of the employers' organisations and the firms.[20]

5. The transition from higher education to employment

In view of the initiatives for vocational orientation of the students actually during their courses of study, which were introduced in Chapter 4 – initiatives which are firmly fixed in the curriculum and accompanied by student deans and Career Advice Centres – the transition to employment, with a search period of approx. 2.8 months, does not as a rule represent a serious problem for university graduates under the current economic circumstances (see above).

In the academic year 1997/98 42,699 students completed their full-time studies at the universities of professional education, of whom 52.8% were women, and 9,517 their part-time studies, of whom 59.5% were women. Of the total of seven subjects studied, the highest number of full-time students completed their studies in economics (11,921), followed by those in engineering (9,7780), teacher training courses (76,642) and in social work/social services (53,344). While female graduates in economics were almost equally represented, among the graduates in engineering there were only 16.3% women, compared to 83.6% in the field of social work/social services and 75% among the future teachers at primary schools and in the lower secondary schools. As far as part-time study is concerned, the graduates in the courses of study in education formed the largest group, followed by those in social work / social services,

20 Loopbaancentrum Letteren van de Universiteit Leiden: Inventarisatie universitaire (studie)loopvbannbegeleeiding. Leiden, 2000; the results of this survey among the universities can, in general, be applied to the work of the corresponding advisory services at the universities of professional education.

economics and the health professions. In social work / social services and in the courses of study in education the proportion of women here was at least twice as high as that of men. In economics the ratio was exactly opposite, and in engineering the proportion of women only amounted to 10%. In the same year 23,388 students, of whom 49.8% were women, completed their courses of study at the universities in nine subjects. Here, the largest number of graduates were in the social sciences (4,527), followed by economics (3,6774), languages and cultural sciences (3,336), law (3,301), engineering sciences (3,133) and medicine (2,462). The proportion of female graduates was highest in languages and cultural sciences (70.6 %), followed by the social sciences (69.4%), medicine (62.1%). law (53.5%), economics (27.4%) and the engineering sciences (18.5%).[21]

Graduates seeking jobs make use of various opportunities of finding work: apart from using the Career Advice Centres mentioned above, these usually consist of studying the job advertisements in the specialist newspapers and journals, but also in telephone enquiries to personnel departments of businesses „on the off chance". In addition, various associations, such as AIESEC or the STEP Foundation, offer their services in seeking employment. In contrast, the State Employment Office (*Landelijk Bureau Arbeidsvoor-zieningen*) is seldom consulted.[22]

Based on the survey of alumni conducted by the universities of professional education and universities in 1998 it can be stated that most of the graduates from universities of professional education and universities already start seeking jobs before completing their studies, making use of the orientation

---

21   Centraal Bureau voor de Statistiek: Afstudeerden hoger onderwijs per sector (hbo) en Hoop-gebied (wo) naar geslacht. (05/11/1999), (www.cbs.hl./nl/cijfers/kencijfers/soz4745a.htm).

22   Berner; Giesen; Schreiterer; Wolf; Zünkeler: Euro-Challenge. International Career Guide for Students and Graduates. Cologne, 3rd Edition 1998, p. 267ff. (Staufenbiel-Institut für Studien- und Berufsberatung).

opportunities already mentioned that are offered within and outside the university. Whereas graduates from universities of professional education do this while being fully aware that the first job will not be their last one, and in so far will only serve for further orientation, „job-hopping" among university graduates is not so widespread. Almost all the graduates from universities of professional education and universities have found firm employment in the immediate vicinity, although approx. 20% of them are partly involuntarily in part-time jobs with less than 33 hours per week. 80% of all the graduates from universities of professional education find work which, with regard to the level of qualification and the course of study, follows on directly from their studies. No less than 40% of the university graduates have jobs – mainly in the fields of economics, the social sciences and languages and cultural science, for which no university study is required but for which a degree from a university of professional education is required. These graduates are more frequently found in areas of work that do not follow on directly from their chosen course of study. In addition to specialist knowledge it is generally the case that so-called key skills are expected from the graduates. Roughly 80% of the graduates from universities of professional education – figures of this kind do not exist for university graduates – are content with the choice of the subject they studied, even after four years of employment. However, despite the good fit of the course of study with the later occupation most of the graduates are of the opinion that the challenges made on them during their studies could have been greater, and the content of their courses could have been more up-to-date; more skills and qualifications ought to have been taught and practised.

Poland

Heidi Hein

The political upheavals in 1989[1] together with the collapse of the socialist system of the People's Republic and the establishment of democratic structures in the so-called "Third Republic" were accompanied by far-reaching transformation processes in every sphere of the state, the economy and society. They made it possible not only to embody the principles of a constitutional state founded on the rule of law in the political system in general and in the educational system in particular, and to introduce a market-orientated economic system, but they also facilitated the development of a new attitude to and shape for the social institution called "science".[2]

Roughly ten years after these political upheavals Poland still faces the task, on the one hand, of completing the transformation processes and, on the other hand, of laying down guidelines for the 21st century with regard to further political, social and economic changes, and last but not least, changes in education policy.[3] In doing so it has to face up to the different processes of globalisation and modernisation and, at the same time, to prepare for membership of the European Union. In the end this means that these multi-layered processes of change must be brought into and kept in harmony.

---

1   See the overview by S. Grabowski, Der demokratische Umbruch in Polen, in: Formen der Demokratie 13 (1998) and A. Kojder, Systemic Transformation in Poland: 1989-1997, in: Polish Sociological Review 3 (1998), pp. 247-266.

2   Cf. S. Baske, Erziehung, Bildung und Jugend, in: Länderbericht Polen, ed. W. Wöhlke, Bonn 1991 (= Studien zur Geschichte und Politik. Schriftenreihe der Bundeszentrale für Politische Bildung Vol. 29), pp. 374-392, here p. 393.

3   It was only the government coalition elected in 1997, consisting of *Akcja Wyborcza "Solidarnosc" ("Solidarnosc"* Election Campaign, AWS) and *Unia Wolnosci* (Freedom Union, UW), that tackled important reforms, such as that of the administrative structure, social insurance, health insurance and the education system.

1. The System of Higher Education and its Place Within the Education System as a Whole

1.1 An outline of the tasks of the higher education system in the People's Republic of Poland and in the "Third Republic"

Since universities have to provide higher education and thus to train an educational elite as well as (up-and-coming) leaders, in the socialist states of Eastern Europe they had to fulfil exact guidelines in order to do justice to economic demands and those of social policy defined by the planned economy. Changes to the goals within higher education were brought about by the political and economic situation and the associated change in the demands of social policy.[4] With its structure, tasks and organisation partially altered by various Higher Education Acts, the development of higher education since the Second World War thus reflects the political and social development of the People's Republic and runs parallel to the important political phases of upheaval or social crises.[5]

The sovietization of Poland found expression in the orientation of the Polish higher education system toward that of the USSR: this included the fundamental measure of splitting the academic community into three sections in accordance with the principle of "divide and rule": basic research, which was to be guaranteed by the *Polska Akademia Nauk* (Polish Academy of

---

4   Cf. U.J.v.Beek, the Case of Poland, in: Transformation mittel- und osteuropäischer Wissenschaftssysteme. Länderberichte, ed. R. Mayntz et al., Opladen 1995, pp. 256-301 and I.R. Wrompel, Einleitende Kommentierung der Gesetzestexte: aktueller und geschichtlicher Kontext, in: Das polnische Hochschulgesetz vom 12. September 1990, translated and commented on by I.R. Wrompel, Bonn 1991 (= Dokumente zur Hochschulreform 71/1991), pp. 3-56, here p. 14.

5   On this cf. L. Revesz, Studenten im Sozialismus, Vienna et al. 1981, chapter on Poland, pp. 79-121. Cf. also V. Grabe, Wissenschaft, in: Länderbericht Polen, ed. W. Wöhlke, Bonn 1991 (= Studien zur Geschichte und Politik. Schriftenreihe der Bundeszentrale für Politische Bildung Vol. 296), pp. 393-398.

Sciences, PAN), practical research, i.e. research orientated towards special requirements, with numerous research institutions and centres under the control of the relevant ministries, and the field of teaching at the institutions of higher education.[6] This principle of the separation of research and teaching, which is still essentially valid today and is in need of reform, was, however, not completely achieved, so that the Polish universities, partly thanks to personal connections with the academies, could maintain a relatively large amount of independence and a comparatively high level in teaching and research.[7]

The Polish Higher Education Act of December 15th, 1951, abolished the autonomy of higher education institutions. The rectors, deans and individual professors from among the lecturers without a habilitation were appointed by the Minister for Higher Education, and entry to higher education was restricted. Individual faculties were removed from universities, so that new types of higher education institutions, such as medical academies, polytechnics and schools of economics, as well as colleges of physical education, came into existence, and they were under the control both of the relevant ministries and the Education Ministry. Since the curricula had to be orientated toward the needs of industry and business and toward the necessity of rapidly integrating graduates into the work process, after the end of the 1940s it was more and more the case that largely specialised courses of study split into two levels were introduced (vocational courses lasting between 3 and 3.5 years and an academic graduate course lasting 1.5 years leading to the Master's degree). This system was abandoned in the second half of the 1950s with the

---

6   Cf. S. Steier-Jordan, Bildungssystem und Bildungsreform in Polen. Wandel und Kontinui-
     tät, in: Osteuropa 49 (1999), pp. 130-144; Z. Flisowski, Transformation of Polish Higher
     Education – Trends and Problems in 1993, in: Perspectives on the Reform of Higher
     Education in Central and Eastern Europe. Conference held by the German Rectors'
     Conference at the Villa Vigoni Mennagio, Italy 18th to 21st July, 1993, Ed. E. Mühle, Bonn
     1944 (= Dokumente zur Hochschulreform 90/1994), pp. 17-21, here p. 17. On the education
     system see S. Baske (note 2).
7   Z. Flisowski, p. 18.

introduction of a uniform Master's course. However, since the demand for jobs was not met in this way, 1964 saw the establishment of differentiation into a three to four-year vocational course of study (*licencjat* as a specialist diploma degree, e.g. at schools of engineering) and a five to six-year Master's degree which, after the amendment of the Higher Education Act, was valid between 1973 and 1990. Finally, continuing education courses were also developed in order to make the employment of graduates as effective as possible.

As in other socialist countries, after the end of the 1940s there were also evening courses, extramural and distance learning courses in order to train qualified cadres for business and industry. These courses were developed due to the necessity of enabling people to obtain qualifications without withdrawing labour from the production process.[8] When compared with the Soviet Union, however, the geography of the institutions of higher education was less centralised, since centres of higher education and science centres also existed at the periphery.

Under the conditions of the socialist regime, science and higher education as a whole were closely connected with the Marxist-Leninist ideology and subordinated to its needs until 1989. The sciences and institutions of higher education had to serve the establishment of the socialist state and society. To this end the curricula were standardised and, as a consequence, they became inflexible. The natural and technical sciences represented an important factor in the planned economy,[9] while the arts and social sciences had to provide the ideological justification for the policy

---

8   In the 1950s and 1960s the proportion of students participating in evening and distance learning courses amounted to roughly 30.5% of those studying, and at the end of the 1970s it was even as high as 38.7%. After that, however, it fell again due to the high economic and social costs and its low level of efficiency.

9   Z. Flisowski, ibid., p. 17, stresses, however, that a barrier was erected between the scientific community and business and industry.

realised. This fundamental socio-political instrumentalisation meant that the higher education facilities were institutionally dependent on the regime, and this led to a certain intellectual lethargy.[10]

As a result of the close links with the ruling regime, in 1989 the "Round Table" recognized the necessity of reforming the higher education system, and it was given a new form in the Higher Education Act of September 12th, 1990.[11] The goal of these reforms was to increase the number of students, to reintroduce vocational training parallel to academic training and to reintroduce a multi-layered open system of higher education, to strengthen the importance of basic knowledge at the expense of the number of restricted fields of study, to achieve the international comparability of degree courses, to permit the use of foreign languages as the language of instruction, and also to aim at the removal of the separation of research and teaching through the integration of universities and other academic institutions within a town, as well as to rationalise the expenditure of the state budget in this respect.[12]

---

10   Cf. ibid., p. 17f.
11   On the transformation of higher education and the economic system see, in addition to the historical outline by I.R. Wrompel, Z. Fliskowski and U.J. v. Beek; M. Severynski, Main Results of the Reforms in Higher Education in Poland since 1989, in: Perspectives on the Reform of Higher Education in Central and Eastern Europe. Conference held by the German Rectors' Conference at the Villa Vigoni Mennagio, Italy 18th to 21st July, 1993, Ed. E. Mühle, Bonn 1994 (= Dokumente zur Hochschulreform 90/1994), pp. 22-23; St. Dzida, Geist und Wissenschaft im politischen Widerstand in Polen, in: Geist und Wissenschaft im politischen Aufbruch Mitteleuropas. Beiträge zum Österreichischen Wissenschaftstag 1990, ed. by M. Peterlik/W. Waldhäusl, Vienna et al. 1991 (= Studien zu Politik und Verwaltung Vol. 30), pp. 95-98. On higher education after 1990 cf. E. Mühle, Polen, in: Handbuch der Hochschulen. Ostmittel-, Südosteuropa und Gemeinschaft Unabhängiger Staaten, ed. by the German Rectors' Conference, revised by E. Mühle/R. Smolarczyk, Bad Honnef 1995.
12   Cf. Z. Flisowski, p. 19.

The present higher education system is thus essentially a result of the social and political upheavals in Poland.[13] The universities were given back their full autonomy, so that only the question of the financial provision of the universities gave the Ministry of Popular Education (*Ministerstwo Edukacji Narodowej*) an opportunity to exert any influence. Since the end of 1991 the *Komitet Badan Naukowych* (Committee of Scientific Research), which works on behalf of the Ministry and is answerable to it, has been responsible for all scientific policy. Apart from this, a number of specialised higher education institutions are answerable to the appropriate ministries, which have to finance them.[14] In addition, this law permits the founding of private (commonly termed "non-state" in Polish) higher education institutions, provided that they fulfil certain staffing standards.

The 1990 Higher Education Act stresses the freedom of research, teaching and artistic activity. In accordance with Art. 3, Para. 3 the educational task consists of educating the students in the name of human rights, social responsibility, democracy and patriotism. Special emphasis is laid on the efforts for nurturing the truth, mutual respect and the duty to work conscientiously. In view of the economic reforms, the law considers the vocational training of the students as the up-and-coming labour force for business and industry to be the most important task.[15] The research work and the creative artistic activity of the higher education institution are to continue to serve the development of the national culture, technical progress and the preparation of the new generation of academics. The duty of participating in the medical welfare services for the population was additionally introduced for the schools of medicine. Finally, the law aims at closer cooperation between the secondary schools and their academic guidance.

13   Cf. I.R. Wrompel, p. 12f.
14   Cf. E. Mühle, p. 108.
15   Cf. I.R. Wrompel, p. 19.

At the present time Polish higher education is undergoing a serious crisis, which is to be solved by a new and currently controversial Higher Education Act which, if possible, is to come into force for the 2000/2001 academic year. Since professors and academics are not appropriately remunerated they are forced to seek second and third jobs at other higher education institutions. The quality of teaching and research suffers considerably from this, even if it is possible at all under these conditions; the mostly poor material equipment of the state institutions of higher education makes matters even worse. Although there were almost three times as many students in Poland in 1997 as in 1989, only marginally more young academics received their doctorate (2600 compared with 2020), and the number of those receiving their habilitation only rose from 653 to 685. This crisis can be attributed to the considerable underfinancing of the entire sphere of education and higher education. For several years Poland has been spending a distinctly smaller proportion of the gross domestic product on this sector than other European countries.[16]

1.2 The integration of institutions of higher education into the education system

Until the end of the 1990s the structure of the education system was laid down by the law on the development of the education system of July 15th, 1961.[17] Since the Polish education system was antiquated, the pupils had not so far been trained to act independently, and the situation of the teachers is poor, the education system was increasingly criticised. It was only in 1999

---

16   In 1995 this amounted to 0.74%, and in 1999 0.76% of the GDP. The pro capita expenditure in this field amounted to only 10% of the funds spent in Germany and France, while the Czech Republic, which is also undergoing a process of transformation, spent almost three times as much. Cf. (N.N.), Deutscher Akademischer Austauschdienst. Außenstelle Warschau. Jahresbericht 1998 (in the following: DAAD 1998), p. 12f. There is very little outside funding by business and industry (cf. Wprost of 12/12/1999).

17   On the education system see S. Baske (note 2).

that the government coalition consisting of AWS *(Akcja Wyborcza Solidarnosci/* Solidarity Election Campaign and UW *(Unia Wolnosci/* Freedom Union) were able to push through school reforms in order to raise the general standard of education which, however, especially among the teaching staff, is meeting with considerable resistance, for instance due to the new teaching methods.

The education system developed in accordance with the laws of 1991 and 1999 usually involves twelve-year education at primary and secondary schools, which can be followed by a course at an institution of higher education lasting either three or five years. The education system valid until 1999 provided for attendance at an elementary school *(szkola podstawowa)* for eight years, followed by various secondary schools: four-year general high schools, four to five-year vocational middle schools *(srednie szkoly zawodowe)*, which as technical colleges or vocational high schools lead both to the standard requirement for entry to higher education and to a middle vocational qualification, basic vocational schools *(zasadnicza szkola zawodowa,* two to three years) or schools providing a preparatory course (two years). Only attendance at the general high school or the technical college enabled a pupil to obtain the *matura*, which is the standard requirement for entry to higher education.

The basis of the current, more differentiated education system, which was introduced at the beginning of the 1999/2000 school year, is the six-year primary school, which is attended by children from the age of seven.[18] This is followed for all pupils by three-year attendance at a grammar school, which ends with selective examinations.

The ministry's plans are that roughly 20% of the approximately 16-year-old pupils should subsequently attend the vocational school *(szkola*

18   For the new education system introduced after September 1st, 1999, see: Gazeta Bankowa of 20-26/2/1999: Ustrój szkólny [The school system], p. 14.

zadwodowa) for two years. This can be followed by attendance at a so-called advanced high school (*liceum uzupelniajace*), at which the requirement for entry to higher education can be obtained.

Roughly 80% of the pupils are to attend a so-called "profiled high school" (*liceum profilowane*), at which they can obtain the requirement for entry to higher education after three years. Approximately 50% of these high-school graduates are then to be able to start studying without an entrance examination. The other half can attend advanced colleges (*kolegia*[19] and *szkoly policealne*). This reform has introduced "project-related" learning into the primary schools, and not learning differentiated by subject. Differentiation by subject starts only in the grammar school, in which, to a certain extent, achievement-related and interest-related groups can be formed.[20] The vocational schools are to provide a broad education in order to achieve flexibility among the workforce. The high schools, which are to prepare pupils for higher education and for participation in the life of society are, in contrast, to develop different profiles (humanist, technical-natural science, economic), and here only certain subjects are compulsory for all pupils.

At the universities one can study the "classic" arts subjects as well as those of the social and natural sciences. One can study engineering sciences at the polytechnics *(polytechnika)*, some of which also offer degree courses

---

19   The colleges established after 1989 (*kolegia*, 6 technical colleges, 32 language colleges, as of Sept. 1994) cannot be considered as being part of the higher education system. Under the supervision of the universities they train teachers in two-year courses.

20   The creation of grammar schools is an important point in the reform programme, since they are to complement the frequently very unsatisfactory education in rural areas and help the pupils from these regions to obtain equal opportunities. In 1980 one school leaver in fourteen from primary schools in rural areas succeeded in studying at an institution of higher education, and at present only one in 140 manages it. Cf. H. Golombek, Deutscher Akademischer Austauschdienst. Außenstelle Warschau. Jahresbericht 1999, 3/2/2000 (in the following DAAD 1999), p. 8.

in economics, a few of them also offering courses in the natural sciences. In addition, there are medical schools, colleges of education, theological colleges, as well as colleges of fine and dramatic arts,[21] schools of business, agricultural colleges and colleges of physical education. Since 1998 universities of applied sciences have been founded after the German model. Like most of the private courses in higher education, they lead only to the *licencjat*, but there is also the opportunity to attend advanced courses at a university which can lead to the Master's degree.

In addition to the Master's degree course, which usually takes five years (for all subjects) it is also possible to complete a three to four-year career-related course leading to the so-called *licencjat* (vocational diploma, "Bachelor") or to the diploma degree in engineering *(inżynier)*. As far as medicine is concerned, the professional title of "Doctor" *(lekarz)* is awarded after the successful completion of five years of study (six years for dentistry). *Licencjat* graduates can obtain the Master's degree after a further two years of advanced study. A doctoral programme can be started only after obtaining the degree of Master or "Doctor" *(lekarz)*, and after the doctorate the title of "habilitated doctor" ("Dr. habil.") can be aspired to. In accordance with the international models ("BA" – "MA") it is becoming increasingly common to split what is designed as a five-year course into two phases. The *licencjat* and advanced or postgraduate courses fulfil the need for courses which provide career-orientated graduates for the labour market. In addition to the courses with normal full-time attendance (customarily called "daytime study" in Poland) the evening and distance learning courses continue, and are becoming increasingly popular. They enable a person to obtain further qualifications while pursuing a career.

---

21   Colleges of music (8), academies of fine art (6) and colleges of drama (3).

The most important requirement for entry to a state institution of higher education is generally, in addition to the university entry level certificate, an entrance examination at the beginning of the course of study.[22] Full acceptance as a student is completed after matriculation and after the new student has taken a solemn vow.

The degree course is divided into academic years, which mostly last from October 1st until September 30th. An academic year is split into periods when there are classes (semesters), when class attendance is compulsory, examination periods totalling approx. 6 weeks per year at the end of the semesters and above all at the end of the academic year, practical work experience as required, and the winter, spring and summer vacations totalling at least six weeks. Before the beginning of each academic year the students receive a detailed timetable and calendar of events with a list of all the subjects, practicals and other events to be attended.[23] Overall, it can be stated that the majority of Polish students complete their studies after twelve years of schooling and after five or six (Master's) years of study at most, and are available to the labour market at the age of 24 or 25.

Roughly 800,000 of the 1.3 million students paid for their training in 1999.[24] In accordance with the Constitution of 1997 study at state institutions of higher education is basically free of charge, but not "additional services". Since 1990 the universities have been permitted to demand fees for the entrance examinations.[25] Payment for evening classes and distance learning were an

22 The selection procedure is laid down by each individual senate.
23 Cf. I.R. Wrompel, p. 48.
24 In 1998 the Polish state spent roughly 4 billion zloty on higher education, while the students paid a total of approx. 3.2 billion zloty in tuition fees. Cf. Wprost of 5/9/1999: Rachunek za studia (The bill for studying).
25 The amount of the fee is laid down by the Ministry. However, one problem here is that some university professors offer preparatory courses for which they charge fees, and that at the same time they administer the entrance examinations.

additional "back door", but this has now been declared to be unconstitutional. As a result of the practice until now some state institutions of higher education were able to finance 10% and others 50% of their annual expenditure by means of these fees.[26]

Thus the Polish government is faced with a dilemma that is to be solved by the new Higher Education Act. On the one hand, it definitely wants to maintain the high quota of young people studying, in order to bring the level of education up to that of the EU member states. On the other hand, however, the funds for this are insufficient. At the present time there is a discussion about whether or not "paedagogical services", such as issuing certificates and carrying out examinations must be paid for. Since these "services" must be used by every student the possibility of a monthly fee amounting to 10% of the average monthly income in Poland (1400 zloty, just under DM 700) is one of the solutions being discussed, while second full-time university courses must be paid for as a matter of principle.[27]

The private institutions of higher education demand tuition fees for attendance. The magazine *Wprost* worked out an average sum of between 4,000 and 8,000 zloty that the students had to pay for their course of study at a non-state institution of higher education in 1998.[28]

---

26   Cf. DAAD 1998, p. 13. According to information provided by the University of Warsaw, for an academic year it demanded 5,400 zloty for an evening course in Law, and 1,400 in Journalism, 2,400 zloty for a distance learning course in Journalism and 2,000 zloty for one in Polish Studies. In 1999 1,000 zloty were demanded for a distance learning course in Biology at the Adam Mickiewicz University in Poznan.
27   Cf. DAAD 1999, p. 14 and Wprost of 5/9/1999.
28   Cf. Wprost of 20/12/1998. In 1999 full-time study at the private Warsaw *Wyzsza Szkola Dziennikarska* (School of Journalism) cost 9,200 zloty as a daytime course, as an evening course it cost 7,200, and as a distance learning course 6,000 zloty; at the private *Wyzsza Szkola Bankowosci, Finansów i Zarzadzania* (Academy for Banking, Finance and Adminstration) it cost 5,300 zloty (daytime course) and 4,400 zloty (evening course).

As a result of these enormous costs for students a system was created for financing the study of students from socially weaker families. Since October 1998 roughly 112,000 students have been receiving state support (as a loan) amounting to 400 zloty per month. This loan has to be paid off after completion of the course, and here the state takes over part of the interest due. Particularly good results lead to a reduction of the sum to be repaid.[29]

In addition, there is a differentiated scholarship system in Poland. So-called social scholarships (*stipendia socjlne*) averaging 100 zloty are provided for students from families who per capita income is not higher than 400 zloty. A single payment of 500 zloty is made as support in emergency situations (accident, illness). In addition, there are scholarships of 200 zloty for students who have completed their first year of study with a "4" (third best mark). For the best students, who also have to show their ability outside their degree programme, e.g in the form of publications in popular scientific journals, the Ministry of Science awards scholarships of 550 zloty.[30]

1.3 Data on Polish institutions of higher education and on students

The process of transformation was accompanied not only by a large qualitative change in the higher education landscape but also by a quantitative one. In 1990 there was a total of 112 institutions of higher education with roughly 403,000 students, while in 1997/98 roughly 1.09 million students

---

29   Cf. DAAD 1998, p. 13f. A credit of this kind with a favourable interest rate is granted for a maximum of six years and paid out in 10 monthly instalments.

30   As a comparison: a room in a student hostel (three people sharing) cost 160 zloty (per person) in Warsaw in 1999, the best equipped rooms cost 220 zloty, a two-bedded room in Kraków 120-140 zloty (per person), and a single room 280 zloty. A flat in the centre of Warsaw even costs around US $300. A comfortable room in a hostel of the private *Wyzsza Szkola Nauk Humanistycznych* (College of Humanist Sciences) in Putulsk with its own sanitary installations costs between 300 and 350 zloty. Cf. Polityka. Dodatck specjalny (5/1999), p. 7.

were attending 246 state and private institutions of higher education. In 1999 the total was 259.[31] The marked increase in the number of institutions of higher education is due, above all, to the founding of 88 Schools of Economics. There are also some (1994: 17) Military and Police Academies in addition to the institutions of higher education open to the public at large.

Since there is a large and increasing demand for higher education the Polish government has started to increase the density of state institutions of higher education, and thus the universities and institutions of higher education are permitted to found branch institutions with at least two faculties in other cities. Ten of these branch institutions of higher education had been founded by 1998. One of these measures is the founding of universities of applied sciences (*wyższe szkoły zawodowe* – 10 had been founded by 1999). It is characteristic of the foundation of institutions of higher education of this kind that they were established in cities where no such institution had previously existed and in regions where higher education had not been widespread so far. The goal is that they should contribute to the economic development and the raising of the general level of education in the region in question. In this case, the universities of applied sciences[32] cater to the needs of business and industry in the region and, in their turn, business and industry are required to make placements available. Despite this regional decentralisation, the institutions of higher education are concentrated in Warsaw, Kraków, Lódz, Poznan, Gdansk, Lublin, Wroclaw and Upper Silesia.[33]

---

31   State: 99, private: 136, church or ones associated with religious groups: 14, state universities of applied sciences 10 (cf. DAAD 1999, p. 19).

32   People with a habilitation, doctorate or Master's degree work here. It is frequently a second job for them, since they are employed at a neighbouring university.

33   Cf. U.J. v. Beek, p. 275.

Table 1: Comparison of the number of Polish state and private higher education institutions (HE) in 1990/91 and 1997/98

	1990/91	1997/98	state HE inst. 1998
Total HE institutions	112	246	91
Universities	11	13	13
Technical colleges	30	30	20
Agricultural colleges	9	10	9
Schools of economics	5	93	5
Colleges of education	10	19	9
Medical schools	12	11	10
Schools of navigation	3	3	2
Physical education colleges	6	6	6
Colleges of art	17	20	17
Theological colleges	7	16	2
Other HE institutions	2	25	0

Source: Wprost. Supplement of 30/5/1999, p. 10 and DAAD 1998, p. 9f.

Despite the founding of new state higher education institutions[34] and an increase in the capacity of existing ones, the demand for higher education could not be satisfied by state higher education institutions. That is why 140 private institutions of higher education had been established by 1999 in accordance with legal regulations. The Ministry of Education has to register and permit them to be set up. It has been possible for private institutions of higher education to become established even in medium-sized towns like Koszalin,[35] predominantly with courses in Economics.[36] Only few of them (1998: 21) also offer the Master's degree in addition to *Licencjat* courses. 82 offered only one subject; the broadest range is provided by the *Wyzsza*

---

34   Two new universities were founded in 1999: The Warsaw Academy for Catholic Theology became the Cardinal Wyszynski University, while in Olsztyn the College of Education and the Agricultural College were united to form the University of Ermlamd and Mazury.

Szkola Humanistyczno-Przyrodnicza (Higher Education Institution for Humanities and Natural Sciences) in Sandomierz, which has nine subjects. Overall, the success of the private institutions of higher education are not only proof of the "thirst for education" of young Polish people, but also of the serious crisis of the state higher education system.

The number of students rose from 403,000 to 1,091,800 between 1990/91 and 1997/98. In 1999 1.26 million Poles were studying, 57% of them women. All types of higher education institution are involved. However, there are especially distinct increases in the number of university students and students studying at technical and business institutions. Roughly 934,000 students were studying at state institutions of higher education in 1999, 308,000 at private ones, and 23,000 at church ones. It is remarkable that in 1998/99 for the first time more new students were matriculated at private institutions of higher education than at state ones. The large increase in the number of students overall is due to the strong growth in the number of distance learning students. For the first time their number (616,000) lay above that of full-time students (roughly 586,700), while roughly 62,700 students were matriculated in evening courses.[37]

35   The *Baltycki Wyzsza Szkola Humanistyczna* (Humanist Academy of the Baltic) is located there: it offers Master's courses (Education, (public) Administration, History) and *Licjencjat* courses (Polish Philology, Administration and Marketing, Education and History). With 7,000 students (1998) it is the largest private institution of higher education. Here the matriculation fees are 250 zloty for full-time courses and 350 zloty for distance learning courses. The course in Public Administration currently costs 1,000 zloty for full-time and distance learning courses, the History course 1,350 zloty and 1,000 zloty respectively, Education 1,350 zloty and 1,000 zloty respectively, and Marketing and (Business) Management 1650 zloty and 1,000 zloty respectively (all figures are per semester).

36   In 1997 more than half the total of 200,000 students at private institutions of higher education were studying an Economics subject. (cf. DAAD 1998, p. 11f). In the meantime there are also numerous private institutions of higher education offering subjects not related to Economics.

Table 2: Comparison between the number of students at Polish higher education institutions in 1990/91 and 1997/98 (in thousands)

	1990/91	1997/98
Total HE institutions	403,6	1091,8
Universities	11,1	334,0
Technical colleges	84,0	241,0
Agricultural colleges	36,4	77,3
Schools of economics	24,0	201,5
Colleges of education	47,6	121,2
Medical schools	38,7	26,3
Schools of navigation	2,5	7,0
Physical education colleges	14,6	19,9
Colleges of art	8,2	10,7
Theological colleges	6,7	14,9
Other HE institutions	4,1	8,7

Source: Wprost. Supplement of 30/5/1999, p. 10.

The figures in Table 2 point to the fact that the majority of Polish students prefer business and technical courses of study. However, education, humanist (= arts subjects), social science and medical courses are popular with the students. It can nevertheless be stated that in 1997/98 fewer students put their names down for humanist, social science or medical courses and mathematics/ computer science, while the number of students rose in the technical and business subjects. In the "fashionable subjects" like Psychology, Political Science, "International Relations" and the courses of study in Business there are considerably more applicants than places, while competition in the philological subjects and law was less intense. In contrast, there are frequently more places than applicants in many technical and natural science subjects.[38] Since in 1999 only 130,000 free full-time places were offered at the state higher education institutions to the roughly 343,000 young people who had qualified for university entry, the

---

37   Cf. DAAD 1999, p. 12 and the statistical appendix: p. 19ff.

applicants who were turned down can take up an evening or distance learning course costing approx. DM 1000-2000 in tuition fees per academic year at state higher education institutions. The best of these can succeed in obtaining a free place after their first year of study.

Table 3: Comparison between the number of students at Polish higher education institutions in 1990/91 and 1997/98 (in thousands) by subject

	1990/91	1997/98
Education	14,1	13,8
Art	2,4	1,2
Humanities	10,9	8,6
Theology	2,3	1,6
Social Sciences	4,3	11,8
Economics/Administration	14,8	23,9
Law	4,7	4,9
Natural Sciences	3,1	2,4
Mathematics/Computer Science	2,0	1,9
Medicine	10,1	3,1
Engineering Science	16,5	17,6
Architecture	1,1	0,7
Agriculture	7,0	3,2
Transport/Traffic	0,7	1,0
Media	1,0	0,6

Source: Wprost. Supplement of 30/5/1999, p. 10.

1.4 The labour market for higher education graduates

The labour market collapsed as a result of the breakdown of the communist economic system and the beginning transformation. Since full employment officially existed in the People's Republic, unemployment statistics were introduced for the first time in 1990.

Between 1992 and 1998 Poland had the strongest economic growth among the large Central and Eastern European countries undergoing transformation, and therefore the economic upswing after 1994 was noticeable on the labour market. This upswing phase on the labour market ended in the second half of 1998 due to a clearly noticeable economic decline, so that the unemployment rate of 10.4% (December 1998) rose to 13% (December 1999).[39]

It is characteristic of the Polish labour market that the main centres of unemployment are largely dependent on the geographical location and the economic structure, particularly since the "town-country" conflict regarding the infrastructure and culture is still strongly marked. It is correspondingly high in the agriculturally orientated voivodeships in the north of Poland and in the cities whose economic structure during the People's Republic depended solely on one large industry (e.g. Nowa Huta near Kraków) or was marked by unprofitable branches of industry like the textile industry (e.g. Lódz) or mining (e.g. Walbrzych). This means that long-term, structurally caused unemployment in the various regions brings about the increasing poverty of the population.[40]

The unemployment rate is comparatively low in the large urban centres, in which the service sector is concentrated, and in which the most foreign capital was/is being invested.[41]

---

38   Cf. DAAD 1999, p. 11.
39   Cf. PlanEcon. Data Supplement, vol. XVI, No. 2 (2000), in: Bundesinstitut für Ost-
      wissenschaftliche und Internationale Studien (Cologne), p. 24.
40   Cf. Rzeczpospolita of 22/1/2000: P. Apanowicz, 13 procent bez pracy (13 percent
      without work).
41   Cf. J.W. Tkaczynski, Von der "polnischen Wirtschaft" zum "polnischen Tiger" Europas?, in:
      Osteuropa-Wirtschaft 42 (1997), pp. 275-292, here: p. 287f. On the significance of joining
      the EU for the Polish labour market cf. Z. Wisniewski, Effekte des EU-Beitritts auf den
      Arbeitsmarkt in Polen, in: Osteuropa-Wirtschaft 42 (1997), pp. 293-300.

Women[42] and young people[43] are above-averagely affected by unemployment. In 1997 the proportion of 18-24 year-olds was 35%, most of whom are comparatively badly trained.[44] Overall, 83,500 graduates (of a total of 1.6 million unemployed), i.e. roughly 5.2%, were unemployed in 1998.[45] However, the number has been considerably reduced, since in March 1999 only 1.5% of the unemployed were graduates from higher education institutions, which makes it clear that higher education offers better opportunities.[46] This is connected with the fact that in Poland vocational training still continues to predominate: in 1992/93 72% of elementary school leavers had vocational training (38% basic vocational school, 34% middle vocational school), and in contrast only 28% had attended a *liceum*. In 1995 a mere 6.8%, and in 1998 13% of the population more than 15 years old had attended higher education institutions.[47]

A survey by the *Instytut Spraw Pracy* (Institute for Labour Affairs, ISP) of employers from all branches and in the field of the public administration in Warsaw, which has a low unemployment rate, and in Lódz, which has a high unemployment rate, makes clear which degree subjects are particularly sought after by employers: 25% were seeking engineers of all types, 19% economists, 5% lawyers and 4% were seeking marketing experts and computer scientists, while only 3% were seeking arts graduates, 2% doctors and 1% natural scientists.

---

42   In 1998 61.5% of all the unemployed were women. Cf. Rzeczpospolita of 28/8/1998: A. Kowalik, Najdotliwsze dla kobiet i mlodziezy (Most painful for women and young people).
43   In 1998 20% of the unemployed were under 24 years old. Cf. Rzeczpospolita of 15/9/1998: (a.f.t.) Mlode bezrobocie (Young unemployment).
44   Cf. Z. Wisniewski, p. 294.
45   Cf. Rzeczpospolita of 15/9/1998: Mlode bezrobocie (Young unemployment).
46   Cf. E. Banaszak, Sytuacja osób z wyzszym wyksztalceniem na rynku pracy (The situation of people with higher education on the labour market), pp. 5-13 (end of 1999 / beginning of 2000) (this contribution by the employee of the "Career Service" office in Torun was made available to the author by the *Ministerstwo Pracy i Polityki Spolecznej* (Ministry of Labour and Social Policy) in February 2000, but unfortunately without bibliographical information. However, it is of fundamental importance for statements made later).
47   In towns 17% of the population had higher education, while in the countryside the figure does not even reach 4%. Cf. DAAD 1999, pp. 8 and 19 and DAAD 1998, p. 19.

What is amazing about the result is that 37% of the graduates were being sought without more precise details about what kind of subject they had studied.[48]

If one also includes the data provided by the job-finding services associated with the universities, this produces the following consequences for the graduate labour market:

Engineers basically have good career prospects, especially computer scientists and electronics engineers. However, the labour market is more difficult for civil and chemical engineers. In fact, computer scientists do not have to worry about finding a job, but rather which offer they should accept. Although economists continue to be sought after, in towns with a development that is not all too dynamic and in which courses in economics are offered, it can be seen that a certain degree of saturation has been reached in the labour market for graduates in this subject.

It is interesting that the employment prospects for art students are good, provided that they have knowledge of graphics programmes and are prepared to work in advertising.

The survey by the ISDP does not mention the chances of agronomists, which, however, are not bad if they want to work in food technology. On the other hand, the labour market for lawyers proves to be more problematic, above all if they have had no practical experience. The potential employers of lawyers and administration experts are frequently worried about the fact that they will use the job, that in most cases does not correspond with their training profile, merely as a springboard for an appropriate position, and thus will not stay with the firm for long.

---

48   On this and on the following statements cf. E. Banaszak, p. 6.

For graduates from universities and colleges of education (above all graduates in history, biology, chemistry, geography, Russian, Romance languages etc.), who were trained as teachers, the chances of finding a corresponding job are fairly slight. Better knowledge of English, and partially also of German, or a degree in these languages promise to be an exception to this. Since graduates of English studies prefer to aim at better paid and more prestigious careers in industry and business, there is a large shortage of English teachers, and for the same reason to a lesser extent of German teachers as well, so that head teachers frequently offer privileges to teachers of these subjects, such as a government flat. Roughly 82% of teachers are women. Overall, however, the teaching profession is not very prestigious and financially hardly very lucrative, so that talented and committed graduates have so far rather been deterred from taking up this profession.[49] The educational reform of 1999 attempts to counteract this with the introduction of a career structure which is graded according to training, performance and abilities, and where the remuneration differs.

In contrast to the situation in the Western democracies, a career as a scientist or a university professor was not very attractive during the People's Republic and remains so during the "Third Republic".[50] The so-called "brain drain" abroad, and above all into business and industry at home, is large as a result of the low level of pay in higher education, since life in business or industry is generally (financially) more attractive for graduates than a job in academia.[51]

---

49   According to the old pay scales, after 30 years of service an experienced teacher earned only 30% more than a beginner. In 1999 a beginner in the profession received 905 zloty (about DM 450) and a teacher with 30 years of experience approx. DM 680. Thus the raising of the initial salary to DM 610 is one important step in the reform of the education system. Cf. DAAD 1999, p. 9.

50   Negative selection took place during the People's Republic, since the sciences were subject to political restrictions (censorship, which frequently led to self-censorship) and, in addition, politically acceptable people were appointed, frequently without a habilitation, however. These factors, combined with the overall wretched financial and material provision of higher education hardly made the academic's profession attractive.

51   This is why idealists and second-class academics frequently take up a university career.

When no details are given about the course the employees to be recruited should have studied, this means that for the employers it is essential that they should have higher education and additional qualifications ("potential"). There are essentially three reasons that can be given for this attitude:

- The large consulting firms and concerns, which mostly work internationally, usually "cream off" the best graduates each year immediately after they have completed their studies. The firms attach particular importance to the results of their examinations, scholarships, prizes and awards, social aspects, i.e. involvement, placements, fluent foreign languages and periods abroad. The consulting firms seek especially educated people in order subsequently to provide them with further training for a particular job.
- Job offers which provide jobs in "new spheres of employment" are typical of the transformation of Polish economic life. Numerous "new spheres of employment" (e.g. public relations and logistics), for which there are sometimes not even any expressions in the Polish language,[52] cannot avail themselves of graduates with a degree in the appropriate subject because this subject did not exist during the time of the People's Republic. This is why the missing specialists are to be replaced by people who, as a result of their abilities, their knowledge and experience, e.g. in related jobs or subjects, can make up for their lack of specialisation.
- Finally, graduates are sought who have preferably had training in economics and polytechnical subjects, and who have held management positions for several years.

Overall it can be stated that although graduates continue to have very good career prospects they nevertheless frequently work in fields that do not correspond to the subjects they have studied. As a result of the educational

---

52   This is noted by E. Banaszak, p. 9.

structure of the Polish population and the simultaneous process of economic growth and modernisation, these opportunities will still remain, at least in the medium term, provided that the graduates are prepared to equip themselves with such "key abilities" as foreign languages and computer knowledge.

2. Linking Higher Education and the Employment System

The necessity for orientation toward the labour market was postponed by the state institutions of higher education by referring to their autonomy. At the present time, however, because of the pressure of society and the competition from the universities of applied sciences and the private institutions of higher education, there are indications that they are beginning to modify their curricula in order to relate to the needs of business and industry. The degree to which their graduates are integrated into economic life is essential for the reputation of an institution of higher education, since one of its primary tasks is to train the rising generation of experts and managers.[53]

As far as the modernisation of the curricula is concerned, it is, above all, the newer state and private institutions of higher education that are prominent, since they are less bound by tradition. Thus, for example, they offer new subjects and combinations of subjects, such as Chemistry with Marketing, Public Relations or International Relations as degree courses.

Since graduates with knowledge of several subjects have better career chances, some universities offer interdisciplinary courses[54] and the opportunity of choosing additional subjects to complement their main course of study.

---

53   The ranking lists regularly published in magazines help school leavers in their choice of higher education institution. As a rule, the universities in Warsaw, Kraków and Poznan and the technical universities in Warsaw, Kraków and Wroclaw are to be found at the top of the list. The Warsaw School of Commerce leads among the business schools; private institutions of higher education are also frequently to be found among the best.

The participation of the universities in specialist exchange programmes is also important in providing students with the opportunity to gain experience abroad. Since the international comparability of degrees is being aimed at, the institutions of higher education are increasingly introducing a credit-point system along the lines of the international model, in particular for courses in Economics.

In order to provide students with additional knowledge in data processing, the universities, colleges and academies are setting up special training centres. They are also trying to adapt the teaching programmes to the needs. In addition, they are participating in the organisation of practicals outside the institution of higher education, since these does not only provide the students with work experience. Apart from this, the societies founded by the universities are significant, since they are to facilitate contacts between students and graduates already integrated into the world of work.

3. Career Orientation during the Course of Study

With the exception of a few subjects in which work experience is compulsory, career orientation during the course of study is generally left to the initiative and involvement of the students themselves. An important role is played here by (voluntary) practical work and part-time jobs, which frequently lead to contacts with the later employer.

The Career Services Offices (*biura karier*) established along the lines of the British and Dutch models are often situated at the interface with working life. The first pilot project was established at the Nicolas Copernicus

---

54 Thus there are interdisciplinary (*miedzywydzialowe*), individual humanist (= arts) and mathematical-natural science degree courses at the universities in Warsaw, Katowice and Torun, as well as an interdisciplinary course in Environmental Protection in Warsaw. Cf. Polityka. Dodatek specjalny (5/1999), p. 2.

University in Torun (*Biuro Zawodowej Promocji Studentów i Absolwentów UMK*) in 1993. There were nine[55] Career Offices of this kind in Poland in 1999; additional ones are currently being established. Their basic task is to provide students and graduates with orientation and to advise them individually so that they can shape their studies and their search for a job as creatively and flexibly as possible. Their task is thus to help in the choice of career and to provide information about jobs available and about the various careers, employers and the labour market situation, as well as about graduate and advanced studies. To this end they also work together with possible employers and place graduates with them. In addition, they offer "workshops", at which students can learn to write their curriculum vitae and letters of motivation and also practice interviews. Apart from this, the teaching institutions can reexamine their training structure and programmes on the basis of the experience gained by the Career Office. They also provide help in finding placements and vocation programmes for younger students.[56]

The international unions of students provide important involvement with regard to career orientation. AIESEC and BEST, for example, organize annual job markets etc., usually in cooperation with the Career Services Offices, while ELSA invites representatives from various legal professions to the institutions of higher education to inform law students about their career opportunities. Each of these student organizations arranges practicals in firms during the vacation, most of which are sponsored by the individual organization.

---

55   Apart from in Torun, Career Offices existed in the following cities: Poznan (Adam Mickiewicz University), Lublin (Marie Sklodowska Curie University) Wroclaw (University and Polytechnic), Katowice (Academy of Economics), Warsaw (Main Agricultural College), Kraków, Gliwice and Kielce (Polytechnics).

56   On the tasks of a Career Services Office of this kind see, for example, the homepage of the *biuro karier* at the Copernicus University: (www.torun.pl/BiuroKarier/). The funding of this particular Career Services Office is guaranteed through the cooperation of the University with the Employment Office of the voivodeship in Torun. The advisers here were trained in Poland and Great Britain.

Further help with students' orientation is provided by the involvement of the Chambers of Industry and Commerce and the employers. The later provide information in the institutions of higher education about their recruitment methods and publish special prospectuses for graduates etc. Programmes like *"grasz o staz"* ("you play for a STAGE / preparatory time?") are popular. They are a kind of competition for finding much sought-after placements in the large firms.

4. The Transition from Higher Education to Employment

In accordance with the increase in the number of students, the number of graduates from Polish institutions of higher education rose from 56,100 in 1990/91 to 142,760 in 1998.[57] Of these, 133,817 graduated from a university (70,774 with a Master's degree, 43,153 with a *Licencjat*), 25,808 from private institutions of higher education (583 with a Master's degree, 25,225 with a *Licencjat*) and 3,135 from church institutions of higher education (2,215 with a Master's degree, 920 with a *Licencjat*).[58]

Table 4 reflects the number of graduates by subject in 1990/91 and 1997/98. It shows that in 1997/98 mainly graduates in Education, Economics, Arts and Social Sciences joined the labour market. It is also clear here that the number of Economics students rose extremely rapidly after the political upheaval and the beginning of the process of economic transformation, which can be put down to the hopes of new students for a good job and a career in the changing industrial and business sector.

---

57   Cf. DAAD 1999, statistical overview, p. 19f. In contrast, Wprost, Supplement of 30/5/1999, p. 10 gives the figure of 146,300 for the academic year 1997/98.
58   Cf. DAAD 1999, statistical overview, p. 20.

Table 4: Comparison between the number of graduates in 1990/91 and 1997/98 (in thousands) by subject

	1997/98	1990/91
Education	17,5	26,8
Arts studies	2,4	1,2
Humanities	9,6	9,1
Theology	1,8	1,3
Social Sciences	3,7	8,5
Economics/Administration	9,8	19,0
Law	3,9	3,6
Natural Sciences	4,1	2,3
Mathematics/Computer Science	1,8	1,6
Medicine	10,2	3,9
Engineering Science	19,4	12,8
Architecture	0,7	0,4
Agriculture	7,7	3,1
Transport/Traffic	0,7	0,4
Media	0,9	0,5

Source: Wprost. Supplement of 30/5/1999, p. 10.

It is especially difficult for graduates to find their first job. Thus 7,342 of the graduates from the academic year 1997/98 were still unemployed in March 1999. By comparison only 3,705 graduates from the previous year were still unemployed in March 1998. There are various reasons for this, and they lie both in the structural and economic fields as well as in the personal field.

The slowing down of the development of the labour market for graduates can be explained only to a slight extent by the introduction of social insurance, while it is probably the slackening of the economy which was the decisive factor.[59]

Problems arise as a result of the differing economic growth rates in the different regions, as well as from the contrast between town and country that is still large, and from the low mobility level. Wherever the growth rate is high it is easy to find employment, while in regions with low economic strength it is difficult even for the highly qualified to find work. Few graduates are prepared to leave the place where they have lived and studied, even though, above all, the receptive Warsaw labour market still provides opportunities, and even though it is precisely in the provinces that large international firms have established branches due, among other things, to the tax advantages, and they require academically trained personnel. However, the latter are frequently not prepared to move to the countryside.[60] On the other hand, the traffic infrastructure has largely not been expanded, so that daily commuting a great distance between home and work is possible only with great difficulty over a longer period of time. In addition, there is still often a lack of willingness to change jobs more frequently.

Further reasons lie in the education system, since pupils and students are frequently "overloaded" with facts, but are rarely trained to work or act independently or creatively. It is thus frequently the case that graduates do not know how to seek work, or which "new jobs" are available with good career prospects. Additional problems include a lack of work experience, which can

---

59   Cf. Rzeczpospolita of 22/1/2000: P. Apanowicz, 13 procent bez pracy (13 percent without work) confirms this trend. According to this, 22,840 graduates were registered with the Employment Offices (urząd pracy) in December 1999, but roughly 7,000 graduates fewer found a job than in the previous month. The Centrum Analiz Społeczno-Ekonomicznych (Centre for Socio-economic Analyses) predicts that work can now be found only for the roughly 200,000 graduates from this academic year.

60   Cf. E. Banaszak, p. 13.

be provided by placements etc. The fact that most of the graduates have had no social experience through social, cultural and/or political involvement makes things even more difficult for this group of people seeking employment.

The essential precondition for integration into working life is the learning of "key abilities"[61] such as data processing and foreign languages. In addition, graduates are required to be in a position to acquire knowledge quickly and solve problems independently. They are to be committed and loyal to their employer, but also sociable. Apart from that, employers require them to be young and that they can prove that they have had some work experience.[62] It is also of considerable importance that their only slight knowledge of the Polish labour market is improved and that the graduates are given the opportunity to become easily adaptable to it. The latter also includes the exact planning of further training measures after completion of their studies. As a result, huge numbers of graduates take advantage of the provision of graduate and advanced courses (for which a charge is made),[63] the majority of whom, however, are only following the recommendation of the employment offices.

5. Prospects for the Future

Joining the EU will probably mean that the structural and technological unemployment will increase since, in order to achieve greater productivity, technological progress will be accelerated as a result of the heightened competitive situation. Foreign investment will also increase technological progress. In addition,

---

61   Cf. Rzeczpospolita of 31/8/1998: A. Kowalik, Jest popyt na prace (There is a demand for work).
62   Cf. E. Banaszak, p. 9f.
63   These include, for example, MBA courses (Master of Business Administration), which are offered, among others, by the *Główna Szkola Handlowa* in Warsaw, the University and the *Politechnika* (Polytechnic) in Warsaw, the *Akademia Ekonomicza* (School of Economics) in Poznan (cf. zycie gospodarcze of 1-15/4/1998, p. 46ff.).

internationalisation and globalisation, the expansion of information technologies, a change in the value system, the ever-growing importance of the service sector and of environmental protection, and also the employment rate in smaller (medium-sized) firms and independence will increase. This means that a broad general education as the basis for job specialisation, as well as continual further training within the framework of the vocational qualification will become necessary.[64] Since the need for highly trained and specialised staff will increase during the course of the increased productivity and the developments sketched out here, higher education will gain more and more significance for the Polish labour market.[65]

If these developments are taken into account, the labour market will, at least in the medium term, provide good employment opportunities for graduates from institutions of higher education, even though a certain degree of saturation will occur with regard to management personnel. The most important precondition for this is that students should acquire skills and qualifications outside their subject area. However, this can only be provided by a higher education system that both works well and is efficient in the long term, and in which research and teaching are made possible at a high level, so that the success of the reform of higher education will ultimately be an essential precondition for the continued development of the Polish labour market for graduates from institutions of higher education.

---

64   Cf. E. Banaszak, p. 15f.
65   Cf. Z. Wisniewski, p. 296ff. The following training structure is to be aimed at: 20% (compared with the current 34%) basic vocational school, 30% (currently 34%) middle vocational school and 50% (currently 28%) *liceum* providing a general education.

Sri Lanka

Charles Fernando

1. Introduction

Whether one starts in the West from the USA looking, for example, at the roundtables and the research initiated by the National Centre for Public Policy and Higher Education, or in the East with debates in Japan on issues such as quality in the State and the Private Universities; whether one examines the work of the UNESCO World Conference on Higher Education, the recent discussions at ILO on Lifelong Learning, or even the work of the Dearing Committee in the UK; whether one discusses work-based learning in Liverpool, problem-based learning in Maastricht, and moves onto the scenario of the teacher and the student both being forced eventually to becoming permanent learners, or to the prospect and impact of virtualization; whether interest in another critical area such as university links with the World of Work leads one to research by Teichler and the team at Kassel in Germany, and by Neave, De Weert and others at Twente in the Netherlands, ... one is confronted with the fact that universities everywhere are at a crossroad and that the ethos of the traditional university is rapidly changing. In such a challenging situation, when a hundred different issues dealing with Higher Education are being discussed, it doubtless is meaningful to contribute to an ongoing study, even though in a very limited way through the contribution of a country report.[1]

---

1   The author is grateful particularly to Mr. Faizal Salieh, Dr. Premadasa Udagama, Dr. W. M. K. Wijetunga, Prof. P. Wilson and Prof. M. M. Karunanayake. Some of their comments and suggestions helped the thinking process, while others have found their way into the report. Years of experience in the world of study and work in Sri Lanka and abroad, and fifteen years of total reflective involvement and commitment to Higher Education and student experience therein in both the state and private sectors has convinced the author of the need for serious review of Higher Education in the state sector in Sri Lanka. Any comment made along those lines is solely the author's responsibility, and is in the hope that this may lead to discussion and debate and eventually to meaningful change.

2. Higher Education in Sri Lanka

Education systems differ widely. There is also no doubt that even a term such as „Higher Education" (or „Tertiary Education" often used as equivalent) is interpreted in different ways in different contexts. In theory, Higher/Tertiary Education could be taken as covering all education and training leading to some qualification beyond the Upper Secondary level, but in practice other distinctions tend to be made.

This was, for instance, what prompted UNESCO to attempt ISCED (International Standard Classification of Education) to facilitate some level of international comparison in the compilation and interpretation of data. ISCED clearly distinguishes between pre-primary, primary, secondary and tertiary as part of mainstream education, although it accepts the possibility of some instances of post-secondary which could be non-tertiary. (It is accepted that non-formal, special, adult etc. fall outside what is considered mainstream education.)

In Sri Lanka three terms are commonly in use identifying three sectors in the field of education and training:

1. General Education (conducted in schools)
2. Higher Education (in institutions offering programmes of study leading to higher diplomas and degrees) and
3. Technical Education and Vocational Training (in other post-secondary institutions).

General Education and Higher Education come within the purview of the national Ministry of Education and Higher Education, though much responsibility in the General Education area is devolved to the Provincial Governments which came into existence about a decade back. The apex body responsible for the formulation of policy in the two sectors is the National Education Commission (NEC).

The assignment of responsibility for Technical Education and Vocational Training is more dispersed than in the two sectors above, due partly to the way it developed historically and also to the desire of various government ministries to hold on to institutions that grew up within their domains. (See Appendix B for further details.) The Tertiary and Vocational Education Commission (TVEC) functions as the apex policy-setting body for the Technical Education and Vocational Training (TEVT) sector. The role of the TEVT sector is being recognised even more than in the past and its status is in the process of being strengthened.

The White Paper on Education presented to Parliament in 1981 distinguished three segments of education in a different manner: 1. General Education; 2. University Education; and 3. Tertiary (Vocational, Technical and Professional) Education. One notes that in '2' the state sector was implied. The Appendix shows how the lack of clarity in these matters (combined with implications of the Universities Act of 1978 which limited the use of the term 'university' to the State Universities) has led in reality to an anomalous situation where the TVEC of the TEVT sector appears to be dealing in isolation with matters of policy regarding university level teaching in the private sector.

Such lack of clarity is evident in many other areas. Simply because some aspects of teacher training are handled in practice within institutions looking after 'general education', the former is thus included within the latter.

It was not possible to find some classification scheme for the broad post-secondary area which showed how the different players in the field fitted together. The author has therefore attempted a grid / graphical representation which might be a starting point for discussion on such a classification. This is provided as Figure B-1 in Appendix B.

Problems exist with regard to access to data, too, even though Sri Lanka is generally recognised as a country that maintains and publishes reasonably reliable data and statistics. One notes that the widely available publications, such as those from the Central Bank of Sri Lanka and the Department of Census and Statistics of the Ministry of Finance and Planning, provide extensive data for the general education sector and the state university sector. On the latter, good statistics were made available in the past by the University Grants Commission, even though information available now appears to be a little more restricted. As for the Technical and Vocational sectors, some information is available in the earlier mentioned sources about just one institution, the Department of Technical Education and Training that has within its purview the Technical Colleges. Thus information on the broader 'Tertiary Education' sector is very limited.

One underlying cause of a number of such problems (including administrative ones, such as the multiplicity of Government Ministries dealing with this area and the absence of coordinated action) is the lack of a clearly accepted definition of "Higher Education". It is used broadly as including all of post-secondary education or as consisting of three segments: University Education, Teacher Education, and Advanced Technical Education. At other times it is interpreted as being limited to the universities, or even in a further restricted manner as limited to the State Universities.

This report adopts this last interpretation partly for reasons of practicality and the availability of data. Even though it is a very limited proportion (less than 3% as seen in Appendix A) of Sri Lankan youth who have the opportunity of studying for a degree locally, over 85% (of the said 3%) have access only to this „State University System". It is thus assumed that information provided here will be relevant and will also permit one to draw conclusions applicable mutatis mutandis also to "Higher Education" in the broader sense.

2.1 The domain for this report

The „State University System" consists (at the moment) of 13 units: 12 universities and the Open University of Sri Lanka. Figure 1 gives an idea of the geographical location of the universities. As will be explained below, the study is to limit itself to the 12 national universities.

2.2 What precedes higher education – general education

Appendix A describes the Sri Lankan educational system in more detail. With a minimum age of entry to the school system set at 5 years, Sri Lanka currently has a 5+3+3+2 pattern at school level. Grades 1-5 constitute the „Primary", grades 6-8 the „Junior Secondary" and grades 9-11 the „Senior Secondary". The centralised and nationally conducted General Certificate of Education (Ordinary Level) – GCE (O/L) for short – examination is taken at the end of grade 11 (thus typically around age 16). A little over 30% qualify to move on to the next level. Grades 12-13 are the „Collegiate" and end with the national examination General Certificate of Education (Advanced Level) generally referred to as the GCE (A/L). The „Collegiate" is, in the minds of the students and their parents, a period of study for university entrance. The target of all (except for about 2-3% who could hope for or afford an opportunity to go abroad for higher studies) is to obtain a place in the university system.

About 60% of those who sit the GCE (A/L) reach the level required by the local state universities, but it is only about 16% of those that the universities do, in fact, admit to the degree programmes. Appendix A shows that finally only about 2.75% of those who begin primary education (and so are taken to

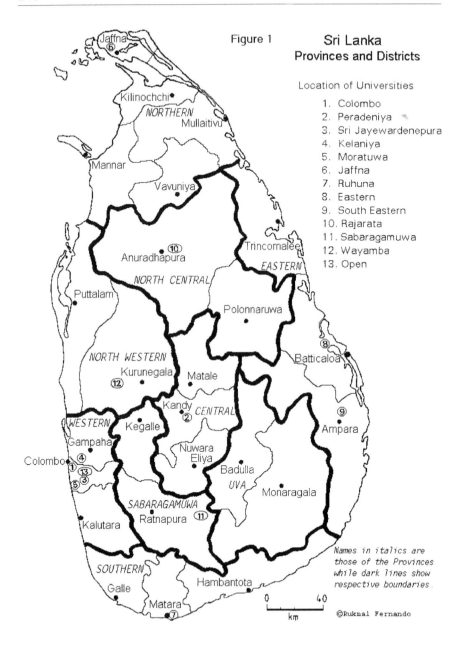

Figure 1   **Sri Lanka**
                  Provinces and Districts

Location of Universities

1. Colombo
2. Peradeniya
3. Sri Jayewardenepura
4. Kelaniya
5. Moratuwa
6. Jaffna
7. Ruhuna
8. Eastern
9. South Eastern
10. Rajarata
11. Sabaragamuwa
12. Wayamba
13. Open

Names in italics are
those of the Provinces
while dark lines show
respective boundaries.

©Rukmal Fernando

be within the same age group) enter the Sri Lankan university system in the end. The same appendix examines the context of what finally is a „written examination based" (biased towards cognitive skills of the type linked to the memorisation of facts) filtering system as well as the consequences of such a process. The broader process of selection for university, too, is dealt with in that appendix. Reference is also made there to Educational Reforms being implemented and the hope that things may change somewhat in the future.

2.3 The broader post-secondary sector

Appendix B takes this subject up in some detail and Figure B-1 was designed to give a summary view of the situation. It is clear that in addition to the "State Universities" many stakeholders are involved. There are the various educational and training institutes that have grown up within the state sector that have been recognised for degree-awarding purposes. Private sector institutions do not have the same privilege, but have an option of offering degrees from abroad in franchised or external modes. The same appendix hints that with private sector involvement growing in this manner (and the products of some of those institutions being in demand in business and industry), some official recognition (e.g. as "degree-awarding" or as "Affiliated University Institutes") will only be a matter of time.

The provision of facilities for external degrees is not new. Gratiaen (1933) refers to how the Colombo Academy (a leading secondary school of the time) offered the possibility of qualifications from the University of Calcutta in 1859, years before the Ceylon Medical College was set up in 1870. Wijetunga (1983) refers to how such qualifications from the University of London became available. De Silva & Peiris (1995) refer to two institutions outside state control, Aquinas College in Colombo and Jaffna College in Jaffna that prepared students for external examinations of the University of London in the 1960s. Professional bodies (Sri Lankan, or local chapters of foreign ones) offer professional qualifications, some of which are considered equivalent to degrees.

The State is heavily involved in (and bears the burden of) the TEVT (Technical Education and Vocational Training) sector, the importance of which has been recognised in the context of the problem of unemployment and underemployment, and the need for qualified employees, given the developments in the labour market and some growth in industrial development and foreign investment. Apart from the contribution of many religious and non-governmental groups, private sector involvement has so far mainly been either in in-house training of one's employees by business and industry or in the more lucrative areas such as computer-related training.

What Appendix B indicates as the growth of initiatives in both state and private sectors including the voluntary in the broad post-secondary / tertiary sector (beyond the traditional "degree / degree-equivalent" level is, however, a positive fact worthy of note.

3. Universities in Sri Lanka

For reasons explained earlier, from this point onwards the term University is to refer to whatever is part of the "State University System" functioning within the framework of the Ministry of Higher Education and the University Grants Commission (UGC).

The UGC describes itself as the apex body in the university system that allocates funds to the universities and institutes involved, serves as the central admission agency for undergraduate degree courses, reviews the working of the university system with a view to maintaining standards, and implements national policies in respect of higher university education.

3.1 The institutions within the state university sector

Table 1: The Sri Lankan universities (within the state system)

Name (Abbreviation)	Started	Number of Faculties	Students currently enrolled	Affiliated Institutes
University of Colombo (CBO)	1942*	7	6203	5
University of Peradeniya (PDN)	1942*	7	7461	2
University of Sri Jayewardenepura (SJP)	1959	5	7212	1
University of Kelaniya (KLN)	1959	6	6146	4
University of Moratuwa (MRT)	1972	2	1803	
University of Jaffna (JAF)	1974	6	2525	
University of Ruhuna (RUH)	1984	5	3705	
Eastern Univ. of Sri Lanka (EUSL)	1986	4	1004	
South Eastern Univ. of Sri Lanka (SEUSL)	1995	3	572	
Rajarata Univ. of Sri Lanka (RUSL)	1995	4	934	
Sabaragamuwa Univ. of Sri Lanka (SUSL)	1995	4	1029	
Wayamba Univ. of Sri Lanka (WUSL)	1999	2	200	
Open Univ. of Sri Lanka (OUSL)	1980	3	5072°	

Source: Data published by the UGC.

Comments:
* The two universities are intimately connected with the University of Ceylon founded in Colombo in 1942 the shifting of which to Peradeniya commenced in 1952.
** Students currently enrolled.
° While some information is provided about the Open University, one notes that it is not considered in the report. In addition to the undergraduates referred to in the table, it has 9000 odd students in Certificate and Diploma programmes and close to 2400 in postgraduate programmes.

As the criteria for admission and the mode of study (with some level of distance education involved) etc. are different, and as most students can be expected to be studying while in some employment, the Open University, though mentioned above, will not be considered in the analysis. Some universities award "External Degrees" where private tuition is offered by external parties. This is done mainly by individuals (including academic staff of universities) and organisations outside the state sector. Currently about 104,000 are reported to be enrolled on "external" programmes at five universities. The total output of graduates is around 2300 per year (UGC, 2000). This sector, too, is not considered in the report, given that here, too, a good portion of the students can be expected to be in employment.

The 12 universities have 6 institutes affiliated to them at the undergraduate level and 6 others at the postgraduate level. The postgraduate institutes are not considered here. Among the institutes at the undergraduate level, the Institute of Workers' Education opened in 1975 merits special mention, particularly because of the concern with adult/continuing education that its creation manifested (See Wijetunga, 2000). While two institutes dealing with indigenous / ayurveda medicine set up in 1977 and 1995 reflect relevant concerns, the Institute of Computer Technology set up in 1986 was a response within the university system to today's needs (to be seen together with other initiatives outside the university sector as shown in Appendix B). The recruitment processes are different from those applied to the standard universities, and while qualifications are available at different levels, the output of graduates as such from all such institutes is marginal. In the report, graduates will mean those from the 12 universities (of the 13) whose undergraduate level enrolments are included in Table 1.

3.2 The evolution of the universities

Table 2 shows the evolution of the universities during the period 1986 to 1998. The Wayamba University, started in 1999, raised the current total number of Universities to 12 (leaving out the 'Open University' not considered here). As Sri Lankan universities went through a crisis period with the second southern youth rebellion around 1987-89 when the universities were closed much of the time, double batches and intensive programmes with some shortening of the academic years etc have been used as mechanisms to clear the backlog. In addition, academic years are not yet standard among universities since the disruption of that time. One must therefore be careful not to read too much into the figures but to understand and appreciate the trend. While some have questions about the maintenance of standards, quality and other implications, what needs to be noted as very clear is that there has been an expansion of the system.

Table 2: The evolution of the universities 1986-1998

	1986	1990	1994	1998
Number of Universities	8	8	8	11
Number of Undergraduates	18217	29471	30764	38594
Number of Teachers	1808	2040	2525	3719
New Admissions	5630	6463	8015	11658
Number Graduated	4179	4476	5750	6738
Arts *	1764	1759	1977	2513
Commerce / Management	718	772	1022	1219
Law	61	88	183	182
Science	759	814	1187	882
Engineering	286	454	652	496
Medicine	338	314	399	1023
Dentistry	63	27	41	56
Agriculture	142	175	190	201
Veterinary Science	20	34	31	36
Architecture **	28	39	68	130
Expenditure (total) Rupees Millions	1058	1379	2597	3227
Capital Expenditure	663	423	548	1100
Recurrent Expenditure	395	956	2049	4327

Source: Data published by the UGC.

(*)   Arts includes Oriental Studies, Humanities, Social Sciences etc.
(**)   Quantity Surveying has been counted within Architecture.

While Table 2 also provides an idea of the broad areas within which graduates have been produced, Table 3 shows what is foreseen for the immediate future. The consequences of a 'rationalisation of resources' exercise carried out in the early Seventies are still apparent, as not every field of study is available at each university. Table 3 should thus also provide an idea of the broader subject areas each university is currently involved in.

Table 3: Distribution of the university intake proposed for academic year 2000/01

University / Subject Area	CBO	PDN	SJP	KLN	MRT	JAF	RUH	EUSL	SEUSL	RUSL	SUSL	WUSL	Special Intake	Total
Medicine	190	175	150	160		100	125							900
Dentistry		75												75
Veterinary Science		75												75
Agriculture		200				50	150	50		50	75	125		700
Food & Nutrition												125		125
Bio Science	125	150	80	120		100	130	75	30					810
Engineering		320			500		100							920
Physical Science	190	280	100	220		200	210	75	30					1305
Computer Science	50													50
Surveying Science											75			75
Management	125		615	250		220		50	50	100	150	80		1640
Commerce	165		180	150		150	200	50	55					950
Law	200													200
Arts	550	600	500	550		350	350	150	150	110	175		650	4135
Architecture & QS					125									125
Applied Science						50				75	90	100		315
Total	1595	1875	1625	1450	625	1220	1265	450	315	335	565	430	650	12400

Source: UGC.

Notes: - *Arts includes Oriental Studies, Humanities, Social Sciences etc. The 'Special Intake' is distributed amongst universities depending on the availability of places in some subject areas.*

- *'QS' stands for quantity surveying.*

- *It has been proposed that the annual intake be 20000 students by the year 2005. The proposed number 12400 above 11658 reported in Table 2 can be taken as indicative of the trend.*

In addition to growth in numbers and subject areas covered, the Sri Lankan Universities have gone through various phases of growth and shifts in modalities of control since formal inception in 1942. The year 1956 marked an important change in the national political climate with a more populist-nationalist swing. Pressure to expand the university system and to open it up to larger numbers was mounting, but the traditional university set-up was not that sensitive to such issues. The government thus raised two centres of Buddhist learning (Vidyodaya Pirivena and Vidyalankara Pirivena) to university status in 1959, and that was the start of what currently are the Universities of Sri Jayewardenepura and Kelaniya. While such broadening of opportunity was most laudable, seeds of potential problems were also sewn during this period. One was the abandoning of English as a language of instruction in most areas of study and its loss of importance within higher education with the switch-over to the vernacular. The other was the excessive intake (four-fold increase between 1960 and 1965) of students into the Arts stream.

Given the political context, government control continued to increase particularly through the Higher Education Act of 1966. Following the first southern insurrection of youth in 1971, in which university students had played a key role with other young people particularly from the under-privileged rural areas, more centralisation resulted. All universities became campuses of one university, resulting finally in over-centralization of decision-making etc., which led to considerable dissatisfaction within the university community. However, some reforms were effected. Jaffna and Moratuwa were established as within the university system during this period. Centralised admission procedures led to a limitation to the intake of arts students, and a conscious attempt at increasing the intake into science-based courses.

Though contested, for example by Gamage (1996), the Universities Act of 1978 has been interpreted as an attempt at the partial restoration of autonomy that the universities had lost over the years. Thus each campus (of the then one central university) was granted independent status within the framework of overall coordination and resource allocation assigned to a new agency, the University Grants Commission.

A new Universities Act is in draft form. It is said to favour an increase in university autonomy. The question of importance needs to be "Autonomy for what?". That the Sri Lankan universities suffer from a deep malaise is an accepted fact for many serious-thinking people outside the system, and for a minority within the system. Whether a new Parliamentary Act would change the situation substantially is doubtful. As seen at the end of Appendix A, change and revolutions have occurred in the past and, albeit very small, there is some hope that the universities may change or be forced to fight for survival in a threatening environment with growing private sector involvement in Higher Education and a tendency of the private sector to prefer graduates coming out of such programmes.

3.3 Funding for the universities

University education is government-directed and government-funded. Table 2 provides some information on the quantum of state funding. This works out basically to about 0.4% of the GDP on the university system since about 1980, which is about 14-15% of the total set apart for education as a whole. One notes, however, that student numbers have grown by close to 400% since 1980.

The strain on resources is thus understandable. But leaving material resources aside, recruitment, assessment and control systems as well as salary are typical of the state sector, and the recruitment and retaining of experienced and capable staff is a serious problem. If this is a serious problem in the more established universities, what it is in the new universities established partly for political purposes can be easily imagined.

At the undergraduate level university education is tuition-free, while registration charges are purely nominal. In addition, about 95% of the under-graduate students receive a small allowance for subsistence purposes. Between 40-50% receive hostel accommodation at nominal rates.

Registration and examination fees, which still are relatively very low, are charged in the external degree programmes. Postgraduate programmes are different and are fee-levying. These serve as a marginal source of income for the universities. But apart from that and other marginal receipts, for over 94% of their requirements the universities depend on the State for funds.

4. Unemployment in Sri Lanka

Table 4 provides a summary view of the labour market situation in Sri Lanka. The Labour Force component of the population is the economically active population (i.e. employed + unemployed during the reference period) aged 10 years and over. From another point of view, unemployment would be the excess of labour supply over demand.

Table 4: A summary view of the Sri Lankan labour market (using data for 1998)

Population (x 1000)	Population Rate in Percent	Labour Force Participation Rate in Percent			Unemployment Rate in Percent		
Year Mid-year	Growth	Male	Female	Total	Male	Female	Total
1998 18,774	1.2	67.4	36.2	51.5	6.6	14.7	9.5

Sources: Department of Census and Statistics & The Central Bank of Sri Lanka.

The Labour Force Participation rate may change somewhat in the future as a result of the change in the age structure. The 60+ age group is projected to increase from 8% in 1991 to 18% by the year 2021, whereas the age group below 15 years is expected to fall from 31% to 19%, eventually making the index for the ageing of the population jump from 26 in 1991 to an estimated 95 by 2021 (Central Bank, 2000).

4.1 The pattern of unemployment

The unemployment issue has been a matter of serious concern in Sri Lanka. The rate given in Table 4 of 9.5% (of the labour force) may not appear too serious in itself. In addition, from close to 19% in 1971 through (as shown in Table 5) 15.9 in 1990 it is down to 8.9 in 1999, clearly indicating a fall in the rate of unemployment. During 1990-1999, the male rate is reported to have dropped from 11.8 to 6.7 while the rate for females has manifested a faster decline from 23.4 to 13.0 percent.

Table 5: Unemployment rate 1990-1999

Unemployment rate – percentage of labour force									
1990	1991	1992	1993	1994	1995	1996	1997	1998	1999
15.9	14.7	14.6	13.8	13.1	12.3	11.3	10.5	9.5	8.9

Sources: Quarterly Labour Force Surveys (QLFS) of the Department of Census and Statistics & Reports of the Central Bank of Sri Lanka.

In national statistics, there are occasional changes of definition which lead to a problem of non-comparability in historical data. For the unemployment rate of 8.9% for 1999, the Central Bank (2000) provides the figure of 9.9% to compensate for a change of definition which also affects previous data. A figure of 9.1 would be reached if a longer reference period were used in the survey. But whatever series of figures is used, a clear downward trend is noticeable.

As for factors that contributed to this trend, the Central Bank cites economic growth, some expansion in self-employment and in small-scale business enterprises, as well as the growth of the private sector. For a number of years there had been a decline in the share of the public sector in total employment due to on-going privatisation, restructuring of semi-government institutions, and the expansion of the private sector. The Central Bank, however, admits a reversal of this trend in 1999 with a 3% increase in public sector employment in 1999 over that of 1998. In fact the increase had been 4% in the government institutions with a drop of 1% in semi-government ones.

The World Bank (1999) commends the decline in the rate of unemployment as impressive given Sri Lanka's rapid increase in labour force participation in the 1980s, linked much with the influx of women into the labour market. As for other factors which contributed to the decline, it cites the annual outflow of labour migration which has increased tenfold over the last decade, as well as war-related recruitment mostly from the rural areas.

The World Bank (2000), however, takes a critical look at the public sector which has 12% of the labour force (17% if with the semi-government sector) and judges it as large, costly and suffering from low effectiveness and efficiency. The country is reported to have "the largest bureaucracy per capita in Asia".

Two points relevant to our study are included in the same study. Firstly, it is noted that in the public sector, workers with the lowest levels of education are reported as earning on average double that of their equivalent in the non-public sector. Top policy makers and professionals (among whom we could expect graduates to end up after some years of work and experience) are reported as insufficiently compensated with Sri Lanka having "the lowest salary compression ratio in South Asia". This is then linked to the inability to attract and retain skilled expertise/talent in the public sector. Secondly, a matter linked to education policies and long-term planning is also referred to. It is reported that political interference in the administrative structures is linked to the fact that "public policies have taken a short-term and politically motivated bias, particularly damaging in an environment of frequent electoral cycles". As will be seen later, the public sector has traditionally been the main provider of employment for graduates, and eventual changes will continue to have some bearing on graduate employment.

Even though the overall drop in unemployment rates has been positive, a disturbing feature for decades has been and still is the high concentration of unemployment among the younger age groups. Table 6 shows it to be extremely high for the 15-19 and the 20-24 age groups. The sex differential stands out, too, with the rate for females being higher.

Table 6: Unemployment rate by age group and sex

	All Ages	15-19	20-24	25-29	30-34	35-39	40-44	45 & over
Total	8.5	29.5	23.3	10.9	5.2	3.2	1.6	1.5
Male	6.3	26.5	16.8	7.0	2.0	1.9	1.1	1.7
Female	13.0	34.6	36.8	17.9	11.6	5.2	2.5	0.9
* Total	18.7	40.4	35.3	20.1	11.1	7.4	5.9	

Source: QLFS 1999 2nd Quarter of the Department of Census and Statistics.
*Row marked * is from the Census of Population 1971.*

Table 6 (top section) is based on the Quarterly Labour Force Survey (QLFS) of the 2nd quarter of 1999, for which unemployment rates are available by age and sex. Other data, some even more recent, are available according to other classifications. Table 6 is proposed as sufficiently indicative. The bottom row gives parallel information from the population census of 1971. The concentration of unemployment among young people, as well as the fact that it has been a problem for decades are clear.

When the breakdown by level of education is examined (in Table 7 with 3 sets of slightly differing data), what is referred to in Appendix A as the "filtering-out" process at GCE O/L and GCE A/L (resulting in high percentages around O/L) is apparent.

Table 7: Percentage distribution of the unemployed by level of education

Level	QLFS 1999 (average of 4 quarters)				QLFS mid-98 to mid-99	Demographic Survey '94
	M & F	Male	Female		M & F	M & F
Total	100.0	100.0	100.0		100.0	100.0
No Schooling	0.2	0.2	0.1	No Schooling	0.4	1.6
Grades 1-5	4.2	4.6	3.9			
Grades 6-10	41.9	48.2	35.6	Grades 1-10	47.3	53.8
GCE O/L	29.1	29.1	29.1	GCE O/L	27.8	23.6
GCE A/L & above	24.6	17.9	31.3	GCE A/L	22.5	20.5
				Degree & above	2.0	0.5

Source: Department of Census and Statistics.

Table 7 uses percentage distributions and shows the numerical concentrations of those unemployed among persons with some education as opposed to those without. The raw rates are even more indicative. Over the decades, the rates rise from the category "No Schooling" upwards. While the national rate of unemployment was 8.9% in 1999, the rate for "GCE A/L and above" was 17.4% and that for "GCE O/L" was 12.9% with other rates below the national rate. Leaving the "quality / level" of employment aside, we can thus agree with what is typically assumed in Sri Lanka that the risk of being unemployed rises with education. (Deeper analysis might prompt us to hypothesise that it is perhaps a case of the risk being higher with what education currently is!) Wilson (1976) shows that the risk is comparatively higher in the rural sector.

The graduates are a small component of the population, and so is the number of unemployed graduates when taken relative to all who are unemployed. The fact, however, that they and the community have made high-level investment in education, as well as the implied potential in them as a precious resource, also definitely makes their case too important and critical.

4.2 Unemployment among graduates

Unfortunately, there are no statistics about the unemployed graduates. During the last few years, and particularly when important elections were close, we have had protest campaigns launched by various associations representing them to draw public attention.

10,250 graduates were recruited into the government sector in 1999 under a special programme. A little over 9000 of those are said to be in service still. In a similar programme 8000 were recruited earlier in 1994. Both were linked to national elections and it cannot be denied that these fall into the "short-term and politically motivated" category (see section 4.1, and World Bank, 2000) indicative of ad hoc solutions.

A national newspaper on 5th August 2000 carried a news item that the Central Province Unemployed Graduates' Association had recently launched a protest campaign to exert pressure on the State. The leadership of the association had said that the authorities provided employment as a response to earlier campaigns but that a large number had not been confirmed in their posts and that many others were still awaiting employment. A similar campaign took place recently in the Eastern Province. Some action on these demands appears to have been taken by the State and, in addition, a few hundred are being recruited with Parliamentary Elections set for October 2000.

All this certainly confirms the fact that there are graduates still without jobs, as well as that there is some expectation that jobs will also be offered to them by the State in response to the protests, particularly if these take place at the "appropriate" time.

The sad fact is that no one knows what the situation exactly is. Some estimate the number of unemployed graduates to be 15,000 while others put it around 10,000-12,000. Some state officials estimate it at 6,000. Indraratna (1974,1992) refers to how even in the early 1970s there were different estimates at variance with one another (e.g. 6000-7000, 10000, 12000-14000). Much depends on "what is declared" at surveys, as it is possible that young graduates who are self-employed (e.g. conduct tuition classes. See Section 5 of Appendix A) may say they are unemployed, and a female graduate who has had a child and is busy with family matters may not declare herself as available for work.

An important study with regard to the unemployment problem in Sri Lanka was carried out for the International Labour Organization (1971) by Dudley Seers. This offered the explanation of the "skills mismatch" between supply and demand which has continued to influence action even today. As for the specific problem of graduate unemployment the only study worthy of mention which also included a survey and its analysis was Sanyal et al. (1983) (with the involvement of the IIEP of UNESCO and of Marga Institute, Colombo). Though circumstances have changed much since then, its chapter on "The Graduate Employment Situation" (Philipupillai & Wilson 1983) has contributed to the current study through the provision of valuable insights. Ekanayake et al. (1989) is a very limited study and Gunawardane (1999) provides some ideas. Some discussion took place at a dialogue organised in September 1998 by the Sri Lanka Foundation Institute. It is, however, regrettable that nothing of the type Sanyal et al. (1983) has been done since, and that remains a challenge for the future.

The "skills mismatch" hypothesis already referred to, as well as the "queuing for public sector jobs" hypothesis are among those put in question by the World Bank (1999). Whether or not what the new study proposes as explanatory by way of "strong job preferences" (which when combined with factors such as availability of income support from the family is shown to encourage extended periods of job search) and "labour market segmentation" is totally independent of factors alluded to by the earlier hypotheses and is a matter to be further analysed.

The Ceylon Chamber of Commerce carried out a survey in 1999 and listed a set of attributes expected by today's business and industry of a graduate at entry level. The list tallies well with such lists in other countries. In addition to essential computing, numeracy and communication (not merely in the vernacular but in English, too) skills, general knowledge (world affairs and wide interests) is included. A critical thinking ability combined with an open / positive / practical mindset; the willingness to learn from a wide cross-section of people; good interpersonal skills; the ability to work with different people and in different teams; the ability to lead a team and achieve results within a given timeframe were stated as required. Other attributes in the list were the ability to prioritize and organize time productively; the ability to adapt to changing work situations; the ability to use initiative; and the ability to take risks.

In general it is apparent that subject/technical skills are referred to when the "skills mismatch" is discussed within typical university circles, but as in many other places around the world what is interesting to note is that in the case of graduates the world of work tends to see a mismatch in the softer/ transferable skills.

It is important to note that due to occasional disruptions (and particularly the 2nd southern youth revolt. See Section 2.2) the academic calendars of the universities were seriously affected. The accumulated backlog of batches of students has not been totally cleared. In addition, the post-A/L selection processes normally imply a two-year wait for university entrance. As a result the minimum age at which a graduate can expect to complete his or her studies is around 25 years, while it can become more in the case of those who have, for instance, attempted A/L more than once to succeed in gaining entrance to University. This puts a graduate at a disadvantage with employers preferring A/L qualified persons for reasons of age and other factors such as flexibility. One can imagine what impact this age at qualification, if combined with, say, 2 years of job search, could have on the personality of the graduate, leading possibly to conditions such as a "discouraged-worker effect" and reducing the chances of meaningful employment. Among current university reforms, the reduction of the time for the selection process, and clearing the backlog of batches are ones being pushed energetically, so that the typical student entering the system about 2 years from now may have a chance in the future of graduating around the age of 23-24.

It is noted that the context of graduate employment/unemployment needs to be properly understood for solutions sought as facilitating the transition between Higher Education and the Labour Market to be effective. While seeking such understanding, one must and does move forward even on the basis of limited perceptions and partial explanations.

5. The Transition Between Higher Education and the Labour Market

In Section 4 we have seen some of the key elements with regard to the general problem of unemployment in Sri Lanka, and moved on to some consideration of how it affects the graduates.

The reverse side of the coin is the subject of graduate employment, and consideration of where the employed graduates are and what they do. It is well known that up to about 1965 there was more or less an automatic provision for any graduate to be taken into the teaching profession within the State school system, and that female graduates had a strong preference for this career path. Within the public sector there were also opportunities in the Sri Lanka Administrative Service and in the semi-governmental sector (i.e. Corporations, Boards, National Banks etc.). Sanyal et al. (1983) have some information about the situation in the 1960s and the 1970s. They show that for doctors, engineers and scientists the demand continued to be there within the country and also abroad (with in the Seventies managers, accountants and other professionals, too, beginning to be part of the outflow). At that time there was no serious mismatch between supply and demand either in the case of categories such as dentists, veterinary surgeons, agriculturalists and architects. But from the early 1970s danger signals were already there, beginning with regard to graduates from the Arts stream.

Things have changed much since then. The Socio-Economic Survey 1996/97 (Central Bank 1999a) shows that with 90.7 of the graduates being employed, 73.2% were in regular employment, 8.5% self-employed, 2.4% were employers, and about 6% were in the contract/casual categories. As for the expected occupation, the main preference of the unemployed graduates was for "professional, technical & related" jobs (82.7%), while 13% indicated "clerical and related". Other than for such summary information or what is available resulting from an occasional gathering of data on a cohort from a specific academic department, no systematic study has yet been done on the destination of graduates, what they do etc. This is therefore a task for the future.

Though not directly connected with "transition" as such, one cannot ignore the element of manpower/education planning. For about a decade from the mid 1980s the University Grants Commission had a tradition of a rolling five-year Corporate Plan which has been ignored since then (though there is now some talk of reviving it). The available information was used to work out a projected demand for graduates in broad subject areas, and then to estimate the intake. Even if the estimates were not totally accurate, the exercise manifested some element of a demand-driven culture and was therefore fully worthwhile. One notes that recent studies have posed the question as to whether government agencies charged with the planning of the national economy and socioeconomic sectors, and the collection and management of labour market data have been fully up to the task and are not working in isolation.

Getting back to the issue of "transition" we note that it is facilitated through a number of initiatives both within and outside the universities. We deal with that next.

5.1 Facilities subsequent to graduation

Facilitating job search and job placement: A certain amount of this has been done for many years from within the university at a personal level by academic staff and at a somewhat formal level by academic departments on the basis of contact with the world of work outside. It is sometimes the organisation that contacts the university / department and asks for graduates of a certain type or from within a subject stream.

Providing further training: In the 1980s there existed a unit called the Graduate Placement Service. This contributed to placing graduates in employment, provided employment counselling and conducted training programmes aimed at improving their employability. On the basis of his experience there, Kumaradasa (1995), who was in charge of the programme, has presented a cause and effect diagram for the unemployment problem of graduates (Figure 2). In an interesting initiative, the University of Colombo provides a one-year conversion programme on which graduates can enroll with a view to migrating into the IT sector, which currently offers employment prospects.

Figure 2: Cause and effect diagram for the unemployment problem of graduates

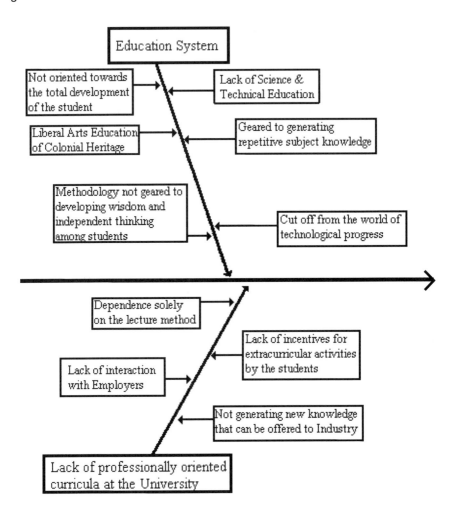

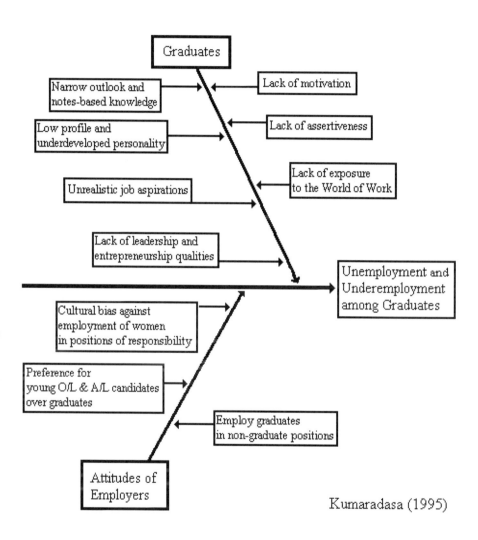

Kumaradasa (1995)

Source: Kumaradasa (1995).

Facilitating post-graduation work experience: An innovative programme "Tharuna Aruna", funded by the State and managed by the private sector was set up in 1997 at the request of the State by four leading Chambers of Commerce and Industry to help reduce the level of unemployment among educated young people, primarily the graduates. This offers a 16-month placement in the private sector during which period the State also pays the graduate a small monthly allowance. While some success has been achieved, with a little over 260 obtaining jobs in the institutions they were placed in and another percentage succeeding elsewhere, the dropout rate has been very high. It is noted that when the government offered jobs to over 10,000 graduates in 1999 (see Section 4.2), many who were in placement in the private sector left to join the public sector. In spite of that set-back (which needs analysis in itself) the development of the initiative is worth watching.

5.2 Facilities available during studies

Job-orientated courses: Around the late 1960s, the problem of the unemployment of graduates began to be felt especially with regard to graduates from the Arts / Humanities. The early 1970s saw an attempt to diversify with an emphasis on applied studies. Thus courses in or programmes of study leading to degrees in Public Finance and Taxation, Estate Management and Valuation, Education, Development Studies, Mass Communication, and Library Science were commenced. Most were eventually discontinued due to problems resulting from insufficient attention to the manpower requirements of the country, but some have survived until today. Degree programmes in still other subject areas have, however, been added recently, particularly in Management Studies.

Reform of curricula: This has been done in some programmes of study with a view to making the subjects more relevant to today as well as to offering a limited level of flexibility and multidisciplinarity through modular structures within overall system constraints. In some instances an element of student-centred learning has been brought in too.

Work Experience: Though standard in the more professionally orientated courses (Medicine, Engineering, Accountancy, etc.), this element is now being incorporated in small ways within a number of other study programmes, so that at least some short period of placement is being attempted.

Career Guidance: Even though this was clearly envisaged in the reform proposals of the early 1970s, it got off the ground as a new initiative about 2 years ago. While other universities are also initiating programmes, the Universities of Colombo and of Sri Jayewardenepura have taken the lead with pilot programmes. A start has been made with some level of job search services to students and recruitment services to employers. The University of Colombo, geographically located within the commercial capital of Colombo, has built on that strength, drawing on resources of the private sector. Thus executives from the private sector serve as mentors to some groups of students, conduct sessions on job search skills etc. Sri Jayewardenepura, while maintaining somewhat similar activities, is trying out a strategy that seeks to integrate career orientation and career guidance within the academic programmes, and within university culture itself. It seeks to concentrate on contributing to the employability of and capacity building among the undergraduates emphasising the soft / transferable skills. It is moving now into areas such as a) Critical and Creative Thinking; b) Problem Solving; c) Team Work; and d) Interpersonal Relationships. Its objective is to be a centre helping and guiding the undergraduates in their efforts to undertake career education, career exploration, career choice, career planning and career management. With an educational system/culture of the type already described (see Section 4.2 & Appendix A) whose products include graduates who at the end of 3-4 years of free education expect a job to be "provided", such approaches will need a system-wide concerted effort over time.

6. Conclusion

Basically, the whole issue of the transition from Higher Education to Employment, and the inter-linked subject of the relationship between Higher Education and the World of Work, hinges on the understanding of Higher Education and of its mission and objectives. As is seen in Appendix A, one regrets that university reforms as currently envisaged do not have a sufficiently clear focus, and are not supported by the university community. It is clear that one needs to move away from the traditional supply-driven pattern without sufficient concern for skills and outcomes, and away from the assumption that greater concentration on limited subject areas and the practice of "packing" knowledge into the brain is what will contribute to the quality and employability of the graduate. But if Higher Education were to be transformed to inspire / enable / prepare the undergraduates to a) develop to their highest potential through learning and lifelong learning; b) acquire and apply knowledge for the benefit of the economy and society in a manner that serves the needs of a fast-changing knowledge-based economy; and c) play a role in shaping a democratic and inclusive society, then Higher Education can be expected to become and remain a meaningful / dynamic / enriching process and "transition" will tend to be a very limited action as befits its definition. Even though questions exist as to whether reforms are fundamental enough and whether sufficient resources are being committed to the reform effort, Sri Lanka has at least been thinking of and dealing with such issues in some way, and has begun to think afresh. That is a positive sign.

In a fast changing world the implications need to be reviewed all the time. At an ILO-led debate at UNESCO in August 1998, Prof. Ulrich Teichler (well known for his involvement in this area) claimed that "many actors in Higher Education [...] when it comes to issues of higher education itself [...] believe that intelligent amateurism suffices". Thus, as elsewhere, Sri Lanka will need to move on, even reviewing all the activities mentioned as facilitating the "transition". The university and the teachers may need to be guided in order to be more explicit about the conception of their own role, and the theories of learning that might be implicit in such (And so the key role of staff training and development becomes evident.). Auto-critical evaluation, among other things, can contribute to a process of renewal. Sharing with others with a view to learning from one another, as is being done here, is certainly another precious component.

BIBLIOGRAPHY

Central Bank of Sri Lanka (1999a). Report on Consumer Finances and Socio Economic Survey – Sri Lanka 1996/97 Part I. Central Bank of Sri Lanka, Colombo.

Central Bank of Sri Lanka (1999b). Economic and Social Statistics of Sri Lanka 1999. Central Bank of Sri Lanka, Colombo.

Central Bank of Sri Lanka (2000). Annual Report 1999. Central Bank of Sri Lanka, Colombo.

de Silva, K.M. & Peiris, G.H., eds. (1995). The University System of Sri Lanka – Vision and Reality. International Centre for Ethnic Studies, Kandy.

Department of Census and Statistics (2000). Quarterly Report of the Sri Lanka Labour Force Survey – Second Quarter 1999. Department of Census and Statistics, Colombo.

Ekanayake, S.B., Munasinghe, P.K. & Pieris, A. (1989). Employment and Education Linkages in Sri Lanka. National Institute of Education, Maharagama.

Fernando, Charles (1971). Youth in Rebellion. Worldmission 22/4 pp. 39-46, New York.

Gamage, D.T. (1996). Evolution of Universities and Changing Patterns of Governance and Administration. Karunaratne and Sons Ltd., Colombo.

Gratiaen, L.J. (1933). Central School Commission III. Journal of the Royal Asiatic Society No. 86, Colombo.

Gunawardane, R.P. (1999). Graduate Unemployment: Is it Significant in Lanka in Daily News 5-7th May 1999.

ILO – International Labour Organisation (1971). Matching Employment Opportunities and Expectations – A Programme of Action for Ceylon. ILO, Geneva.

Indraratna, A.D.V. de S. (1974). Rationalization and Job-orientation in our University Education in Proceedings of the Twenty Ninth Annual Sessions of the Ceylon Association for the Advancement of Science. Colombo.

Indraratna, A.D.V. de S. (1992). Economics of Higher Education in Sri Lanka. Navrang, New Delhi.

Karunaratne, C. (2000) Women and Management in Higher Education – Local Experience in Daily News 8th March 2000, Colombo.

Kumaradasa, D.L. (1995). Graduate Employment: The Problem and Prospects in National Workshop on Higher Education Policy – Papers Presented. National Education Commission, Colombo.

Ministry of Education and Cultural Affairs (1969). Education in Ceylon, A Centenary Volume. Ministry of Education and Cultural Affairs, Colombo.

Philipupillai. A. & Wilson. P. (1983). The Graduate Employment Situation in Sanyal, B.C. et al. (1983) University Education and Graduate Employment in Sri Lanka. Marga Institute, Colombo.

Sanyal, B.C. et al. (1983). University Education and Graduate Employment in Sri Lanka. Marga Institute, Colombo.

Sumathipala, K.H.M. (1968). History of Education in Ceylon 1796-1965. Tisara Prakasakayo, Dehiwala.

Udagama, P. (1999). Rhetoric and Reality: Education in Sri Lanka after Independence. Amal Publishing Company, Colombo.

UGC (1998). Statistical Hand Book 1997 – Academic Year 1995/96. University Grants Commission, Colombo.

UGC (2000). Sri Lanka Universities Year Book 1999/2000. University Grants Commission, Colombo.

Wijemanne, E.L. (1976). Population Growth and Educational Development in ESCAP (1976) Population of Sri Lanka, ESCAP – United Nations, Bangkok.

Wijetunga, W.M.K. (1983). Development of University Education in Sri Lanka (1942-1980) in Sanyal, B.C. et al. (1983) University Education and Graduate Employment in Sri Lanka. Marga Institute, Colombo.

Wijetunga, W.M.K. (2000). The Relationship between Adult Education Movements and Existing Social, Political and Economic Systems : The University Workers' Movement in Sri Lanka in Cooke, A. & MacSween, A. (eds.) The Rise and Fall of Adult Education Institutions and Social Movements. Peter Lang, Frankfurt.

Wilson, P. (1976). Economic Activity of the Population in ESCAP (1976) Population of Sri Lanka, ESCAP – United Nations, Bangkok.

World Bank (1999). Sri Lanka – A Fresh Look at Unemployment. The World Bank, Washington D.C.

World Bank (2000). Sri Lanka – Recapturing Missed Opportunities. The World Bank, Washington D.C.

Appendix A – Background Note on Education in Sri Lanka

1. From the past ... to today

Sri Lanka (formerly Ceylon), the small pear-shaped island at the southern tip of India is roughly twice the size of Belgium. The current population is just a little over 19 million. In spite of a multitude of problems it faces, it is recognised as an outlier among developing nations having a tradition of investment in human resources and the promotion of gender equality. Sri Lanka is thus credited with having achieved human development outcomes more consistent with countries that are more developed. The issue today is how Sri Lanka can move on from there, without being forced downwards.

As for the topic considered in the main report, even if one does not go into a detailed analysis of the history of education in Sri Lanka, it is thought that a few glimpses would provide the context within which issues related to university education might be better understood.

Numerous studies exist. While Sumathipala (1968) looks at the History of Education in Ceylon during the period 1796 to 1965 from a "Buddhist-Nationalist" perspective, through contributions by a multitude of authors the Centenary Volume of the Ministry of Education and Cultural Affairs (1969) provides extensive coverage of the history of education in Sri Lanka since the establishment in 1868-69 by the British of the Department of Public Instruction, now named the Department of Education. Wijemanne (1976) places issues within a population perspective.

As in the case of a number of countries in the East and elsewhere, there was a long tradition of education nurtured by a monastic tradition, emanating in the case of Sri Lanka primarily from Buddhism, which has flourished in Sri Lanka since its establishment by the Buddhist missionaries sent by King Asoka of India in the 3rd century BC. True, the early Buddhist temple schools (pirivena) were primarily for the monks, but a few laymen from the better-off families who could afford the time benefited from the institution. For the masses the process of socialisation was more informal, with training for the vocational roles being provided within the family, in caste-based occupational groups, or in the form of apprenticeship under recognised master practitioners. But the temple played a key role in society.

Sri Lanka's colonial history spans about 450 years, beginning with the arrival of the Portuguese in 1505. They, the Dutch, and finally the British had roughly 150 years each here until independence in 1948. Small schools were started in the parishes. Reading, writing and religion were the concern. Some see here the beginning of the link between "certificate" and "employment", for the school certificate with an indication of competence to read and write in the Portuguese language had become a key to employment in the "formal / government" sector. The Dutch contributed strongly to the creation of a formal missionary school system where the study of the Dutch language as well as the vernacular (Sinhala / Tamil) and a little arithmetic, too, was recognised. The school, and linked with it the education and adherence to the religion of the rulers, became even more established as the means to seek favours from those in power.

Though education was neglected for a brief period by the British, the school system was quickly revived (with Anglican, Roman Catholic, Wesleyan, Presbyterian and other denominations managing them) as offering possibilities for forming and recruiting suitable people for the public service and, incidentally, also for winning people to Christianity. Similar denominational schools were opened by the Buddhists and Hindus much later. Moslem schools appeared on the scene even later. One needs to highlight the role of the Buddhist Theosophical Society, particularly with regard to the Buddhist schools. After the establishment of the Department of Public Instruction in 1868-69 such schools, too, were eligible to receive grant-in-aid from the State.

In the process a system consisting of two types of schools had come into existence. The English medium schools, fee-levying and accessible to the privileged few, were well resourced. The vernacular schools were non-fee-levying but had poorly qualified teachers and very poor facilities. It is understandable that gradually, and particularly after the introduction of universal franchise in 1931, voices began to be raised on a number of socially disruptive issues and a movement for democratisation of education surfaced. The year 1945 marked the beginning of this change with a policy of free education from kindergarten to university becoming accepted. Dr. C. W. W. Kannangara, who spearheaded the change, is recognised as the "Father of Free Education in Sri Lanka".

After Independence in 1948, the nationalist revival and its reaction against the colonial past gained momentum. Amongst a host of changes ushered in particularly after 1956, one notes within education the impact of the change of the official language from English to Sinhala, and in 1960-61 the nationalisation of all government-aided denominational schools, bringing them under the control of the State, and leaving out only just a few that opted then to be non-fee levying and private.

Since independence, though combined with some positive changes such as those in response to manpower needs of a developing economy (some development in areas such as science education, vocational training), with the increasing politicisation of all aspects of life, politicians in collusion with partisan pundits have also been responsible for ad hoc change to systems (in general education as well as in the tertiary area) every now and again without building up progressively towards clearly identified goals. Some useful insights into the situation are provided in Udagama (1999), while an analysis more focussed on the Universities is to be found in de Silva & Peiris (1995).

The negative aspects aside, as stated at the beginning, Sri Lanka can be proud of having achieved high ratings in human development outcomes in the past, so that even around Independence in 1948 in the matter of literacy rates (with figures for 1946 indicating 70.1 for males and 43.8 for females with an overall rate of 57.8) she was ahead of all South Asian countries and most East Asian countries as well. The 1997 figures are 94.3 for males, 89.4 for females with an overall of 91.8. With a life expectancy of 69.5 for males and 74.2 for females and other such Human Development Indicators, Sri Lanka stands far ahead of others in the region. All this is certainly proof of the tremendous potential in its people. Even though a war is raging due to the involvement of extremist elements unprepared for a process of give and take, though unfinished, much is already real among the people as such by way of unity in a context rich in ethnic, linguistic, religious, and cultural diversity.

And yet, paradoxically Sri Lanka remains caught up in a number of complex problems for which more and more honest-thinking people are beginning to point an accusing finger at politicians and the political system of the last 2-3 decades. Though crushed at great cost including much loss of life, the two southern uprisings by the young people (in 1971 and in 1987-89) were clearly indicative of the country's problems. The other rebellion, still raging in the north has led the country to an internal war, which no doubt contributes to aggravating current problems. These issues have been dealt with in a number of books and articles. The author of the current report analysed the 1971 rebellion in Fernando (1971).

Sri Lanka is stated to have reached a per capita income level of US$ 820 and is said to be becoming a middle-income country. But the Country Strategy Outline of the World Food Programme (1998) states that the real per capita income in dollar terms has declined from 294$ in 1981-85 through 233$ in 1986-90 to 188$ in 1991-96, and other reports indicate a widening of income disparities. The same report indicates that in 1995, 38% of Sri Lankan children in the age group 3-59 months were underweight (when the WHO considers 20% very high), that 24% of the children were stunted, that nearly one out of five children had low birth weight and that 33% of expectant mothers were anaemic. We need therefore to note that this, too, is Sri Lanka, and that this generation will be the input into the educational processes of tomorrow.

The latest report on Sri Lanka from the World Bank (2000) entitled "Sri Lanka: Recapturing Missed Opportunities" while accepting the growth in per capita income warns that social discontent is high among younger Sri Lankans, who feel excluded from the country's economic benefits and processes. Regional poverty disparities are reported to have widened between 1990 and 1996. The gradual deterioration in the public sector that started in the early 1970s, the erosion of institutional capacity and economic governance, the weakening of accountability, and Sri Lanka's low ranking in Asia in governance are all referred to. The politicization of recruitment by successive governments is shown as one cause, while the politicization even of poverty alleviation programmes is taken up. The report itself refers to discontent among young people, and these factors cannot be ignored, since they have a serious impact on education and employment.

While admitting that due consideration needs to be given to good governance within a country as a variable of importance, given, however, that the World Bank prescriptions are what have been applied during the past few decades, what is referred to in the two paragraphs above is an indication that there is some justification for what some do, in at least questioning the rationale for the uniform application of the magic formulas emanating from international organisations such as the IMF/World Bank and more recently the WTO, as well as the unreserved acceptance of the "credo" of the benefits of globalization.

2. The general education scene

Some relevant aspects of the current situation with regard to the general education sector is presented in the Table that follows, based on the 1997 figures.

Of what is referred to as Private Schools, about 50% are those that opted to be private in 1960-61 at the nationalisation of assisted schools. This category follows the national curriculum and adheres to other rules and regulations issued by the national Ministry of Education.

	Number	Pupils	Teachers
Total Schools	10,983	4,260,989	187,539
Government Schools	10,358	4,124,108	179,589
Other Schools	625	136,881	7,950
Pirivenas	550	50,991	4,298
Private Schools	75	85,890	3,652

Roughly the other 50% is of a new type ("International Schools") opened over the last 10 years or so under the open economy promoted since the late seventies. These provide facilities for students to sit for foreign (mainly British) examinations marking the end of secondary level. Questions have been raised about the quality of at least some of these, but the Ministry of Education does not seem to have any supervisory or regulatory power over them.

While noting that it is the schools with Grading 1A or 1B or 1C (i.e. about 24% of the schools) that prepare students for the tertiary level (in the universities, professional institutions and the higher technical schools), an idea is provided below of

how the Government schools (i.e. 94.3% of all Sri Lankan schools) are classified on
the basis of resources available. It is clear that science education at GCE (A/L) is
available in only 590 out of over ten thousand schools.

Grading	With resources for holding classes up to	Schools	Pupils
1A & 1B	Grade 13 / GCE (A/L) including Science	590	1,041,038
1C	Grade 13 / GCE (A/L) only Arts/Commerce	1,867	1,360,056
2	Grade 11 / GCE (O/L)	3,744	1,184,549
3	Grade 5	4,157	538,465
All grades		10,358	4,124,108

with GCE = General Certificate of Education; O/L = Ordinary Level; and A/L = Advanced Level

Pre-primary schooling of the nursery / "Montessori" type is quite popular even in the
rural areas (though not necessarily in the very remote areas). The State is not involved.
The quality of the programmes varies, and so do the prices charged.

At the moment the minimum age of entry to the school system is 5 years. Grades
1-5 constitute the "Primary", Grades 6-8 the Junior Secondary and Grades 9-11 Senior
Secondary. Collegiate is in Grades 12-13. And so we have 13 years of schooling as a
possibility with a 5+3+3+2 pattern.

Things have not been clear and consistent all the time, and in fact may not be so
even in the future. One notes that between 1964 and 1985 the school structure was
changed 5 times. At one point the minimum age of entry was raised to 6 years. All
this has created problems in nomenclature and, worse, the understanding of trends
and patterns. Many were forced to question the purpose and the result of such
exercises. As for the immediate future, yet one more change appears to be on the
cards envisaging the creation of Junior Schools (for grades 1-9) and Senior Secondary
(for grades 10-13) with the compulsory period of education (ages 5-14) looked after
by the Junior Schools.

Schooling is compulsory between the ages 5 to 14. No legal action is, however,
taken and the approach has been to encourage attendance. It can be said that the
rates of non-attendance and drop-outs have been on the decline. The "Annual School
Census" (by its very nature) has no information on non-attendance. While a study of
trends in the decennial "Population Census" suggests that currently about 70% of
those in the age-group 70 years and above might report "no schooling", the figure for
the age group 15-19 would be around 10-12% only. It can be assumed that those
within this last group who report "no schooling" would include a good portion of
those who did some years of schooling but dropped out.

The latest Socio-Economic Survey (1999) gives a figure of 8.8% for school avoidance. As about 65% of those counted within this are those who had not completed the age of 5 years at the beginning of the school year, the figure needs to be interpreted as around 3% in reality. Thus avoidance of schooling exists, but at a relatively low level. The reasons for such behaviour need, however, to be looked at. For about 35% it is the inability to provide the basic requirements, while disability or poor health account for about 25%. Home / family / other work is the reason in the case of about 9%, while the non availability of a convenient school is cited by 5%.

For an indication of some details concerning those who do attend, one notes that in 1997 of all students enrolled 76.4% were in the Sinhala medium while 23.6% were in the Tamil medium. 50.1% were female whereas 49.9% were male.

At the end of Grade 11 students face the first public national examination "GCE (O/L)" (Ordinary Level), and in order to move to the next grade a specified minimum levels of marks needs to be achieved. The curriculum at this level is fairly standard and permits only a few options. At this examination candidates typically offer 8 subjects. Failure rates at public examinations are relatively high and major differentials in performance are noticeable between urban and rural schools, with higher failure rates in the latter in subjects such as Science, Mathematics and English. And so in spite of the long tradition of education and attempts at the improvement of quality, problems remain and a large number of young people leave after 11 years of schooling without any nationally recognised qualification as such.

At the O/L examination of 1997, of 360,026 candidates (including first-time repeaters) from the schools plus 141,479 private candidates (who can be taken as mostly repeaters of the type second-time and beyond), just a little over 32% qualified to move on to the next step within the structure which is the "GCE (A/L)" (Advanced Level).

The GCE (AL) is prepared for in grades 12 and 13. It is considered pre-university, and the dream of all those getting to this stage is to enter the university and obtain a degree. Students choose one of three areas: Science, Arts and Commerce. Their choice is, however, restricted since minimum criteria need to be satisfied by way of scores in specified subjects at the GCE (O/L). It is essential to note that in the case of the typical Sri Lankan student, a crucial decision about one's future is made at this stage. The choice between the three streams is dependent mainly on the marks one obtained at GCE (O/L) and partly on the school one is in or can afford to attend (as less than 6% of the schools offer Science education at this level). However, this choice totally determines the broad area of study one can join if one were to get an opportunity of entry into a Sri Lankan State University and this it indirectly determines one's future.

At the end of Grade 13 the students face the second public national examination the GCE (A/L) (Advanced Level). In 1998, of a total of 114,628 school candidates (including first-time repeaters) plus 33,223 private candidates (who can be taken as mostly repeaters of the type second-time and beyond), about 8% failed in all 4 subjects they had to offer. Of the school candidates 52% reached minimum eligibility levels for university entry whereas the figure for private candidates was less than 41%.

3. Entry into the standard university system – hurdle one

We come now to a critical issue concerning University education in Sri Lanka. The tradition of free education makes the participation of children and young students excellent in Grades 1 to 11, and among those qualifying for such a level, extremely high in Grades 12 to 13. But paradoxically less than 3% have the opportunity to enter the University. For the purpose of illustration, and simplifying in many ways we take a hypothetical cohort:

Grade	Number	Status	Left out
One	400,000	enter school[1]	Marginal
Eleven	360,000	sit GCE (O/L)[2]	40,000
Twelve	116,000	enrol[3]	244,000
Thirteen	115,000	sit GCE (A/L)	1,000
Post Secondary	70,000	qualify for university entrance[4]	45,000
	25,000	apply to enter University	45,000
	11,000	taken in by the State Universities as standard students	14,000

[1] (current figures slightly lower due to change of age structure of population)
[2] (figure on right is due to non-attendance & dropouts)
[3] (though 118,000 may have qualified)
[4] (most from cohort but some repeaters too)

This makes it clear that about 2.75% of those who begin primary education (and so are taken to be within the relevant age group) finally enter the Sri Lankan university system and over 97% are left out. However, things would not be complex if the mark achieved were consistently the criterion for selection to University (leaving out of consideration whether it is a fair indicator of capability). Other factors intervene, and they are referred to in the next section.

But what happens to those who are filtered out? Even if one leaves the rest out of consideration, one is justified in thinking that the '116,000' who began grade 12 had the intention of attempting to enter the university. When about 9% of them actually enter the university, the fate of the rest is a matter worth examining. Even though specific studies have not been done, about 18-20% may be expected to have found some opportunity for post-secondary education (e.g. about 9% in state sector Advanced Technical Institutes, the Open University, etc.; 8% in Private Institutes that locally offer courses leading to foreign degrees and professional qualifications; and about 2% into post-secondary education abroad). While another 30-35% may have found some employment, anything between 45-50% can be expected to be waiting/floating (with most having to depend on the family for survival).

The social repercussions of this mad struggle for success in examinations, the rigid selection process and the final outcome are, to say the least, explosive. There is, however, one ray of hope. Even though "a degree" and the resultant "white collar job" was the dream of many in the past, the growth of the private sector and the employment opportunities in it is leading to a change of attitude. One is beginning to see for instance that a technical job in the private sector could bring in more money than a clerical job in the state sector without much loss in "status" for oneself or one's family. Within such a context one notes that even though the development of technical and vocational education has been discussed for decades and plans drawn up, various innovative projects started and abandoned, action is finally being taken to effectively develop the technical and vocational sector in order to open up opportunities and to prepare the skilled workforce at least for tomorrow.

4. Entry into the standard university system – hurdle two

Success in the GCE (A/L) examination by obtaining marks satisfying the minimum requirements for entry into the university system is only a first step. (The shift in the number satisfying such minimum requirements from 1997/98 onwards leaves room for a question as to the cause of such change.) Actual selection to university is based on additional criteria.

Academic Year	Number Qualified (satisfying minimum entry requirements)	Number Selected	Number Selected as Percentage of Number Qualified
1994/95	55126	8851	16%
1995/96	59292	9460	16%
1996/97	56740	9787	17%
1997/98	70379	11200	16%
1998/99	71814	11658	16%
1999/00	73563	11901	16%
2000/01	73347	12400	17%

Prior to 1965, the universities conducted their own entrance examinations which included theory and practical components. By 1966 the aggregate of raw marks obtained at the GCE A/L examination was used as the basis for selection by merit. By 1970, marks were standardised according to the language medium within which one was enrolled. By 1974 the order of merit of standardised marks was combined with quotas assigned to districts in proportion to their population. 1976 saw the mechanism of selection of 70% on merit, and 30% on a district quota basis, with half of that percentage to 10 districts judged educationally underprivileged. By 1978 standardisation was abandoned and raw marks were used again. District quotas were changed and the number of underprivileged districts rose, with even a previously highly privileged district such as Jaffna having to be classed as underprivileged due to disruption and problems created by the northern war.

In the case of Arts subjects (where inter-district disparities in educational facilities are considered as relatively low), admissions are determined on an all-island merit basis, which is in the order of marks compiled for the country as a whole. However, a level of admission is maintained by ensuring that the total number admitted from any district is not less than that of the academic year 1993/1994.

In the case of all other courses of study (i.e. other than Arts) the admissions are assigned:

(a) 40% on an all-island merit basis

(b) 55% to the 25 districts in proportion to the population in each district (the ratio of district population to the national population).

(c) 5% to 13 districts considered educationally disadvantaged on the basis of population (the ratio of the district population to the total population of the 13 districts). These districts are: Nuwara Eliya, Ampara, Badulla, Hambantota, Anuradhapura, Polonnaruwa, Mannar, Monaragala, Trincomalee, Kilinochchi, Mullaitivu, Jaffna and Vavuniya.

Given the demand, this process of selection has led to much debate. It is emotionally charged, too, as some minorities and the privileged classes in the urban areas claim that they would have had a better deal if merit based on the GCE A/L examination were the only criterion. The various changes of scheme effected over the past 35 years are, however, an indication of the concern.

Studies have shown that, for example, in 1948, as many as 75% of the students at the University came from two provinces (i.e. Western 60.8% and Northern 14.2%). In fact they came from schools concentrated in a few small areas within those provinces. By 1968 this proportion had dropped to 41.9% (33.3% and 8.6% respectively) which implied that people from other areas had begun to gain access to the universities. In 1948, the Buddhists accounted for 43.2% and the Christians for 41%, whereas in 66-70 the figures were in the 74-77% and 7-9% range while the respective population status currently is around 69+% and 7+% within the country. In 1956, the proportion of Sinhalese and Tamil students at university was 60% and 34% respectively. Current statistics on the ethnic basis are not available, but the figure for 1995/96 indicates that university students were 78% Sinhalese and 17% Tamil with the proportion of population currently being 74% for Sinhalese, 12.6% for Sri Lankan Tamil and 5.5% for Indian Tamils.

Ethnicity and religion are not directly considered in the selection process, but in it there is doubtlessly a clear and positive bias in favour of the disadvantaged areas. It is most interesting to study the merit and quota components for entry into fields such as Medicine, Engineering, Science and Management and to notice that a number of districts would not have had a single student coming into the university system if "merit" based on examination were the only criterion.

No process is perfect, and review is needed in the light of changing conditions. Unfortunately, Sri Lanka continues to be a country where facilities are concentrated in the populous urban areas. If one therefore looks at the issue in the historical and socio-political context, the current approach needs to be credited as incorporating elements of "affirmative action".

Sex is not considered in the selection process either. Of the total students in general education (i.e. the school sector) in 1998, females were 50.1% while the males were 49.9%. At the university level in the year 1997 for which the breakdown is available, the female-male proportions for new entrants were 64:36 for Arts, 46:54 for Commerce/Management and 32:68 for the sciences area. For the total student population enrolled in that year the overall figure was 44:56. Karunaratne (2000) shows the current figure to be 52:48.

5. Repercussions on the university system

Leaving out of consideration the repercussions of the above on the young people involved and on society as a whole, it is worth considering the impact on the university sector.

It is unfortunate that already from about grade 3 or 4, pressure is brought on the children to succeed at examinations. This is because of what is known as the "Scholarship Examination" held in Grade 5, through which a limited number of children who do well have the opportunity to move on to a "better" school (While the objective is desirable, the mechanism is questionable.). The fever hots up again even more intensely from Grade 8-9 onwards and continues until the end of Grade 13. If one is to have a chance one must succeed in the GCE (O/L) and GCE (A/L) examinations.

And so the tradition has been for the teachers to lecture, where most of the time one helps to transfer the contents of old textbooks into the notebooks of the students, and hopefully into their memories. Presentation of target / anticipated questions for the examinations, and the "correct / model" answer for such is what the students wish to have.

In a country that values "free education", in order that their children succeed at GCE (O/L) and GCE (A/L) parents pay to keep alive a multi-million rupee highly organised "tuition industry" that has grown up parallel to the education system. Even many university academics find it more attractive to concentrate on this area of A/L tuition than on what they should be doing otherwise. Be it after school or at weekends, students are away for "tuition", with those who can afford it having individual tuition or small-group classes, while the hoi polloi go to sessions where hundreds are packed together in halls while teaching is through public address systems.

In the past with the university system being the "supplier" of graduates to the public sector with its centralised/bureaucratic recruiting systems, the "paper qualification" was what mattered and so a rigid written examinations system had become the only way to identify the few to be chosen for university and later for public service.

In an information society where knowledge is out there to be discovered and where navigational skills combined with analytical and judgmental skills (and other transferable skills) are what is going to count, we paradoxically still treasure a system that attempts to pack "knowledge" into the brain or "facts and standard answers" into memory cells. The examination system appears to be testing the ability to retrieve such stored data. The efficacy/impartiality of other systems would perhaps be questionable too, but the net result may be that we are making a mockery of the entire education system and ruining it through a futile exercise designed apparently to concentrate on (*hopefully*) selecting less than 3% of an age group as the cream of it judged suitable for higher education at university (and as future leaders and inno-vators) and ignoring the rest.

It is thus a fact that the "input" into the university process and their attitudes while at the university and with regard to success are seriously conditioned by years of education of a certain type. What is worse is that a good portion of the University teachers may either be forced (due partly to salary issues etc.) to concentrate their energies on other matters or, sadder still, may be unable to see a problem here because they themselves have grown up in this manner.

Thus the concern of some to promote the need to become "demand-driven" and to be working with clear skills and outcomes in view are seen or interpreted as ways of lowering the "quality" of the degree and mixing elements of "professional" with "academic". The overall system may be dysfunctional, too, without a clear vision, targets and policies, and perhaps with mechanisms of the avoidance of responsibility and of "passing the buck" at various levels of authority.

6. And the future?

But once again, there is a ray of hope. Educational reforms, particularly at the primary and the secondary levels, are being effected. It will take years to see the full impact of these, but one is happy that things are moving in a positive direction once again and one can only hope that this movement will be sustained.

The situation is different with regard to the universities. The Central Bank of Sri Lanka (in its latest) Annual Report 1999 states: "General education reforms, implemented on a pilot basis in 1998, were carried out islandwide in 1999 and are progressing satisfactorily, although there were some problems relating to resource constraints and training. Implementation of university education reforms was rather slow due to lack of adequate response from the universities". In another place it states: "The progress of university education reforms has been slow as there was much diversity in the responses to the proposals for university education reforms".

The Education Reform Proposals of 1971 or of 1981, proposals of the Human Resources Development Council, the 1995 Report of a Presidential Committee appointed to identify and study the problems of the university system and to make recommendations, the recommendations coming from various bodies representative of Business and Industry, or the work of the National Education Commission, to mention just a few, all indicate that something radical has to happen. But what are being currently pushed as reforms are not sufficiently radical, have been thought out by a few people, do not have support across the political spectrum and are unfortunately not even really supported by the "University Community". This certainly is sad.

The World Bank, in its latest report on Sri Lanka already referred to, has in its conclusion a clear message that Sri Lanka needs to be very clear about her priorities, and that solutions must be designed with the full collaboration of all the stakeholders, even though stakeholder consultations tend to be often long and complicated. That should certainly be valid for the university sector with (in spite of problems referred to) a wealth of relatively valuable stock regarding teachers and students. In the context of inordinate politicisation of the public sector, one also believes that a bipartisan, or preferably multi-party, approach has necessarily to be incorporated if change is to be achieved and dynamically continued.

Change and revolutions have happened in the past. Isolated instances of rethinking and attempts at change are certainly not absent. There is some slight hope that a deep, fundamental and system-wide reform process rather than a cosmetic one may be initiated and carried through, so that the universities will become and remain demand-driven, catering to the needs of and leading the way in a fast changing world, a knowledge-centred economy and a learning society.

Appendix B – Additional Note on the Post-Secondary Sector

1. Post-secondary education and training opportunities up to degree level

In this appendix we are concerned with some aspects of the opportunities within the range post-secondary to degree level (leaving the post-graduate area out of consideration).

It has not been possible to find a clear classification scheme which permits one to see how the different players in the broader post-secondary field fit in together. The author has therefore attempted a grid / graphical representation in Figure B-1, which for want of a better tool is expected to help place things in context.

2. The beginnings of the development of the post-secondary sector

During the British colonial period, around the year 1859 the Colombo Academy (and later the Queen's College set up by it) prepared students for higher examinations of the University of Calcutta. However, Sri Lanka's first Committee of Inquiry into Education in its report dated 1867 recommended the abolition of the Queen's College and the granting instead of scholarships to a few of the best students to undertake studies in England.

The major breakthrough came in 1870 with the establishment of the Ceylon Medical College which provided an elementary training in medicine and surgery through a 3-year programme, extended gradually to 4 years and then 5 years. By 1888 fully qualified medical practitioners were being produced by the Medical College. Not long afterwards came the next development. The Ceylon Law College was started in 1874 and was managed by the Council for Legal Education. It has continued to this day as an autonomous self-financed institution within the state sector.

While "Medicine" and "Law" were typically for the elite, some opening up of broader opportunities was realised in 1893 when the Government Technical School (later Ceylon Technical College) was opened with 25 students for the purpose of training junior technical officers for the state sector. This does merit some special comment. This institution later developed a centre for science education, and the training of science teachers was undertaken (with that centre later becoming integrated into the Ceylon University College started in 1921). The Technical College began preparing students for the external degree in engineering of the University of London, which it continued to do until about 1950 when the Faculty of Engineering of the University of Ceylon became functional. As early as in 1908, commerce education was available at the Technical College. A professional course in accounting was available by 1943, and degree-equivalent programmes in commerce were available by 1946 as students were offered the opportunity to sit for external examinations of British professional institutes. It can thus be said that the Technical

College played a pioneering role in opening up higher educational opportunities to the people of Sri Lanka.

The First Teacher Training College was started in 1903. This and the Technical College were under the Ministry of Education.

1921 marked the beginning of the Ceylon University College affiliated to the University of London. There were then 115 students. The Ceylon Medical College and the Ceylon University College were merged in 1942 and the University of Ceylon was born. There were then 904 students, out of whom 250 were in Medicine. Wijetunga (1983) and de Silva & Peiris (1995) provide useful information on the development of university education from 1942 onwards.

It is thus clear that the foundation of what we have today as opportunities for post-secondary education and training were laid during that period prior to independence in 1948.

3. Post-secondary education and training today

Institutions referred to in Box A of Figure B-1 are the subject area of the main report. The University Act of 1978 had ensured that no institute other than these could use the term "university", or grant their own degrees.

Beginning in 1981 with the Buddhist and Pali University there has been a gradual change with other institutions being given degree-awarding status by Act of Parliament. The NIE is noteworthy as it offers programmes to teachers in general education going up to Masters level. The NITE is also much centred on the training of trainers / teachers. Some institutions do not award qualifications at degree level as yet but have the authorisation to do so. All such institutions given degree-awarding status by Act of Parliament so far are listed in Box B.

The University Act was amended in 1985 making it possible to grant degree-awarding status to other recognized tertiary institutions outside the state sector. Thus a Private Medical College was granted such a status in 1988, but partly due to mechanisms adopted by that institution to profit from state sector facilities and recognition, and due partly also to the fact that this institution was seen as a threat to "free education" held sacrosanct by the student body of state universities, the government was forced to vest the same in the state later in 1989 and it became part of the University of Kelaniya. The Institute of Technological Studies in Box D was granted such degree awarding status for one of its degrees (a degree in Computer Studies) in 1989. It is noted that the state has not granted such degree-awarding status to any private sector organisation since then. However, institutions in Box B

Figure B-1: Post-secondary education and training opportunities up to degree level

STATE SECTOR
Funded by the State   ◁- - - - - - - - - -- - - - - ▷   OUTSIDE THE STATE SECTOR
charging 'nominal' fees   Fee-levying

Degree or Professional Qualification

A

12 national Universities and connected Institutes

1 Open University

(within the framework of the Ministry of Higher Education & the University Grants Commission)

B

Pali and Buddhist University
Buddhasravaka Bhiksu University
Kotelawala Defence Academy (KDA)
Institute of Surveying and Mapping
National Institute of Education (NIE)
National Institute of Technical Education(NITE)
National Institute of Social Development
National Institute of Fisheries
     and Aquatic Engineering

C
Institute of Chartered Accountants of Sri Lanka (ICA)
Chartered Institute of Management Accountants (CIMA)
Chartered Institute of Marketing (CIM)
Institution of Engineers - Sri Lanka (IESL)
Institute of Chemistry - Ceylon (ICC)
etc.

D
Institute of Technological Studies (ITS)
Informatics Institute of Technology (IIT)
Royal Institute (RI)
Institute of Data Management (IDM)
(Plus NIBM*)
etc.

E | Sri Lanka Law College |

National Diploma / Higher National Diploma / Certificate

F
Department of Technical Education and Training (DTET)
National Apprentice and Industrial Training Authority (NAITA)
Sri Lanka Institute of Advanced Technical Education (SLIATE)
Vocational Training Authority (VTA)

G
Many other state-sector Institutes *such as* the following
(under various Government Ministries and Agencies):
   Teacher Training Colleges / Colleges of Education
   National Institute of Business Management (NIBM)
   Sri Lanka Institute of Development Administration (SLIDA)
   Sri Lanka Institute of Information Technology (SLIIT)
   The Ceylon German Technical Training Institute (CGTTI)
   The Korea Sri Lanka Technical & Vocational Training Institute
   Sri Lanka Television Training Institute
   Sri Lanka Foundation Institute (SLFI)
   Institute of Construction Training and Development (ICTAD)
   Ceylon Hotel School
   Clothing Industry Training Institute
   National Youth Services Council (NYSC)
PLUS
several hundred Institutes outside the state sector *such as*
   Sri Lanka Business Development Centre (SLBDC)
   Institute of Bankers
   Institute of Personnel Management (IPM)
   Institute of Chartered Secretaries and Administrators
   Sri Jinaratana Educational Institute
   Aquinas College of Higher Studies
   Sarvodaya Development and Educational Institute

and in Box D are an indication that in reality university education went beyond the universities as defined in the Universities Act of 1978, and Indraratne (1992) claims that "with these changes, the State lost its sole monopoly of university education hitherto enjoyed by it under the aegis of the Ministry of Higher Education".

Thus institutions in Box D have only had a 'nihil obstat' and not official recognition from the Ministry of Education & Higher Education. They have been able to build up degree programmes of study as long as the degrees were not local and were offered by universities abroad. ITS and IIT provide some university campus style environment and offer degrees based respectively on the US and UK models. Others, such as RI and IDM, offer tuition and facilities for external degrees of foreign universities. Programmes cost typically 6000-7000 US dollars for 4 years full-time. Some other institutions do exist that provide the possibility of completing some years of a foreign degree locally prior to proceeding abroad to complete the degree.

It is clear that some measure of "legality" for private sector involvement in university-level education has been won. Some of these institutions have been accepted by the state as "investment projects". A further contribution along the line of recognition has been the registration of such institutions by the Tertiary and Vocational Education Commission (TVEC). And in another interesting move, the National Institute of Business Management (NIBM) (a state sector organisation shown in Box G and also in Box D) has entered the same arena, offering a foreign degree in Management Information Systems locally, but at about half of what other locally offered programmes cost.

It is expected that (in spite of the opposition of sections of the students in state sector universities) this trend will continue, particularly because there is a demand for higher education (given the extremely restrictive access currently the norm with regard to state universities) and given also that this permits a foreign degree at a fraction of the cost one would incur if one obtained it abroad. One certainly notes the need for the assurance of quality, given that the balance between the achievement of profit and maintenance of standards is not always satisfactory. It can, however, be expected that at least some of the private sector initiatives more responsive to market needs could be a challenge to the state sector. It is highly probable that this trend, which is apparently irreversible now, and which is quite in line with proposals emanating from the World Bank, will lead some day in the not too distant future to explicit approval for the establishment of private universities in Sri Lanka. It may, in fact, be hypothesized that the lack of information and clarity in these matters is purposeful, designed to allow developments to take place without much ado, so that one would later be in a fait accompli situation.

Box C provides a few examples of professional organisations (local ones or local chapters of foreign ones as is the case, for example, with CIMA – Sri Lanka

Division, and CIM – Sri Lanka Branch) that offer a path to professional qualifications including levels considered equivalent to academic degrees.

The Sri Lanka Law College (Box E) is an interesting case. Established in 1874 and providing professional education to law students incorporating elements of apprenticeship, it turns out fully-qualified attorneys-at-law who can practise in the law courts of Sri Lanka. It remains within the state sector but is not funded by the state and is managed autonomously by the Council for Legal Education composed of 'legal luminaries', and thus leaders of the profession. There have evidently been subsequent developments with universities conducting academic programmes in law, and offering these in the external mode, too.

Box F refers to the Technical Education and Vocational Training (TEVT) sector and lists the key institutions within the state sector.

The pioneering role of the Ceylon Technical College started in 1893, and the opening out beyond the elite that it symbolised has been referred to already. Its work is continued through the Department of Technical Education and Training (DTET), which has a network consisting of 36 technical colleges and other institutions affiliated to it. Spread out at district level, it handles about 16,000 students full time and part time, with about 90% of its programmes accessible to those with GCE (O/L) qualifications (and thus perhaps as the post-secondary non-tertiary category of ISCED). But part of what used to be the old Technical College is now within the Sri Lanka Institute of Advanced Technical Education (SLIATE), which concentrates on National Diploma and Higher National Diploma level qualifications with a programme duration of 2, 3 or 4 years and an annual intake of about 1200.

The Vocational Training Authority (VTA) serves rural youth by way of employment-orientated short courses and on the job training through a network of about 200 rural vocational training centres and through three national training institutes that offer longer-duration certificate level courses. The annual turnover is stated to be around 20,000 students. The National Apprentice and Industrial Training Authority (NAITA) incorporates the apprenticeship element very strongly and has over eighty training institutions spread throughout the country that handle short courses. Three national centres have 3-4 year programmes with apprenticeship evidently incorporated. The capacity of NAITA is reported to be about 20,000 craft, technician and other types of apprentices. The TVEC claims that over 85% of the training provided by the state sector in TEVT is accounted for by the DTET, VTA and NAITA.

SLIATE is within the purview of the Ministry of Higher Education, while NAITA belongs to the Ministry of Science and Technology. DTET and VTA (as well as NITE in Box B) are within the Ministry of Labour and Vocational Training. Some involved in the sector argue that all state sector institutions that are related to Technical Education and Vocational Training (TEVT) should be brought under one government ministry, given the crucial role this sector needs to play and the need for a co-ordinated effort. Others refer to countries such as the UK, where all of education, employment and youth are under one ministry, and ask whether that, too, could not be an option worth considering as one that could offer the possibility of co-ordinated and concerted action.

In such a context, one does also notice some misconceptions or anomalies. Thus, for instance, the apex policy-making body for the sector has been named the Tertiary and Vocational Education Commission (TVEC) where the word 'Technical' would have been more appropriate than 'Tertiary' if one took a more holistic view of post-secondary education.

Just as serious questions are being raised about the Sri Lankan university sector, and its sensitivity to and relevance within the context of the market demands of today, parallel questions have been asked about the TEVT sector. However, some movement and change are noticeable. The importance of this sector has been recognised in the context, on the one hand, of growing unemployment and under-employment, and on the other hand of the need for a qualified workforce, given developments in the labour market, industrial development and foreign investment. Much is therefore being done to promote the sector, with assistance also from international bodies.

While not ignoring the deeper question as to whether the socio-political and economic context encourages it, questions remain as to whether the Sri Lankan private sector is sufficiently broad and mature enough to contribute with long term goals in mind. However, the policy being advocated is for the state to move away from being the main provider of training to becoming its facilitator, coordinator and standard setter, and various initiatives such as the Skills Development programme, where the state and private sectors are collaborating, are already in place.

Box G contains a mix of institutions spread over the grid both horizontally (state sector and outside the state sector, whether linked to a professional body or not) and vertically (dealing with a variety of programmes and paths to qualifications). It is provided just as a sampler and also indicates the role being played by the NGO / Voluntary sector.

Switzerland

Martin Teichgräber

The higher education system

The social system in Switzerland is characterized by its cultural diversity. The four official national languages German, French, Italian and Romansch are an important feature of this diversity. Switzerland is a referendum democracy[1] with a federal state structure, which regulates the dividing of responsibility between the federal government, the 26 cantons and semicantons and their communes. This federalism has effects on the Swiss education system. Responsibility for schools is in the hands of the cantons. The responsibility of the cantons, especially in the compulsory school, "means that not just one, but twenty-six different education systems exist with regard to their form and organisation".[2] In the field of the post-compulsory training at the upper secondary level and in the tertiary field, including the higher education system, the structures are less highly differentiated. Nevertheless, due to the decentralized political structures in Switzerland the responsibility of the federal government is limited. Thus only the two Swiss Federal Institutes of Technology *(Eidgenössische Technische Hochschulen)* are federal establishments. Permission is required from the federal government to establish and run universities of applied sciences *(Fachhochschulen)*, and here, depending on the subject, the distribution of responsibility lies either with the federal government or the cantons. Apart from this, authority for the establishment of additional

---

1 The form of Swiss government, in which elements of direct and indirect democracy exist side by side, is given the term "referendum democracy" or "semi-direct democracy". Cf. Huber, A.: "Staatskunde Lexikon", 4th Ed., Lucerne, 1996, p. 83.

2 Wettstein, E., Lauterbach, U.: "Schweiz" in Lauterbach, U. (Ed.): "Internationales Handbuch der Berufsbildung", Baden-Baden, 1995, p. CH-9.

institutions of higher education lies with the former. Here, however, a form of cooperative federalism has become general accepted, through which the federal government provides financial support for the cantonal institutions of higher education on the basis of the principle of subsidiarity.[3]

In Switzerland, the democratisation of the education system and the change into a knowledge and information society has furthered the diversification of the tertiary educational sector. The transformation of selected Higher Vocational Schools and Colleges, especially Colleges of Engineering and Colleges of Economics and Administration into Universities of Applied Sciences *(Fachhochschulen)*, and their official recognition in 1998, meant the start of the restructuring of the higher education system into a "dual" higher education sector. The following goals are being aimed at with the new type of subject-related and vocation-related higher education institution currently being established: the extension of the provision of higher education institutions by means of vocation-orientated courses of training at the higher education level, the revaluation of these courses of study at the national and international level with a view to the Europe-wide recognition of the diplomas and, finally, the establishment of attractive higher vocational training opportunities for people in employment. At the same time, the founding of the first Italian-language university "Università della Svizzera italiana" (1996) in the canton of Ticino brought about the horizontal extension of the university sector.

The higher education system in Switzerland currently consists of 13 universities or university level institutions and 7 universities of applied sciences *(Fachhochschulen)*. The universities or university level insitutions are the nine cantonal universities (Basle, Bern, Fribourg, Geneva, Lausanne, Neuchâtel,

---

3   Cf. Art. 62, Federal Constitution *(Bundesverfassung)* of 18/04/1999; University Support Law *(Universitätsförderungsgesetz)* of 8/10/1999 and the Universities of Applied Sciences Law *(Bundesgesetz über die Fachhochschulen)* of 6/10/1995.

Zürich, St. Gallen, Svizzera italiana), the two Swiss Federal Institutes of Technology *(Eidgenössische Technische Hochschulen)* in Lausanne and Zürich, the University College of Lucerne (since 21/05/2000 University of Lucerne) and the Pedagogical College of St. Gallen. The Cantonal University in Basle is the oldest university in Switzerland. It was opened in 1460. Most of the cantonal universities were founded in the 19th century: Zürich (1833), Bern (1834), Geneva (1873), Fribourg (1889), Lausanne (1890), St. Gallen (1898). Some of the universities have roots dating back to the Reformation. Thus the University of Zürich is based on a school founded by Ulrich Zwingli (1523), and the University of Geneva on one by Johannes Calvin (1559). In addition, the University of Lausanne (1537) was originally opened as a Protestant Theological Academy. The Swiss Federal Institutes of Technology *(Eidgenössische Technische Hochschulen)* were founded in Zürich in 1855 and in Lausanne in 1969. Since 1998 there have been seven universities of applied sciences: *Berner Fachhochschule, Haute école spécialisée de la Suisse occidentale, Fachhochschule Nordwestschweiz, Fachhochschule Zentralschweiz, Scuola universitaria professionale della Svizzera italiana, Fachhochschule Ostschweiz, Fachhochschule Zürich.*

The establishment of the higher education system in Switzerland was carried out to a large extent under the influence of developments abroad. The founding of the universities took place throughout Switzerland along the lines of the German university structure following Humboldt's concept. Previously, however, in Western Switzerland the influences on education had been distinctly French. As far as the universities were concerned, a certain break with the German model occurred during World War 1. French influences have become greater in the western part of Switzerland since then. The two Swiss Federal Institutes of Technology *(Eidgenössische Technische Hochschulen)* and the University of St. Gallen were established following the French model (École spéciale). In the decades after World War 2 Switzerland increasingly developed its own initiatives with regard to university policy. Within the institutions of the tertiary education sector, training in higher education does not take place in a hierarchical manner along the lines of elite or mass training. Research and teaching are also linked with one another. Due to various influences, however, within the universities it is possible to detect interregional differences between German-speaking Switzerland and Western Switzerland *(French-speaking Switzerland)* as far as the structure of the courses of study is concerned: while it is tightly structured in Western Switzerland, German-speaking Switzerland relies more on the students' own motivation. In addition, numerous practice-orientated courses of training are taught at other educational institutions within the tertiary sector in German-speaking Switzerland, which, however, are to be found in the curricula of the cantonal universities in Western Switzerland, where they have a stronger school-like character.

The minimum period of study for the first degree (*Lizentiat/ Licence* or *Diplom/ Diplôme*) is generally eight semesters, with the exception of a few courses of study in Western Switzerland. Nevertheless, within the framework of the *Troisième cycle* – along the lines of the structure of studies in France – some courses of study award a *Licence* degree after three years and the *Diplôme* after an additional year's study. In addition, the *Habilitation* in unknown at universities in Western Switzerland; a doctorate is sufficient for obtaining a professorship at a university. As a result, a doctoral thesis is extremely extensive in Western Switzerland and is undertaken mainly with a university career in mind.[4]

---

4 The information on the historical developments and those specific to the linguistic regions is taken from a research application for a current project: "Fachkultur und Sprachregion – Sprachregionale Distanzen und Differenzen in wissenschaftlichen Disziplinen" at the University of Bern. The director of the project is Dr. Ursula Streckeisen.

Due to the regional linguistic differences it is possibly rather surprising that the profile of the courses offered at the cantonal universities is comparatively similar. Seven universities (Basle, Bern, Fribourg, Geneva, Lausanne, Neuchâtel and Zürich) provide varied specializations from at least thirteen fields of subjects. The University of St. Gallen lays its main emphasis on Economics, Law and the Social Sciences. The most recent university, the Università della Svizzera italiana concentrates on Media Studies and Economics as well as on Architecture. The profile of the Swiss Federal Institutes of Technology lies in the Exact Sciences (Mathematics, Computer Science, Astronomy, Physics), the Natural Sciences and Engineering Sciences (Civil, Mechanical and Electrical Engineering as well as Agricultural Economics and Forest Management). The University College of Lucerne initially consisted of only one Roman Catholic Theological Faculty. In 1992 it was extended to include a Liberal Arts Faculty with Philosophy and History as its subjects. A plebiscite on 21/05/2000 approved its further expansion into the University of Lucerne with the establishment of a Faculty of Law. The faculty to be newly established will become the most important and largest component part of the University of Lucerne. The focal point of the Pedagogical College of St. Gallen lies in training teachers for the lower secondary stage.

The universities of applied sciences *(Fachhochschulen)* provide job-orientated degree courses in the fields of Engineering, Architecture and Environmental Planning, Chemistry, Agriculture and Forest Management, Economics and Services, and also Design.[5] In addition to the courses of study already mentioned, for which the Federal Government is responsible, degree courses are offered in accordance with cantonal law, especially Social Work, Health, Art, Music and Drama.

---

5   Cf. Art. 1 of the *Verordnung über Aufbau und Führung von Fachhochschulen* (Ordinance on the Structure and Guidance of Universities of Applied Sciences), *Bern, 11/09/1996.*

The requirements for admission to a degree course at a Swiss university or university level institution are fulfilled with the *Maturität* (Maturity Certificate), which is the general university entry qualification. Since the Federal Government determines the content of the admission requirements to study Medicine and of the entry requirements to the Swiss Federal Institutes of Technology, it influences the content of what is taught in the *Maturitätsschulen* (grammar school sixth forms) in the cantons. The Swiss *Maturität*, or the *Maturität* recognized by the Swiss Confederation, which has been awarded so far (*Matura* types A to E)[6] entitles the holder to study at any university. As a result of the Ordinance on the Recognition of Grammar School Leaving Certificates, which was introduced in 1995, the cantonal *Maturitätsschulen* (grammar school sixth forms) are in the middle of reorganising their leaving examinations. The goal of the ordinance is the creation of a standardized type of leaving certificate with seven basic subjects, one specialized subject and one additional subject. An eight-year transition phase is planned for this reorganisation.[7] So far, four of the Swiss cantons (Appenzell-Ausserrhoden, Appenzell-Innerrhoden, Obwalden and Glarus) have introduced the new grammar school leaving examinations.

The entry qualifications for universities of applied sciences *(Fachhoch-schulen)* are obtained with the *Berufsmaturität* (Vocational Maturity Certificate), which was newly introduced in 1993. This consists of a completed apprenticeship and the proof of extended general education, and is awarded after the successful completion of a final examination. Students with the grammar school

---

6   The letters given to the individual *Matura* types reflect the focal points of the grammar school sixth forms: Type A: literature (classical languages: Latin and Greek), Type B: literature (Latin and a modern foreign language), Type C: natural sciences, Type D: modern languages, Type E: economics.
7   Cf. *Verordnung über die Anerkennung von gymnasialen Maturitätsausweisen* (Ordinance on the Recognition of Grammar School Leaving Certificates), Bern, 15/02/1995.

Maturität can start studying at a university of applied sciences after a *Maturandenpraktikum* (work experience) lasting one year.

Table 1 provides an overview of the numerical development of entry qualifications to institutions of higher education, new entrants and student numbers. The absolute numbers of students obtaining higher education entry certificates, the numbers of new entrants and the total number of students, as well as the proportion of pupils obtaining these qualifications and of students taking up their studies at institutions of higher education in perspective to the respective permanent population rose constantly during the Nineties. The proportion of female students also increased during this period. In a regional comparison the proportion of female students at the German-speaking universities rose faster (6.5 percentage points) than at the Francophone universities (4.3 percentage points). In the 1998/99 academic year only the two Swiss Federal Institutes of Technology and the University of St. Gallen had more male than female first-year students. Due to the technical orientation – which is usually less in demand by women – of the Swiss Federal Institutes of Technology, the proportion of women there is comparatively small (16.2% in Zürich and 24.9% in Lausanne). The University of Lucerne had parity between the sexes.

In the universities of applied sciences the proportion of women was 24.0% in the 1999/2000 academic year. Due to the differences in the preferences of men and women with regard to the choice of subject studied the proportion of women in the individual subjects varies greatly – e.g. Health 85% and Technology 3.1%.[8]

---

8   Bundesamt für Statistik: Studierende an den schweizerischen Fachhochschulen 1999/2000, Neuchâtel, 2000; Bundesamt für Statistik: Studierende an den schweizerischen Hochschulen 1998/1999, Neuchâtel, 1999.

Table 1: The development of higher education entry certificates, new entrants and students in total (proportion of women in %)

	1985	1990	1995	1998
Higher education entry certificates (*Maturitäten*):				
Grammar school *Maturität*	12.662 (44,3%)	12.090 (48,6%)	12.932 (50,8%)	15.205 (51,9%)
Grammar school *Maturitäts*-quota[1]	12,2% (11,0%)	13,4% (13,3%)	17,2% (17,6%)	17,7% (18,8%)
Berufsmaturität	—	—	480 (n.n.)	5.638 (31,0%)
Universities:				
New entrants	14.049 (40,4%)	15.688 (44,4%)	15.854 (45,8%)	17.441 (47,6%)
New entrants quota[2]	14,6% (12,4%)	16,1% (14,8%)	18,2% (17,2%)	19,4% (19,0%)
Students	74.806 (35,8%)	85.940 (38,8%)	88.243 (41,8%)	94.695 (43,8%)
Universities of applied sciences:				
New entrants	—	—	—	6.090 (25,3%)
Students[3]	—	—	—	10.945 (22,7%)

1) Grammar school *Maturität*: proportion of pupils obtaining their *Maturität* as a percentage of the permanent population of 19-year-olds.

2) New entrants quota: proportion of students enrolled at a university or university level institution for the first time as a percentage of the permanent population of 21-year-olds.

3) Until that time only students in their 1st and 2nd years of study are included.

Source: Bundesamt für Statistik: Studierende an den schweizerischen Hochschulen 1998/99; Studierende an den schweizerischen Fachhochschulen 1998/99. Neuchâtel, 1999.

Initial situation: the labour market and employment in Switzerland

During the past fifteen years the Swiss labour market has undergone a sustained change. The constant increase in the number of employees in the service sector (3rd sector) contrasts with the decreasing numbers of employees in the industrial sector (2nd sector). While 62.2% of employees of the second

Switzerland

and third sectors were still employed in the service sector in 1985, their proportion was already 70.4% in 1999. In Switzerland, a total of 3.543 million employees were registered in the 2nd and 3rd sectors during the 4th quarter of 1999. Of these, 2.640 million were employed full-time, and 0.903 million part-time.[9]

The phase of economic recession at the beginning and in the middle of the Nineties led to a decline in employment, especially in the industrial sector. Simultaneously, and partly dependent on it, a structural change took place in the Swiss labour market. Both of these facts had an effect on the overall employment situation in Switzerland which, for the first time since the post-war period, thus had a relatively high level of unemployment. This rose from 1.4% (1991) to 3.9% (1997). Nevertheless, when compared with the countries of the European Union, after Luxembourg it still had the second lowest unemployment rate in the Nineties.

The most recent results from the Swiss labour force survey indicate an easing of the labour market and reveal an unemployment rate of 2.6% for 1999.[10] This is essentially the result of two factors: a continued rise in employment in the service sector and a positive development in employment due to the economic recovery in the export-orientated branches of the chemical industry, mechanical engineering and in the building industry.[11]

9   Bundesamt für Statistik: Statistisches Jahrbuch 2000; Bundesamt für Statistik: Weitere Zunahme der Erwerbstätigkeit – Press Release, No. 12/00; Neuchâtel, 2000. The Swiss employment statistics (BESTA) include the employees in firms within the 2nd and 3rd sectors (6 hours and more per week).
10 Bundesamt für Statistik: Schweizerische Arbeitskräfteerhebung – Sonderauswertung, Neuchâtel, 2000.
11 Bundesamt für Statistik: Statistisches Jahrbuch 2000, T3.20, Neuchâtel, 2000; Bundesamt für Statistik: Schweizer Arbeitskräfteerhebung 1999 – Press Release, No. 94/99, Neuchâtel, 1999.

However, the rise in employment in the service sector is not distributed evenly among all the branches of industry. The rise in employment is to be found essentially in the following branches of the service industry: computer services, real estate, the provision of general services for businesses, teaching and health services. In contrast, employment in the retail trade and the credit business is declining.

In general, it is largely not a matter of an increase in employment within the public sector, but in the field of private services. An increasing division of labour is also to be found as a result of this development, and here the number of small and medium-sized businesses in Switzerland is continually increasing. In 1998, for example, 99.7% of all Swiss businesses had fewer than 250 employees.[12]

Due to the structural change, the demands made on the employees have altered in many areas of the employment system. The processes of change in the modern service society, and the economic and technological demands associated with this change, are increasingly requiring "human capital" at a high level in society. Without the necessary abilities, skills and knowledge the modern "post-industrial knowledge society" is not equal to this task, nor to the international competition on the world market that is automatically connected with it.

If one looks at the development of the education of the Swiss population aged between 25 and 64, then one finds a continual rise in the level of education. A change is taking place mainly at the middle educational level. In 1998 58% had completed training up to the level of the upper secondary school certificate. This is an increase of 8 percentage points when compared

---

12   Bundesamt für Statistik: Statistisches Jahrbuch 2000, T3.6, and also Taschenstatistik der Schweiz, Neuchâtel, 2000.

with 1980. The proportion of the population with a "traditional" university training amounted to 10% in 1998, compared with 6% in 1980. Due to the regional differences in the provision of courses by institutions of higher education this proportion was 5 percentage points higher in the French-speaking part of Switzerland than in German-speaking Switzerland. The relatively low percentage of graduates from higher education institutions when compared with other countries is to be increased in the next few years as a result of the reform of higher education into a "dual" system of higher education. In 1998 23% of the population had completed training at the tertiary level, i.e. university training or advanced vocational college training (today's universities of applied sciences).

Table 2: Educational level of the population aged 25-64 in 1980 and 1998 expressed as a percentage

Educational level[1])	1980	1998			
	Switzerland overall	Switzerland overall	German-speaking Switzerland	French-speaking Switzerland	Italian-speaking Switzerland
Compulsory schooling	34	19	18	23	24
Upper secondary level (vocational education)	50**	51	52	44	57
Upper secondary level (general education)	**	7	7	9	8
Tertiary level (non-university)	9	13	14	11	7
Tertiary level (university)	6	10	9	14	5

1) The highest completed training defines the educational level.

** Upper secondary level (vocational and general education)

Source: Bundesamt für Statistik (Schweizer Arbeitskräfteerhebung): Bildungsindikatoren 1999, Neuchâtel, 1999. The figures for 1980 are taken from the Swiss Confederate Census.

The demand by firms specifically for qualified staff is having effects on the unemployment rate. If one splits this up in accordance with the educational level of the unemployed, then it can be seen that those with only low qualifications are increasingly affected by unemployment. People with qualified training have better chances on the labour market, and are thus more seldom unemployed. Here, however, as far as Switzerland is concerned, no distinct differences can be determined between training at the higher education level and advanced vocational training, including the upper secondary level. In 1999 the unemployment rate among graduates from universities or university level institutions was 2.5%.

Table 3: Unemployment rate of the economically active population aged 25-64 by educational level in 1995 and 1999 expressed as a percentage

	Unemployment rate	
Educational level	1995	1999
Compulsory schooling	5,7	5,2
Upper secondary level (general and vocational education) and advanced vocational training	2,4	2,0
University training	2,6	2,5*

* Value not statistically significant in 1999 (confidence interval >+-1)

Source: Bundesamt für Statistik (Schweizerische Arbeitskräfteerhebung) – Sonderauswertung 2000.

A higher educational qualification generally has a positive effect on the employment status. According to the Swiss labour force survey of 1998, 59.8% of those employed in managerial positions – senior management of firms or section managers – had tertiary level training, 36.3% had training at the upper secondary level, and merely 17.2% had training at the lower secondary level.[13]

13   Bundesamt für Statistik: Schweizer Arbeitskräfteerhebung 1998, Neuchâtel, 1999 – (www.statistik.admin.ch/stat_ch/ber03/sake/dsake04.html).

At the current time the demand for well-trained specialists and managers in numerous branches of business cannot be satisfied. According to data of the Swiss employment barometer, in the 4th quarter of 1999 26% of the firms of the 3rd sector complained about an insufficient supply of trained personnel. This proportion was particularly high in the fields of computer services (57%) and aeronautics (80%).[14] As far as education is concerned, there is a shortage of (specialist) teachers at the lower secondary level in some cantons. In order to counter this shortage, some of the German-speaking cantons near the border, for example, employ teachers from Germany. No exact information is available about the current requirement figures in the individual branches of employment, but the current shortage of computer scientists, for example, is estimated as between 10,000 and 20,000.

Linking university training with the employment system

With the reform of the education system, which includes the restructuring of the higher education system, Switzerland has reacted to the democratisation of the education system, the change from the industrial to the service society and the altered demands for qualifications associated with it. In this way the federal government is trying to play its part in future developments by means of a series of new statutory regulations and recommendations concerning the shaping of higher education structures.

The diversification of the higher education system was brought about by the introduction of universities of applied sciences *(Fachhochschulen)*, and it is characterised today by a "dual" higher education sector. At the same time, the revised versions of university laws – including the law for the universities

---

14   Cf. Bundesamt für Statistik: Beschäftigungsbarometer 4. Quartal 1999 – Press Release, 12/00, Neuchâtel, 2000.

of applied sciences, – has strengthened the autonomy of higher education institutions (including the higher education institutions' legal status and global budget). By setting the course in this way the federal government and the cantons are trying to do justice to the increasing demands of the economy for highly qualified people and, in the age of globalisation and internationalisation, to strengthen the economic position of Switzerland on a permanent basis.

The following points are of particular interest with regard to the increasing interlinking of the higher education system with the employment system:

The essential goal of the universities of applied sciences is the introduction of professionally qualifying training at a higher education institution which corresponds to the growing demand by business and industry for highly qualified personnel. The practice-orientated courses are to prepare students for professional activities that require the application of scientific knowledge and methods.[15] Here, above all, newer specializations seem to have a high status. In the objectives laid down by the federal government for the second stage of expansion of the universities of applied sciences (1996-2003), some of the specializations mentioned in the field of engineering are: Microelectronics, Microsystems Engineering, Biotechnology, Construction Methods. Those mentioned in the field of economics and services include Production and Management Concepts.[16]

In the long term it is hoped that a more effective and more efficient division of tasks between the two types of higher education institutions that now exist can be achieved. In addition, from the quantitative point of view the

---

15   Cf. Art. 3, Universities of Applied Sciences Law of 6/10/1995, Bern.
16   Cf. the Appendix to Art. 11, *Verordnung über Aufbau und Führung von Fachhochschulen* (Ordinance on the Structure and Guidance of Universities of Applied Sciences), Bern, 11/09/1996.

creation of a "ceiling" for student numbers at the universities, university level institutions and the two Swiss Federal Institutes of Technology and an increase in the student numbers at universities of applied sciences are to be achieved.

With regard to the further diversification of job-orientated degree courses and their remodelling, the Swiss *Wissenschaftsrat* (Advisory Council on Science and Academic Affairs)[17] recommends the possible introduction of courses of study from universities of applied sciences at universities, the transfer of existing courses from universities to universities of applied sciences and the possibility of the dual provision of the same degree courses at universities of applied sciences and universities, but with different profiles.[18]

In addition, the Swiss *Wissenschaftsrat* recommends that the institutions of higher education should reexamine and possibly restructure and revise their existing courses along the lines of a 3-stage model:

Stage A: basic stage, Stage B: advanced stage (*Lizentiat* or *Diplom* examination) and Stage C: (postgraduate stage: job-orientated special diploma and academic post-diploma training). The goal of this is to fulfil the different educational tasks of the institutions of higher education – "e.g. training with specialised, vocation-based subjects versus general academic and cultural education; the opening up and democratisation of university training versus academic training for an elite etc." In stages A and B prime importance is attached to the training of graduates qualified for a job who will be able to take over a broad range of tasks. This is to be achieved, among other things, through the teaching of sound specialised knowledge, through the teaching

---

17　The *Wissenschaftsrat* (Swiss Science Council) is the advisory body of the Federal Council on questions of policy concerning science, research and technology.

18　Cf. Wissenschaftsrat: "Zielvorstellungen für die Entwicklung der schweizerischen Hochschulen – Periode 2000-2003, 1997, Bern, p. 22ff. and p. 41ff.

of interdisciplinary knowledge and abilities as well as by practical research experience. Stage C is split into job-orientated and academic studies. Specialised and cross-sectional knowledge for special demands made by the labour market and for special segments of the market is to be taught in the job-orientated postgraduate course, and here the "teaching of new scientific knowledge" is to be given special emphasis. Postgraduate study can take place immediately after completion of the first degree course, after a phase at work or while working, and it can be full-time or part-time. The academic goal of Stage C includes the doctorate, postdoctorate and the habilitation, which, however, is restricted more and more to the humanities. The main target here is to cater for the new generation of academics. Special graduate and postdoctorate programmes are to provide the incentives for this. In addition, the attractiveness of a university career is to be improved. Suggestions for this include the levelling out of the hierarchical stages, greater differentiation in the planning of posts, the revaluation of individual career steps and the establishment of career-related posts (tenure track system).[19]

Increasing globalisation requires the international orientation of higher education. With the signing of the Declaration of Bologna the federal government supports the creation of a European area of higher education and the associated demand for internationally recognized training cycles and university degrees. For the establishment of the European area of higher education the declaration considers the following, among others, to have priority: the adoption of a system of study essentially based on two cycles – one up to the first degree (undergraduate) and one after the first degree (graduate) – as well as the introduction of a credit point system for the recognition and equivalency of successfully completed classes. It is intended that the first degree should confirm

19   Cf. Wissenschaftsrat, loc. cit., p. 36 and p. 55ff., and also Wissenschaftsrat: Zielvorstellun-
      gen für die Entwicklung der schweizerischen Hochschulen – Horizont 2000. 1993, Bern,
      p. 20 and p. 24ff.

a level of qualification relevant to the European labour market. The admission requirements for the second cycle require the successful completion of the first cycle, which lasts for at least three years. The "graduate cycle" ought to be completed with a master's degree or a doctorate.[20]

As before, the central tasks of the universities and universities of applied sciences are seen to lie in the fields of training, research and services – services for the community, the solution of problems of the state and society, and the linking of teaching and research activities with economic innovation and employment. In its recommendations for the development of the institutions of higher education the *Wissenschaftsrat* calls the term "services" unsatisfactory and, instead, formulates the expression "partnership – higher education institution – society – business." The institutions of higher education are seen here as a part-system with multi-dimensional relationships with the various systems. Linking of this kind is to be established to a greater extent between business and the higher education sector. The *Wissenschaftsrat* thus states: "The contribution of the universities to local and regional life by assuming a broader training and service function (e.g. continuing education courses, the creation of technological parks, innovation centres, spin-off enterprises) has increased and continues to be expected from the businesses."[21] The linking of the higher education institution and business takes place in joint work within problem and practice-orientated research projects. Here, the main emphasis of the universities of applied sciences *(Fachhochschulen)* lies in practice-orientated research, i.e. at the interface between science and business. For this purpose the universities of applied sciences are to establish transfer centres which serve companies as the place to go for services and advice.[22]

---

20 Cf. The Declaration of Bologna by the European education and research ministers dated 19/06/1999.
21 Wissenschaftsrat, loc. cit. p. 18.
22 Cf. Appendix to Art. 11, Verordnung über Aufbau und Führung von Fachhochschulen, Bern, 11/09/1996.

In addition, the contacts with business are to be intensified at the institutions of higher education as a whole by means of an "exchange of personnel". This would be possible, for example, through a dual function of the teaching staff at the higher education institution and in business, and through practical work by the students and by their preparing their first-degree or doctoral theses within business.[23]

These efforts towards strengthening the transfer of technology and knowledge between all types of higher education institutions and the business are supported by the federal government with the aid of public funds. The Swiss National Fund promotes basic research at institutions of higher education, and also individual focal support programmes of practice-orientated research. The Commission for Technology and Innovation specially supports the transfer of practice-orientated knowledge and technology and the establishment of national competence networks at the universities of applied sciences.

The political consensus of the federal government for strengthening the interaction between the institutions of higher education and business does not meet with approval everywhere, and it is sceptically viewed by some actors in the higher education sector. In contrast, the transfer of knowledge and technology at the two Swiss Federal Institutes of Technology *(Eidgenössische Technische Hochschulen)* and at the University of St. Gallen has largely become a model for these universities. Networking of this kind can be found especially in some fields in the natural sciences and technical subjects. Here the teaching staff have a dual function in the university and in business. In addition to the professional work of the teaching staff within business – e.g. advisory and research tasks – a number of professors have, in the meantime, also founded their own enterprises. In this connection, mention must also be made of the initiatives of the universities

---

23   Cf. Wissenschaftsrat: Ziele für die schweizerische Forschungspolitik – Periode 2000-2003. Bern, 1997, p. 15ff.

towards promoting and supporting the founding of businesses both for graduates and teaching staff from the universities – e.g. the founding initiative of the Swiss Federal Institute of Technology in Zürich (called: ETH Tools).

For the students this means that, on the basis of existing contacts, jobs can be found in business for new graduates, and the joint funding of places for doctoral students is made possible by outside funding. In contrast, in the remaining fields of study – especially within the humanities – a development of this kind is distinctly less marked or is lacking entirely.

Vocational orientation during the degree course

What expectations do employers have of graduates from institutions of higher education? Which skills, profiles, knowledge and methods are demanded of the graduates on the labour market? And which qualification profile promises to be of greater value when compared with other potential competitors for a job? No matter what their specialization is, all new entrants, other students and graduates are confronted with these questions. Of course, the form and shape of these questions will differ according to the specialization and the students' desired field of activity. It can be seen, however, that the demands for qualifications that companies make on employees have become more comprehensive and more differentiated. In addition to detailed specialist knowledge, key qualifications such as the ability to work in a team and the ability to cooperate (social competence) as well as general and interdisciplinary thinking are increasingly required, and these are to be acquired with the aid of practical job experience during a student's course.

What does job-orientation during a student's course actually look like, and what opportunities of practical relevance to the later field of activity are offered to students at the institutions of higher education?

One central requirement that universities of applied sciences impose upon themselves is to make students aware of the close relationship between theory and practice and to train them for their later jobs. As a rule, the courses at universities of applied sciences build on a completed apprenticeship / vocational training – or at least one year of practical work experience – in a job related to the specialization. The programmes leading to the first degree last 3 or 4 years for full-time courses of study, and 4 or 5 years for part-time courses of study: individual degree courses at the universities of applied sciences are offered as full-time and as part-time courses (evening courses), while others are only offered as full-time courses. In the case of part-time study while working, the Law on Universities of Applied Sciences requires that at least 50% of the employment must be within a field of activity related to the degree course. The first degree course is completed with a *Diplom*. The universities of applied sciences offer *Nachdiplom* (postgraduate) courses to further extent and supplement specialized knowledge.

With few exceptions, due to the practical experience which the students have, a compulsory on-the-job semester (practical semester) – as often required by the universities of applied sciences in Germany – is not demanded as an element within the course of study. Practical elements of this kind are provided in a different form. On the one hand, there is the theoretical and functional inclusion of (research) practicals, group projects and the practice-orientated nature of the dissertation. On the other hand, practical references to the later job are provided by the lecturers, who come from "practical work".

Thus, for example, for the 4th and 6th semesters the course timetable for the three-year full-time course in Industrial Economics at the St. Gallen University of Applied Sciences (a part of the *Fachhochschule Ostschweiz*) provides for group projects lasting several weeks, in which a concrete practical task is dealt with. In addition, the dissertation consists of a task from business practice. It is interesting here that the University of Applied Sciences would like to involve business actively in the problems to be dealt with, thus intensifying the exchange between companies and the University. The latter has established a knowledge-transfer office for this purpose. Businesses can hand in problems from their own practice here, and they are then dealt with by students as a group project or as a dissertation. The businesses receive the results, and here the University of Applied Sciences advertises the fact that it guarantees high quality and that the results can be translated into practice.

In this connection, mention must also be made of the increasing involvement of Swiss industry in arranging initial vocational training with regard to the trainees' possibly undertaking a degree course at a university of applied sciences. On the basis of the education reforms carried out and of the changes in the profiles demanded for some fields of activity, the Swiss engineering, electrical engineering and metal producing and working industries are thus offering a two-year "high-tech training course" for the first time in the year 2000. This course is for school-leavers with the grammar school *Maturität*, and is offered in the fields of Electrical and Electronic Engineering, Computer Science, Automation Engineering, Design and Polymechanics. This training opens up the possibility of admission to a university of applied sciences without an additional examination. The goal of this initiative is to secure new opportunities for recruiting young engineers, and here industry hopes that those leaving their jobs in the future will do so in order to start studying Engineering at a university of applied sciences.

At the universities and university level institutions the job-orientation is greatly depending on the individual field of specialization. In addition, there are differences between the universities in some of the courses. These are due partly to the regional differences – which have already been mentioned – within the structure of the courses.

The standard period of study for first degrees at universities varies depending on the subject and on the university, and lasts between 3 years (short university courses in French-speaking Switzerland) and 6 years (Medicine). The degree course is formally undertaken as full-time study. In reality, roughly a third of the students are regularly employed during their courses and in the vacations, and, in fact, actually study only part-time. The possibility of employment is sometimes dependent on the study regulations and traditions in the individual subjects (total number of hours required per week in a semester).[24] The first academic degree, as a rule the *Lizentiat* or *Diplom*, is also the precondition for further vocational or academic qualifications (postgraduate [*Nachdiplom*] or doctorate).

Some subject areas include practical training in the desired field of employment during the course – e.g. Medicine. As a result, practice-orientated training closely connected with the future job is also provided at the universities. However, in other subject areas – e.g. the Humanities – job orientation in the form of practical elements within the course takes place only to a very limited extent. Individual arts faculties offer initiatives in which the students can gather practice-orientated knowledge in order to increase their chances of obtaining a job, e.g. the pilot project at the University of Basle. In the Engineering Sciences and in Economics there are practical elements in the course that are partly laid down in the curriculum, such as work experience placements, industrial placement semesters or dissertations in cooperation with businesses. Thus, for example, the course leading to a degree in Materials Engineering at the Swiss Federal Institute of Technology in Zürich contains compulsory industrial placements in one or more firms: the six-week basic work practical has to be completed before the start of the 3rd semester. The remaining 12 weeks must

---

24   Cf. Diem, M. (Bundesamt für Statistik): Soziale Lage der Studierenden – Eine Repräsentativuntersuchung bei Studentinnen und Studenten der Schweizer Hochschulen 1995, Bern, 1997, p. 36ff.

be completed before the 8th semester, and ought, as far as possible, to be undertaken over a continuous period. The University of St. Gallen, on the other hand, demands that all students on the degree course (*Diplom*) – with the exception of the degree in Law – should show proof of a 6-month period of practical work in business or in public sector employment.

Independent of the compulsory practical elements in the course, all students have the opportunity to gain practical, career-orientated experience through industrial placements. The essential difference, however, lies in the formal degree of obligation. In the case of voluntary work experience placements, no formal examination of the type of work, the length, the time or the agreement with the curricula is provided for.

Student organisations are involved in this field, and they help to find work-experience places mainly in the field of Economics (e.g. AIESEC) and, to a certain extent, in the Engineering Sciences as well (e.g. IAESTE). Their general goal is to enable to students to complement the theoretical knowledge they have gained at the higher education institution with practical work experience. In addition, they organise seminars, workshops and events on subjects connected with starting a job (application training, rhetoric courses) and act as intermediaries between higher education institutions and business.

Job markets are organised at some institutions of higher education as a form of making direct contacts. They provide businesses with the opportunity to present themselves, and they give students a chance to obtain information about obtaining a job. A few universities provide electronic markets for jobs and work experience placements both for graduates and students, e.g. "Telejob" (electronic job market) of the associations of assistants and doctoral students at the two Swiss Federal Institutes of Technology in Zürich and Lausanne.

The transition from higher education to work

The university degree quota[25] in 1998 was 9.2%. Compared with 1985 this is a rise of 2.8 percentage points. Between 1985 and 1998 the university degree quota of women rose more strongly than that of men. Nevertheless, at 7.5% it is still 3.5 percentage points lower than that of male students. Overall, in the 1998/1999 academic year 9,161 *Lizentiat* and *Diplom* degrees and 2,860 doctorates were awarded at the universities. The proportion of women receiving *Lizentiat* and *Diplom* degrees was 41.4%, and with doctorates it was 30.4%.

The largest number of *Lizentiat* and *Diplom* degrees was awarded in the Humanities and Social Sciences (2,471), then follow the Exact Sciences and Natural Sciences (1,508) and Economics (1,347). Due to the differences between the sexes with regard to their preferences for the different subjects of study, the proportion of women is the highest in the Humanities and Social Sciences, with 62% of the *Lizentiat* and *Diplom* degrees gained. In contrast, the proportion in the Technical Sciences is 19%. The subject areas with the highest proportion of women awarded *Lizentiat* and *Diplom* degrees were Interpreting and Translating (84%), Pharmacy (83%), Archaeology (79%) and Psychology and Art History (77% each).

Doctorates were gained primarily in Medicine and Pharmacy (34%). Measured against the overall distribution of the students according to language region – German-speaking Switzerland (57.7%) – the proportion of doctorates awarded at German-speaking universities was well above the average (75%).

---

25   University degree quota: licentiates and diplomas awarded to students at universities or
      university level institutions as a percentage of permanent population of the 27-year-olds.

In addition, 1,118 *Nachdiplom* degrees were awarded. This is almost two-and-a-half times higher than in 1990. These interdisciplinary training courses for advanced and additional studies are offered primarily at the French-speaking university or university level institutions. Overall, 81% of these postgraduate degrees were awarded at three institutions: the University of Geneva (46%), the University of Lausanne (19%) and the Swiss Federal Institute of Technology *(Eidgenössische Technische Hochschule)* in Lausanne (16%).[26] The imbalance in the *Nachdiplom* (postgraduate) degrees and doctorates by language regions can largely be explained by the differences in the structure of the higher education system in Western Switzerland and in German-speaking Switzerland described at the beginning of this paper.

The new universities of applied sciences *(Fachhochschulen)* with their specialized vocational subjects accepted the first newly-enrolled students in degree courses at the university of applied sciences level in the 1997/98 academic year. Due to the three-year or four-year standard course length the first university of applied sciences degrees are being awarded in the year 2000. Until now the students in the relevant subject areas have been awarded the original *Diplom* degrees of the higher vocational schools. The degree courses are, in fact, still being adjusted at the universities of applied sciences; however, the current *Diplom* degrees of the Higher Vocational Schools and Colleges still essentially form the basis for the planned degrees at universities of applied sciences. The following *Diplom* degrees were awarded at Higher Vocational Schools and Colleges: Colleges of Engineering (HTL) (2,176) and Colleges of Economics and Administration (HWV) (860), Higher Vocational Schools for Design (HFG) (154), Higher Vocational Schools for Home Economics (43) and Higher Vocational Schools for Social Service (787).

---

26 Bundesamt für Statistik: Hochschulabschlüsse 1998, Neuchâtel, 1999.

In addition, there were 963 non-academic university degrees, including teacher training. It is planned that teacher training for primary schools and lower secondary schools should be raised to the degree status at universities of applied sciences. Despite this, there is currently a large amount of interlinking of university training and non-university training in the training of teachers, and here the training can take place "depending on the canton, either at the universities [e.g. Bern and Geneva], at other educational institutions, or even at both locations".[27] Due to the responsibility of each canton for education it is precisely within teacher training that numerous exceptions are expected to be made in the individual cantons in future. Most of the *Nachdiplom* degrees at the Higher Vocational Schools were awarded within the fields of Engineering and Architecture (1,078). More than half the courses provided in this field were developed only during the Nineties. Graduate courses with their main emphasis on business studies (e.g. management) are strongly represented here. *Nachdiplom* certificates[28] are awarded in addition to these *Nachdiplom* degrees.

The employment situation of new graduates

The employment situation of new graduates has improved considerably as a result of the economic recovery in Switzerland in the past few years. The current results of the 1999 survey of new graduates from universities and universities of applied sciences[29] confirm the favourable labour market situation

---

27   Bundesamt für Statistik: Bildungsabschlüsse 1998, Neuchâtel, 1999, p. 53.

28   "The *Nachdiplom* certificates differ from the *Nachdiplom* degrees in that they contain fewer units of instruction (at least 150 up to a maximum of 400) and are less institutionalised." Bildungsabschlüsse, loc. cit., p. 59.

29   Cf. Bundesamt für Statistik: Neuabsolventinnen und Neuabsolventen der universitären Hochschulen und der Fachhochschulen – Press Release No. 350-0039; BFS aktuell: Beschäftigungssituation der Neuabsolventinnen und Neuabsolventen: universitäre Hochschulen; BFS aktuell: Beschäftigungssituation der Neuabsolventinnen und Neuabsolventen: Fachhochschulen, Neuchâtel, 2000.

for first-degree graduates. The employment situation of new graduates from universities and university level institutions one year after graduation reveals the following picture: 87.4% in employment, 4.5% not employed and looking for jobs, 2.8% with a job promised, 5.5% do not want to be employed for various reasons (including continuing education, running a home, military service). Compared with 1997, the proportion of those not employed and looking for jobs fell by 3.1 percentage points. Here, however, regional differences and ones specific to the subject are to be found: in general, the employment situation of new graduates in Western Switzerland and in Ticino is less favourable than in German-speaking Switzerland. In 1999 (comparative value 1997), for example, the proportion of unemployed graduates seeking work was merely 2.7% (5.1%) in German-speaking Switzerland, compared with 7.3% (11.3%) in Western Switzerland and 7.6% (9.9%) in Ticino.

The more unstable economic situation and the higher level of academic degrees – together with greater competitive pressure – in Western Switzerland are mentioned as being the essential factors for this. In addition, the training at higher education institutions in this part of the country, which is mostly shorter and organized more along school lines, means that although the graduates are younger they have been able to gather less practical experience in their actual field of activity during their degree course, and this has a negative effect when they are seeking jobs. There are also differences between the various subject areas with regard to obtaining a job. In the case of the Humanities (excluding Theology), the proportion of unemployed graduates seeking employment was 7.6%, and for the Social Sciences it was 7.0%. The new graduates in Medicine and Pharmacy (1.2%), Law (2.1%) and Theology (2.2%) had the smallest transition problems.

Graduates are increasingly finding jobs in the private service sector. While only 10% of the graduates were employed in this field in 1980, the figure in

1999 is 23.4%. The other fields of employment are mainly higher education institutions (18.3%), the health service (11.7%), industry (11.5%) and the legal system (9.9%).

For the new graduates from universities of applied sciences *(Fachhoch-schulen)*[30] the employment situation is even more favourable than for those from universities. One year after graduation 92.3% of the new graduates were in employment, 1.4% had jobs promised, 2.7% were not seeking employment, and merely 3.7% were not employed and looking for jobs. Here, too, the employment situation for graduates seeking their first job has undergone a positive development when compared with recent few years. In particular, the regional differences have been reduced. In Western Switzerland 5.1%, in Ticino 4.2%, and in German-speaking Switzerland 3.1% were seeking jobs. Compared with 1997 this is a drop of 11.2 percentage points in Ticino, 3.7 percentage points in Western Switzerland and 1.4 percentage points in German-speaking Switzerland. The most frequent problems with the transition from the universities of applied sciences to the employment system were to be found among the new graduates from the field of Art and Design. 8.9% of them were seeking jobs.

More than half (54%) of the graduates from universities of applied sciences were given jobs as employees without management functions. Other jobs were as employees with management functions (23%), advisers or teachers (12%), and 2.7% were self-employed. In a comparison with the universities of applied sciences the employment situation of graduates from universities or

---

30   In the study attention is drawn to the fact that those questioned include not only new graduates from the universities of applied sciences recognized until now by the Federal Government, but also cantonal universities of applied sciences, and/or higher vocational schools and colleges.

university level institutions assumes a different form. It is true that most of them are also given jobs as employees without management functions, but they more frequently undertake practical training or work as trainees (1997: 15%) or as academic assistants at the university (1997: 14%).[31]

The results from the 1997 survey of new graduates from Swiss universities or university level institutions show that the graduates mostly find their jobs through applying on their own initiative or through job advertisements. Obtaining jobs through employment exchanges seems to play hardly any role and can be ignored as far as the numbers are concerned. The comparatively high level of help given by professors and academic assistants in finding jobs in the Natural Sciences and in Engineering is, however, remarkable.

31   Diem, M. (Bundesamt für Statistik). Die Beschäftigungssituation der Neuabsolventinnen und Neuabsolventen der Schweizer Hochschulen 1997, Neuchâtel, 1998, p. 31.

Table 4: Which search activity was decisive for finding your first job? (Only those who sought employment) According to groups of subjects, expressed as a percentage

Search criteria	Faculty groups[1]								
	Theol.	SoSci.	Econ.	Law	Hum.	NatSci.	Eng.	Med.	Tot.
Reply to job advertisement	27	28	23	20	27	23	24	14	22
Application to employer without advertisement	20	21	29	50	19	26	30	48	32
Contacts from work as a student	15	13	9	5	14	9	10	14	10
Jobs found with the aid of friends, acquaintances	8	8	6	8	8	7	7	3	7
Jobs found with the aid of professors and academic assistants	5	7	3	5	9	18	14	8	9
Jobs found with the aid of fellow students and colleagues	6	6	3	4	8	4	5	5	5
Jobs found with the aid of private employment and personnel agencies	1	4	9	1	4	2	2	1	3
Jobs found with the aid of the employment exchange	—	3	1	1	3	2	1	—	2
Jobs found with the aid of relatives	—	2	3	4	2	2	1	2	2
Others	18	8	14	3	6	7	6	5	8

1) Abbreviations: Theol.= Theology; SoSci.= Social Sciences; Econ.= Economics; Hum.= Humanities; NatSci.= Natural Sciences; Eng.= Engineering Sciences; Med.= Medicine; Tot.= Total.

Source: Bundesamt für Statistik: Die Beschäftigungssituation der Neuabsolventinnen und Neuabsolventen der Schweizer Hochschulen 1997, Neuchâtel, 1998.

A longitudinal section analysis (from 1981 to 1997) on the connection between the content of the course and the actual employment was also carried out in this survey. Here it was possible to determine the "horizontal substitution" of the requirements for the employment of new graduates on the labour market.

This means that a degree in a specific subject is not an absolute precondition for being employed in a particular job. It is much rather the case that graduates from different subjects can take up the job, with the result that "university graduates who have studied different subjects are increasingly competing with each other – regardless of the economic situation".[32]

Table 5: Employment requirements according to groups of subjects in 1997 and (1981) expressed as a percentage.

groups of subjects	Was there a graduation required by the employer?		
	yes, in my subject	yes, but not especially in my subject	no
Theology	74 (78)	6 (4)	21 (13)
Social Sciences	33 (42)	33 (29)	35 (29)
Economics	34 (36)	45 (33)	21 (31)
Law	87 (79)	7 (10)	6 (10)
Humanities	35 (49)	29 (24)	37 (27)
Natural Sciences	36 (60)	45 (33)	18 (8)
Engineering Sciences	54 (65)	31 (19)	15 (16)
Medicine	90 (94)	9 (5)	1 (2)
Total	51 (66)	30 (20)	19 (15)

Source: Bundesamt für Statistik: Die Beschäftigungssituation der Neuabsolventinnen und Neuabsolventen der Schweizer Hochschulen 1997, Neuchâtel, 1998.

This must be qualified by the remark that especially those areas of specialization which are not directed towards a distinct field of activity are affected by this phenomenon. The demand for students from these subjects is not clearly defined, and this leads to the fact that seeking a job is partly associated with complex transition processes. The situation is different, however, for graduates in Theology, Medicine and Law, whose fields of activity are organized in a

---

32   Diem, M. (Bundesamt für Statistik), loc. cit., p. 30.

comparatively clear manner.[33] These professions have structural stability and
can thus be termed "academically-based professions with a guild structure".[34]

Conclusion

The change into a knowledge society and into a modern service society has
furthered the restructuring of higher education in Switzerland into a "dual"
system. It is the task of the universities and universities of applied sciences by
means of training, research and service to secure the growing demand for
"human capital" at a high level and to push forward scientific and technological
innovations.

Parallel to this, the networking of science and business can be detected,
and this has an effect on the job orientation of the students while studying. It
also contributes towards contacts between students and potential employers.
This new form of the transfer of knowledge is developing mainly in the fields
of the Natural Sciences, Engineering Sciences and Economics. In contrast,
only traces of a development of this kind can be found so far in the Humanities
and Social Sciences. Among the reasons for this is the fact that in these
subjects the fields of activity in which the graduates from these areas will
later work are not clear. As a result, graduates from these degree courses
more frequently have problems when seeking a job. However, the intact
labour market for higher education graduates points to the fact that the demand
for qualified personnel is not restricted merely to a few particular subjects.

---

33   Cf. Streckeisen, U.: Neuabsolventinnen und Neuabsolventen der universitären Hochschu-
     len und der Fachhochschulen: Untersuchung 1999 – Die ersten Egebnisse in fünf Punk-
     ten, Vision 2/2000.
34   Streckeisen, U. Borkowsky, A.: Ende der Beruflichkeit: Mythos oder Realität?, Neue Zür-
     cher Zeitung, Sonderbeilage: "Studieren und Beruf", 09/11/1999.

Evidence of this is to be found in the multi-layered situation with regard to newly developing fields of vocational activity in the modern service society, which frequently cannot be clearly defined, and whose demands for qualifications are not directly designed for the competence in the subject and the methods, or in the social ability within a particular subject. Looking to the future, this can only be met by increasing interdisciplinary links – both regarding content and organization – between subject areas and graduates.

Vitae

Valérie **Canals** is director of studies at the Montpellier Centre for Theoretical and Applied Economics (LAMETA / CNRS). She is attached to the CNRS centre Changes in European Countries and teaches Economics. Her research deals with the transformations of the process of the transition to employment, as well as the link between the formatory periods during the course of an individual's life: initial formation, the formatory effect of transition and continued formation.

Heidi **Cordier**: Consultant at the Ministry of Schools and Continuing Education, Science and Research of the State of North Rhine-Westphalia. Currently working as an adviser on higher education management in Beira / Mozambique.

Claude **Diebolt** carries out research at CNRS, he is a Research Fellow at the Humboldt University in Berlin and Joint Director of the Montpellier Centre for Theoretical and Applied Economics (LAMETA / CNRS). He teaches economic history and the economics of education in Montpellier and Berlin. His research programme is organised around two topics: „Education, salaries and economic growth" and „Education, salaries and labour markets".

Holger **Ehlert**, M.A. – German Studies and Philosophy. Academic staff member, Coordinating Office for Reform in Higher Education at the Heinrich-Heine-University Düsseldorf. Project manager of the THELM research project. Most recent publications on the subject:
- Perborat und Silikat, Hochschule und Öffentlichkeit. Panorama einer

Zusammenarbeit für die Universität von morgen. In: Die reformierte Germanistik. Ed. by Ulrich Welbers and Michael Preuss. Grupello, 2000.
- Handbuch Praxisinitiativen an Hochschulen. Holger Ehlert and Ulrich Welbers (eds.) Luchterhand, 1998.

Charles **Fernando** a graduate of UCL-Louvain, Belgium is Senior Lecturer at the University of Sri Jayewardenepura, Sri Lanka. Atypical within the Sri Lankan University system, he had 17 years of wide and extended experience at grassroots and national levels in Sri Lanka and experience abroad prior to joining it. More recently he completed a 10-year assignment as Consultant for setting up and expanding a private „university" Institute (*a market leader referred to as IIT in the article*) offering Computing and Business Degrees from the UK. He was also Director of that Institute prior to accepting greater responsibilities at the University since 1998 as Director of the Career Guidance Unit to set up and develop that service.

Lorenzo **Fischer**: 1980-1988 Lecturer in Sociology. Since 1989 working as a Lecturer in Education at the Faculty of Political Science of the University of Turin. Since 1996 Head of the Interdisciplinary Institute for Didactic Research and Continuing Education in Teaching, and Deputy Head of IFTS, the Scientific Institute for Student Advice and Reform Projects in Teaching and Continuing Education in Technical and Scientific Subjects.

Conor **Geiselbrechtinger** was born in Munich in 1974 to a German father and an Irish mother. He moved to Ireland in 1978 and lived there until 1999. He attended school in Dublin and took the Leaving Certificate in 1993 after which he studied German and History at the University College in Dublin. He worked as a German lecturer in the Dublin Institute of Technology and is a „Lektor" in the Department of English in Düsseldorf since 1999.

Dr. phil. Heidi **Hein**: born 1969, studied Eastern European History, Modern History, Political Science 1989-1994 in Düsseldorf; 1995-2000 doctoral programme in Eastern European History, Modern History and Yiddish Studies. Completed with doctoral thesis on „The Pilsudski Cult and its Importance for the Polish State 1962-1939". Periods of research in Warsaw, Cracow and New York. Heidi Hein teaches introductory seminars at the Heinrich Heine University Düsseldorf on the history of Eastern Europe in the Middle Ages and in modern times, as well as language classes in Polish for historians.

Hugh **Langridge** M.A., P.G.C.E. Studied German and French at the University of Cambridge, Education at the University of London. Worked in industry 1964-66. Lektor at the English Department, University of Hanover 1967-1992. Currently Akademischer Oberrat. Main fields of teaching and research: British and American Cultural Studies, Translation Methodology.

Dr. Roland **Richter** is senior research associate at the Wissenschaftliches Sekretariat für die Studienreform im Land Nordrhein-Westfalen (Academic Reforms Advisory Board in the state North-Rhine Westphalia), Bochum, Germany. He holds a doctorate in German studies and history from Bochum University. Since 1990 he has published several books and some forty articles on issues of higher education policies in the Netherlands. Since the early nineties he has also been a member of a cross-border network and a number of cross-border working groups aiming at an improved collaboration of the Dutch, Flemish and German ministries and higher education institutions towards a more harmonized higher education policy.

Dr. Kerstin **Teicher**, born 1967. Doctorate 1995 on interpersonal mobility in Japan in the context of change in personnel policy. Most recent publication on the subject:

- Der Übergang von der Hochschule in die Berufstätigkeit in Japan. Ed. by Kerstin Teicher and Ulrich Teichler, Leske und Büderich, Opladen, 2000.
- Bildung und Beschäftigung in der japanischen Forschungsliteratur. Ifo-Inst. für Wirtschaftsforschung. Ed. by Kerstin Teicher et al.

Martin **Teichgräber**, Master of Arts – Political Science, Diplom in Public Administration; since 1996 Research Assistant at the *Hochschul-Informations-System*, Hanover, Germany.

Teichler, Ulrich, Prof. Dr., Director of the Scientific Centre for Vocational and Higher Education Research at the Comprehensive University Kassel.
Publications (selection): Europäische Hochschulsysteme. Frankfurt a.m.: Campus 1990; Der Hochschullehrerberuf. (Ed. with Jürgen Enders). Neuwied: Luchterhand 1995; Brennpunkt Hochschule. (Ed. with Hans-Dieter Daniel and Jürgen Enders) Frankfurt a.m.: Campus 1998; Das ERASMUS-Programm. (With Friedhelm Maiwarm and Martina Schotte-Kmoch). Bonn: BMBW 1999; Higher Education Research. (Ed. with Jan Sadleak). Oxford: IAU Press/Pergamon 2000.

Peter Lang · Europäischer Verlag der Wissenschaften

Peter Runia

Das soziale Kapital auf dem Arbeitsmarkt

Beziehungen in Stellensuche, Personalrekrutierung und Beförderung

Frankfurt/M., Berlin, Bern, Bruxelles, New York, Oxford, Wien, 2002. XVI, 244 S., 14 Abb.
Europäische Hochschulschriften: Reihe 22, Soziologie. Bd. 366
ISBN 3-631-38679-6 · br. € 40.40*

„Beziehungen" - umgangssprachlich „Vitamin B" - sind im Prinzip jedem bekannt. Ihre Existenz wird in der gegenwärtigen Leistungsgesellschaft jedoch häufig geleugnet oder tabuisiert. Viel diskutiert wird das Problem der „Beziehungen", wenn es um Arbeitsmarktprozesse geht, weil hier am deutlichsten sichtbar wird, ob eine Position aufgrund von „Beziehungen" oder allein auf der Grundlage von Leistungskriterien erreicht wurde. Die Arbeit beschäftigt sich mit diesem Problem und untersucht die Rolle von „Beziehungen" auf beiden Seiten des Arbeitsmarktes sowie bei Beförderungen. Als theoretische Grundlage der Erfassung von „Beziehungen" dient der Begriff „soziales Kapital". Der Untersuchung liegt eine Verbindung von ökonomischer und soziologischer Analyse zugrunde. Die Ergebnisse der Arbeit weisen darauf hin, dass soziales Kapital vor allem im Wechselspiel mit anderen arbeitsmarktrelevanten Kriterien seine volle Wirkung entfaltet.

Aus dem Inhalt: Soziales Kapital · Soziale Netzwerke · Individualismus, Kommunitarismus, Gemeinschaft und Gesellschaft · Humankapital · Arbeitsmarkttheorien · Karriere · Stellensuche · Personalrekrutierung · Beförderung · Personalberatung · Soziale Ungleichheit

Frankfurt/M · Berlin · Bern · Bruxelles · New York · Oxford · Wien
Distribution: Verlag Peter Lang AG
Jupiterstr. 15, CH-3000 Bern 15
Telefax (004131) 9402131

*incl. value added tax, the current german tax rate is applied
Prices are subject to change without notice
Homepage http://www.peterlang.de